Lyn Allison

Y0-CLB-508

IMPERIAL ROME

TIME
LIFE
BOOKS®

Other Publications:

THE GOOD COOK

THE SEAFARERS

THE ENCYCLOPEDIA OF COLLECTIBLES

THE GREAT CITIES

WORLD WAR II

HOME REPAIR AND IMPROVEMENT

THE WORLD'S WILD PLACES

THE TIME-LIFE LIBRARY OF BOATING

HUMAN BEHAVIOR

THE ART OF SEWING

THE OLD WEST

THE EMERGENCE OF MAN

THE AMERICAN WILDERNESS

THE TIME-LIFE ENCYCLOPEDIA OF GARDENING

LIFE LIBRARY OF PHOTOGRAPHY

THIS FABULOUS CENTURY

FOODS OF THE WORLD

TIME-LIFE LIBRARY OF AMERICA

TIME-LIFE LIBRARY OF ART

LIFE SCIENCE LIBRARY

THE LIFE HISTORY OF THE UNITED STATES

TIME READING PROGRAM

LIFE NATURE LIBRARY

LIFE WORLD LIBRARY

FAMILY LIBRARY:
   HOW THINGS WORK IN YOUR HOME
   THE TIME-LIFE BOOK OF THE FAMILY CAR
   THE TIME-LIFE FAMILY LEGAL GUIDE
   THE TIME-LIFE BOOK OF FAMILY FINANCE

GREAT AGES OF MAN

A History of the World's Cultures

IMPERIAL ROME

by

MOSES HADAS

and

The Editors of TIME-LIFE BOOKS

TIME-LIFE BOOKS, ALEXANDRIA, VIRGINIA

Time-Life Books Inc.
is a wholly owned subsidiary of
TIME INCORPORATED

FOUNDER: Henry R. Luce 1898-1967

Editor-in-Chief: Hedley Donovan
Chairman of the Board: Andrew Heiskell
President: James R. Shepley
Vice Chairmen: Roy E. Larsen, Arthur Temple
Corporate Editors: Ralph Graves,
Henry Anatole Grunwald

TIME-LIFE BOOKS INC.
MANAGING EDITOR: Jerry Korn
Executive Editor: David Maness
Assistant Managing Editors: Dale M. Brown,
Martin Mann, John Paul Porter
Art Director: Tom Suzuki
Chief of Research: David L. Harrison
Director of Photography: Robert G. Mason
Planning Director: Thomas Flaherty (acting)
Senior Text Editor: Diana Hirsh
Assistant Art Director: Arnold C. Holeywell
Assistant Chief of Research: Carolyn L. Sackett
Assistant Director of Photography:
Dolores A. Littles

CHAIRMAN: Joan D. Manley
President: John D. McSweeney
Executive Vice Presidents: Carl G. Jaeger,
John Steven Maxwell, David J. Walsh
Vice Presidents: Peter G. Barnes (Comptroller),
Nicholas Benton (Public Relations),
John L. Canova (Sales), Nicholas J. C. Ingleton (Asia),
James L. Mercer (Europe/South Pacific),
Herbert Sorkin (Production), Paul R. Stewart
(Promotion)
Personnel Director: Beatrice T. Dobie
Consumer Affairs Director: Carol Flaumenhaft

GREAT AGES OF MAN
SERIES EDITOR: Russell Bourne
Editorial Staff for *Imperial Rome:*
EDITOR: Harold C. Field
Assistant to the Editor: Peter Meyerson
Text Editors: Betsy Frankel, Leon Greene
Designer: Norman Snyder
Staff Writer: Paul Trachtman
Chief Researcher: Carlotta Kerwin
Researchers: Elizabeth Collins, Patricia Skinner,
Lilla Zabriskie, Linda Wolfe, Theo Pascal

EDITORIAL PRODUCTION
Production Editor: Douglas B. Graham
Operations Manager: Gennaro C. Esposito
Assistant Production Editor: Feliciano Madrid
Quality Control: Robert L. Young (director),
James J. Cox (assistant), Michael G. Wight
(associate)
Art Coordinator: Anne B. Landry
Copy Staff: Susan B. Galloway (chief),
Barbara Hults, Florence Keith, Celia Beattie
Picture Department: Joan Lynch
Traffic: Jeanne Potter

THE AUTHOR: The late Moses Hadas, long regarded as one of America's foremost authorities on the ancient world, began teaching at Columbia University in 1925. He was twice chairman of the Department of Greek and Latin at Columbia and held the distinguished title of Jay Professor of Greek. His books include *Hellenistic Culture, Ancilla to Classical Reading* and *Humanism,* as well as editions of works by Tacitus and Cicero. Dr. Hadas' radio and television appearances brought him a wide audience both within and outside the academic community.

THE CONSULTING EDITOR: Leonard Krieger, University Professor of History at the University of Chicago, was formerly Professor of History at Columbia and Yale Universities. Dr. Krieger is the author of *The German Idea of Freedom* and *The Politics of Discretion,* and co-author of *History,* written in collaboration with John Higham and Felix Gilbert.

THE COVER: A relief from Trajan's Column in Rome shows the enthroned Emperor and his entourage receiving pleas for clemency from the defeated Dacians.

CORRESPONDENTS: Elisabeth Kraemer (Bonn); Margot Hapgood, Dorothy Bacon (London); Susan Jonas, Lucy T. Voulgaris (New York); Maria Vincenza Aloisi, Josephine du Brusle (Paris); Ann Natanson (Rome). Valuable assistance was also provided by: Katharine Sachs (London); Franz Spelman (Munich); Carolyn T. Chubet, Miriam Hsia (New York); Joseph Harris (Paris); Erik Amfitheatrof, Joseph Pilcher (Rome); Traudl Lessing (Vienna).

© 1965 Time-Life Books Inc. All rights reserved.
No part of this book may be reproduced in any form or by any electronic or mechanical means, including information storage and retrieval devices or systems, without prior written permission from the publisher, except that brief passages may be quoted for reviews.
Ninth printing. Revised 1979.
Published simultaneously in Canada.
Library of Congress catalogue card number 65-24363.
School and library distribution by
Silver Burdett Company, Morristown, New Jersey.

CONTENTS

INTRODUCTION	7
1 THE SOBER ROMAN	10
Picture Essay: THE WORLD CITY	17
2 FROM VILLAGE TO EMPIRE	34
Picture Essay: ROMAN HOLIDAYS WITHOUT END	45
3 THE PAX ROMANA	56
Picture Essay: AUGUSTUS, FIRST EMPEROR	69
4 THE RITUAL OF DAILY LIFE	78
Picture Essay: MASTERS OF WAR	89
5 POETS AND PROPAGANDISTS	102
Picture Essay: HOMAGE TO ITALY	111
6 THE GODS OF ROME	120
Picture Essay: POMPEII: A SELF-PORTRAIT	129
7 END OF GREATNESS	140
Picture Essay: THE METROPOLIS	147
8 A PERSISTENT PRESENCE	156
Picture Essay: SEEDBED OF CHRISTIANITY	167
APPENDIX	179
Chronologies, 179; Immortal Romans, 182	
BIBLIOGRAPHY, ACKNOWLEDGMENTS AND CREDITS	184
INDEX	186

INTRODUCTION

"Not to know what happened before we were born," wrote Cicero, "is to remain perpetually a child. For what is the worth of a human life unless it is woven into the life of our ancestors by the records of history?" In these volumes on The Great Ages of Man an honored place is rightfully given to Rome, which emphasized so greatly the importance of history and tradition.

During the years in which Rome grew from a collection of prehistoric villages near a crossing of the Tiber to a worldwide empire, there matured the strong sense of order which was the mark of her state and her society. Into this she infused the many cultural and technical achievements of other peoples which she assimilated, preserved and universalized. Tradition and personal achievement, the demand for conformity with ancient ways and the individual's search for glory, continued in dynamic tension throughout her career. They gave shape to the administration of state and empire, and to the development of the law. They were formative elements in a literature deeply concerned with a people's history and a people's mission.

The continuity from which arose the idea of Rome the Eternal may well be studied with more than mere nostalgia in the uncertain world of today. In a time when world agreement is so necessary and yet so hard to realize, Rome recalls the one period when it was almost realized, a period which Gibbon considered the happiest in human history. How did this achievement come to pass, despite the brutalities of war, conquest and exploitation? Rome put no pressure on the manifold peoples of the Empire to conform, destroyed no cultural traditions, and suppressed no difference of language. Instead, she imposed the way of peace, and built up the institutional framework which all men then took for granted as they went about their daily concerns. She allowed her former subjects to participate in her government and to satisfy their ambitions within her system. She won them by the prestige so gained. Even in the days of Rome's decline a Gothic chieftain who intended to destroy her and substitute a "Gothia where a Romania had been" so admired the structure of a state that rested on laws "without which," he said, "a state is not a state," that he turned his efforts instead to the restoration of Roman power by means of Gothic arms.

We too, whose Constitution was shaped by men who knew their Roman authors well, should consider Rome's enduring influence. From the Romans we learned of humane studies and interest in man, Cicero's *humanitas*. If such terms as natural right, equality before the law, government for the good of the governed, have become commonplaces, it is because our Roman heritage has made them so.

This book in the TIME-LIFE series on The Great Ages of Man makes an excellent contribution to our understanding of Roman achievement and Roman influence. It is fortunate in the choice of Professor Hadas as its author. The experience of many years devoted to the study of the history and the literatures of Greece and Rome has enabled him to penetrate deeply into the Roman mind and to present with liveliness and sympathy the many aspects of the Roman record and the Roman character.

T. ROBERT S. BROUGHTON
Paddison Professor of Latin Emeritus,
University of North Carolina

NORTH SEA
BALTIC SEA
Dniepe
Vistula R.
Oder R.
Elbe R.
Dniester R.
GERMANIA
CARPATHIAN MTS.
Eburacum
(York)
BRITAIN
Thames R.
Londinium
(London)
Colonia Agrippina
(Cologne)
Rhine R.
Augusta Treverorum
(Trier)
Vindobona
(Vienna)
Sarmizegethusa
Aquincum
(Budapest)
Viminacium
Danub
Sava R.
Sirmium
Durocortorum
(Rheims)
Seine R.
Lutetia
(Paris)
ALPS
Aquileia
Verona
Mediolanum
(Milan)
PO R.
Bononia
(Bologna)
Salonae
Dyrrhachium
(Durazzo)
ADRIATIC SEA
GAUL
Lugdunum
(Lyons)
Loire R.
Rhone R.
APENNINES
Genua
Tiber R.
Cannae
Brundisium
ITALY
Rome
Ostia
Neapolis
(Naples)
Pompeii
Heraclea
ATLANTIC
OCEAN
Burdigala
(Bordeaux)
Nicaea
(Nice)
Arelate
(Arles)
Narbo
CORSICA
TYRRHENIAN SEA
SARDINIA
Syracuse
SICILY
PYRENEES
Asturica Augusta
Caesaraugusta
(Saragossa)
Ebro R.
Tarraco
Douro R.
Segovia
HISPANIA
Saguntum
BALEARIC ISLANDS
Utica
Carthage
Hippo Regius
Cirta
Zama
Thapsus
Toletum
Tagus R.
Emerita Augusta
(Merida)
Guadiana R.
Guadalquivir R.
Thamugadi
(Timgad)
Caesarea
Carthago Nova
(Cartagena)
Corduba
AFRICA
Olisipo
(Lisbon)
Hispalis
(Seville)
Gades
(Cadiz)
STRAIT OF GIBRALTAR
Tingis
(Tangier)
MAURETANIA
ATLAS MTS.

THE ROMAN WORLD

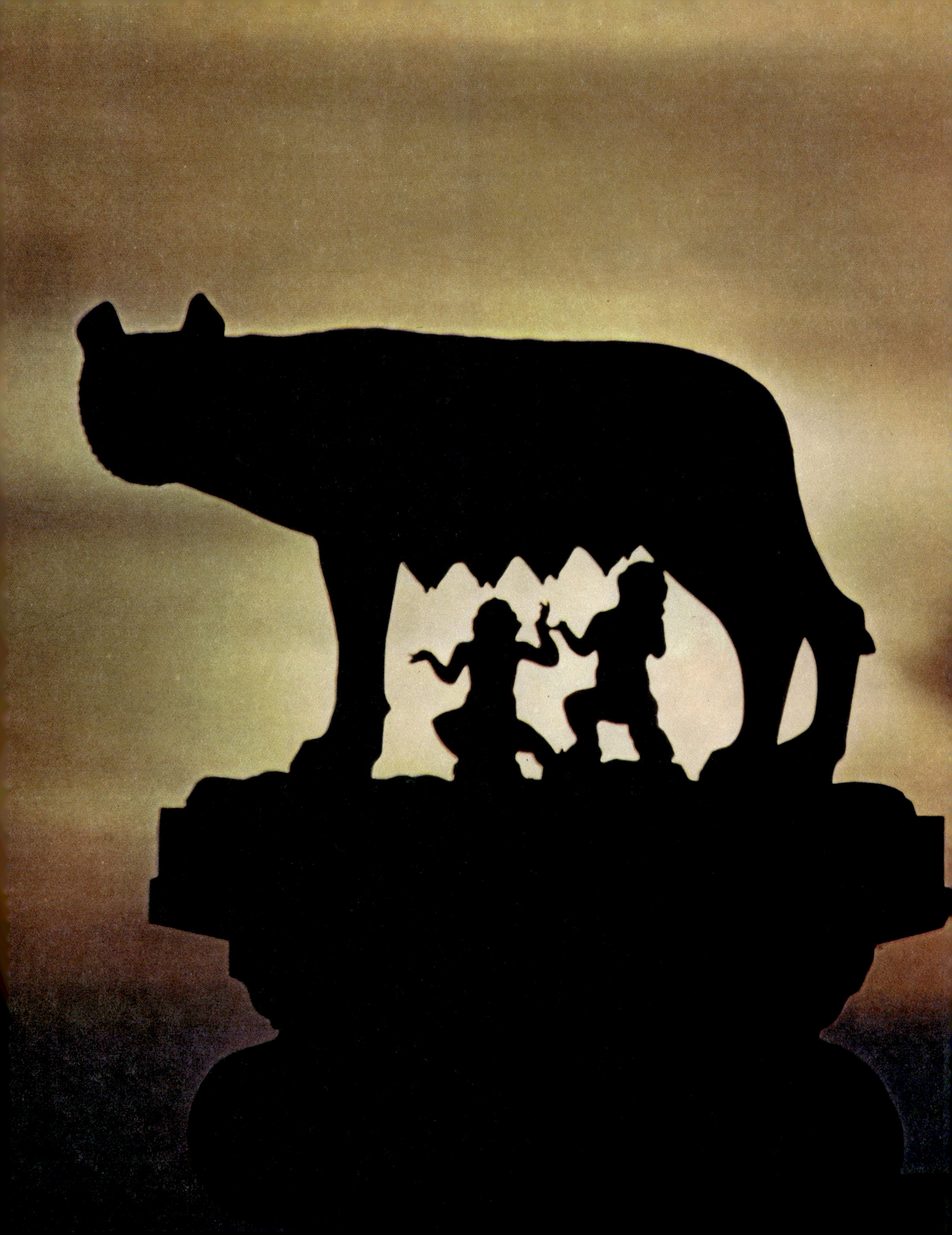

1
THE SOBER ROMAN

LEGENDARY FOUNDERS OF ROME, *the brothers Romulus and Remus were said to have been suckled by a she-wolf. This statue, based on the 2,400-year-old Etruscan original, stands on the Capitoline Hill, site of the city's founding.*

Rome's career spanned a millennium; in that time Rome assembled the greatest empire the world had seen. But the size and stability of the Empire are not the sum of Rome's claim to greatness. A more enduring claim lies in Rome's marked genius in nourishing and embellishing the intellectual and cultural achievements of the Greek world that it conquered, and spreading them across Europe. Roman architecture, art, literature and religion—all showing the influence of Greece—bear the unmistakable stamp of Roman power and assurance. Nevertheless, Horace's statement is true: "Captive Greece took Rome captive."

A tangible legacy of Rome survives in the remains of noble structures built for the ages: the Pantheon and the Colosseum in Rome itself; the mighty aqueducts scattered over three continents; the roads which tied the Empire together. The intangible and more important legacy is the fact that in transforming a fragmented world into a single community, Rome established patterns for public institutions, individual liberty and respect for law that still exist.

Rome's Empire was built by arms and diplomacy and sustained by Rome's intelligent rule of its conquered peoples. There were few nationalist uprisings; most provincials found their new life more than tolerable. In great part, provincials were granted Roman citizenship. Gifted provincials gained honor throughout the Empire; some of Rome's greatest writers and best emperors were provincials. Not all of the Empire's best schools were in Rome: the schools of Gaul, with their Latin curricula, eventually surpassed those of Rome itself.

Rome exacted tribute from the Empire, but it gave much in return: the rule of law within the imperial boundaries, protection against barbarian invasion from without; ready exchange of goods and products, toleration of the cultural differences inevitable within a far-flung dominion. Above all, Rome infused all Romans, provincial or metropolitan, with a positive belief in Rome's own destiny. This belief, firmly established in a time when the pagan gods held sway, survived the dethroning of mighty Jupiter and sustained Christian Rome. Late in the Fourth Century A.D., the Christian poet Prudentius wrote this paean to Roman civilization:

> *... All whom Rhine and Danube water, or gold-bearing Tagus, or great Ebro, all that Hesperian Tiber flows through or Ganges nourishes or the seven mouths of the warm Nile sustains—all these did God teach to become Romans. A shared law made them peers, intertwined them under a single name, brought the vanquished into the bonds of brotherhood. ... Areas geographically remote, shores divided by the sea, now merge in allegiance to a single jurisdiction .... Such was the achievement of the enormous successes and triumphs of Roman power.*

At this remove in time, we can only speculate about final answers to the question: What made the Romans what they were? Up to a point we can analyze the influences that shaped the Roman character and set Rome in the path of world dominion. Certainly Rome's early history played an important part. The earliest Romans were farmers in a hostile land, and no matter how urbanized Rome later became, Roman roots remained firmly fixed in the soil. From their pioneer forebears Romans inherited respect for strength and discipline, for loyalty, industry, frugality and tenacity. These ancient values were formally recognized by the Romans as the *mos maiorum* (ways of the fathers), and always dominated their outlook. The Roman owed his loyalties to the gods, the state and the family. Where the earlier Greeks had cherished their individuality, the Roman always subordinated his personality to greater forces.

In law, the *pater familias*, or head of a family, had absolute power over the members of his household. It was not difficult for the Roman to move from the concept of an authoritarian *pater familias* to that of an authoritarian state and ultimately an all-powerful emperor (called *pater patriae*, father of the country). Thus, while service to the state might be a road to distinction, it was an extension of the obligation that Romans felt toward their families. Cicero, one of Rome's greatest statesmen, wrote:

> *... those whom Nature has endowed with the capacity for administering public affairs should put aside all hesitation, enter the race for public office, and take a hand in directing the government; for in no other way can a government be administered or greatness of spirit be made manifest.*

The earnestness evident in Cicero's advice provides another clue to the Roman character, for a trait which Romans admired was *gravitas*. We translate the word as "dignity," but what it really meant was weightiness. It was this weighty quality, sober, monumental and enduring, which marked the personality of the Roman, his system of government and, indeed, all things Roman. Enduring strength rather than delicacy, power rather than agility, mass rather than beauty, utility rather than grace—these are the hallmarks of Rome. Fact rather than imagination dominates its art; its portraiture is mercilessly realistic, its carved reliefs a solemn record of history. Strength clothed in dignity was the Roman ideal. Swathed in his toga, a well-born Roman never gave the impression of being in a hurry. Always he seemed to be on parade, always conscious of his audience, real or spectral. In thrall to the past, he constantly reminded himself of the eminent forebears whom it was his duty to emulate in every waking action.

Pageantry and ceremonial abounded in Roman life, public and private. Rituals served at times the very useful purpose of bridging the gap between ideal behavior and practical necessity. The Romans prided themselves on their high standards of probity and integrity. When they had to violate these rules, they took pains to contrive a justification, even if they had to make use of what is now called a legal fiction. For example, the ancient ceremony that preceded a Roman declaration of war was performed by a special college of priests called *fetiales*. With great formality, these functionaries would present Rome's grievances, actual or imaginary, to the offending state and demand compensation. If the often exorbitant demands were not met, custom required the *fetiales* to march to the boundary of the other state, invoke the gods to witness that the Roman cause was just, and then cast a weapon into the enemy's territory to symbolize the opening of hostilities.

This worked well in the early days of local wars. But in later years, when it was no longer practical for the *fetiales* to travel to a distant border, an enclosed area on the Campus Martius in Rome was assigned to represent any potential enemy country. Here the *fetiales* could conveniently perform the ritual without which Rome would not go to war. Thus, custom was honored, and ritual-loving Romans could rest easy, comforted by the thought that they had observed the proprieties—at least after a fashion.

Again, the private lives of Roman gentlemen were strictly regulated by a code that defined acceptable and forbidden callings. Cicero, zealous in his efforts to maintain the purity of Roman life, wrote:

> *Public opinion divides the trades and professions into the liberal and the vulgar. We condemn the odious occupation of the collector of customs and the usurer, and the base and menial work of unskilled laborers, for the very wages the laborer receives are a badge of slavery... The work of the mechanic is also degrading; there is nothing noble about a workshop. The least respectable of all trades are those which minister to pleasure, as Terence tells us, "fishmongers, butchers, cooks, sausage-makers." Add to these, if you like, perfumers, dancers, and the actors of the "ludus talarius."*

While virtually all forms of business were closed to them, upper-class Romans had little trouble finding loopholes in the code. One stratagem was to turn over "degrading" businesses to hired agents or trusted slaves. Another was the manufacture of bricks, a very widely used Roman building material: since clay was a product of the earth, brickmaking was considered a branch of "respectable" agriculture. Lawyers, long prohibited from accepting fees for their services, were never known to refuse gifts or bequests from grateful clients. Here, as elsewhere, the letter of the law rather than the spirit, outward appearance rather than inner meaning, were always the important considerations.

By contrast with the earlier Greeks, who were preoccupied with the quest for a speculative morality that would explore the limits of decent action, the Romans rarely concerned themselves with a theoretical definition of ethical ideals. Romans examined a problem, determined what needed to be done, did it and went on to the next task. Hand in hand with the single-minded and unquestioning Roman attitude toward life went Roman conservatism. The Roman justified this resistance to change by his belief that the old ways had been the best ways. He was proud of the discipline enforced by ancient tradition and contemporary regulation. He saw himself as a paragon of sober propriety, and looked down on the more artistic and less inhibited Greeks as frivolous and feckless. With regard to the activities he considered incompatible with dignity, the Roman gentleman strove to create the impression of a reserved spectator: not for him the sweaty rolling in the dust of a gymnasium. He would not play a musical instrument. Nor would he write philosophy—unless he first disclaimed the qualifications of a professional metaphysician.

In his own eyes, then, the Roman was the model of the upright, unsentimental maker of things and mover of events, ever mindful of the importance of established forms, firmly attached to reality. To later generations, however, he has other and less pleasing dimensions. From accounts written by Romans out of firsthand knowledge, he is visible as the personification of ruthlessness, the producer of bloody gladiatorial contests, the practitioner of debauchery in emulation of his monstrous emperors. There is truth in these indictments, and there is an explanation.

The harshness ingrained in Romans was the product of long conflict with man and nature. Like the American pioneers, the early Roman farmer was prepared to leave his plowing and fight his enemies. His character was formed in this hard school, and centuries of rough existence bred in him an acceptance of savagery dealt out and received. Even when later Romans acquired a considerable degree of sophistication, they continued to enjoy holiday entertainments that are horrifying by present standards but which lose much of their horror when they are examined in the light of what was acceptable in those distant times.

Still, there remains the reputation for depravity, which has persistently disfigured the picture of the Romans. This is one of the most damning aspects of the Roman character for modern man, perhaps because it has been given such wide currency in pseudohistorical novels and lurid movies.

But, was Rome so immoral a place? The evidence seems convincing that it was. Suetonius, Juvenal and Tacitus, among others, wrote vividly of the depravity and the corruption of Roman life. But Suetonius was reporting on the life of the most

THE HERO AENEAS, *whose wanderings after the fall of Troy make up the story of the "Aeneid," Vergil's epic poem of the Roman peoples' origins, is shown (top, pointing) arriving in Carthage in this Fourth Century A.D. painting. From this ancient city Aeneas finally crossed the Mediterranean to conquer the Latin tribes.*

sophisticated imperial circles; Juvenal was a satirist who, naturally, used the extremes of conduct for his targets; Tacitus was an unreconstructed republican who yearned for past times. None could be called objective in his choice of subject matter. Other sources tell a different story. They show us the majority of Romans leading responsible and respectable lives. Evil, however, has always made for more exciting reading than virtue, and it is doubtful that Rome will ever escape its aura of sinfulness.

On reflection, however, it becomes evident that if the Roman had been motivated solely by brutality and viciousness, he could never have accomplished his notable deeds or made such a lasting impression on the world. There were dark sides to the Roman, but counteracting these were his deep sense of dignity, his veneration of order, his feeling for history, and his belief in his destiny. The mystique of superiority in which he wrapped himself, the conviction that he was a member of an elite group with a god-given mandate for greatness, was sustained by his familiarity with the legends of the prowess of his forebears. Some of these tales he knew through oral tradition. Others were composed for him, rather late in his history, by writers like Livy, Vergil and Horace. Vergil, for example, describes the early Latins in this passage from the *Aeneid:*

> *Ours is a race from ancestry*
> *Enduring; to the streams we carry down*
> *Our sons at birth, and with harsh frosty*
>   *waves*
> *We harden them. Our boys watch for*
>   *the dawn*
> *To go a-hunting, and they scour the*
>   *woods;*
> *To wheel their steeds their pastime, and*
>   *to aim*
> *Shafts with bent bow. But, patient in*
>   *their toil,*

> *Our youth to scanty ways of life inured*
> *With harrow tame the soil, or else in war*
> *Make towns to tremble.*

Officially accepted Roman history insisted that Romans were invincible. In Livy's history, it is as natural for the Romans to win battles as it is for water to run downhill. It is the occasional reverse which needs to be explained, as divine chastisement for some transgression or merely as a lesson to keep the Romans alert and disciplined. The chronicle of Roman successes was created to serve as a charter for the cult of patriotism. This body of inspirational, nationalistic literature illustrated virtues dear to Romans: bravery, simplicity, morality.

Horatius Cocles, according to Roman belief, saved the city from Lars Porsenna and his Etruscan army that was marching on Rome around 500 B.C. Horatius, standing alone on the far side of the Tiber, held off the invaders while the bridge at his back was being cut down. The wounded Horatius, in the historian Polybius' version, then jumped into the Tiber and "deliberately sacrificed his life, regarding the safety of his country and the glory which in future would attach to his name as of more importance than his present existence. . . ." Livy, in a cheerier ending, says that Horatius safely reached the opposite side, buoyed by the sympathetic Tiber.

Livy introduces the legend of Cincinnatus by stating it "merits the attention of those who despise all human qualities in comparison with riches, and think there is no room for great honors or for worth but amidst a profusion of wealth." During the invasion of the Aequi in 458 B.C., Livy continues, a delegation of Roman officials went to tell Cincinnatus that he had been given dictatorial powers in order to repel the invaders. Cincinnatus, working his modest farm, accepted command of the Roman forces for six months. In just 16 days, however, he had defeated the Aequi, surrendered his dictatorship and was back at his plow.

One of Horace's most famous odes was devoted to the legend of Regulus, a Roman commander who was captured by the Carthaginians during the First Punic War. Sent back to Rome under parole to negotiate peace terms, Regulus instead urged the Senate to carry on the war. Then, true to his Roman word, he returned to Carthage to face death by torture.

The most cherished legend concerned the founding of Rome. In its retelling Roman historians stressed the grandeur of Rome's origins, and paid little heed to accuracy.

Rome, the legend states, was planned by the gods who, after the fall of Troy, ordered the defeated prince Aeneas, a son of Venus, to lead his fellow refugees to a promised land in the West. Surviving many trials and temptations on their roundabout voyage, the Trojans reached Italy. Eventually they joined forces with the Latins and with Aeneas as their king, founded Lavinium, a city near the coast and about 16 miles southeast of the site of Rome. Later, under Aeneas' son Ascanius, they moved a few miles inland to begin a new city, Alba Longa.

In the Eighth Century B.C., the legend continues, the Latin princess Rhea Silvia, sworn to chastity as a Vestal Virgin, gave birth to twin sons fathered by the god Mars. As punishment for the violation of her oath, her uncle, King Amulius, imprisoned her and ordered that the infants, Romulus and Remus, be abandoned to die on the bank of the flooding Tiber. The boys were found by a she-wolf who nursed them until a shepherd discovered them and took them into his home. When they reached manhood, they resolved to build a new city on the Tiber, and Romulus traced the boundaries of Rome with his plow.

When the modern historian attempts to extricate a nugget of fact from the mass of legend, all he can be sure of is that the Romans were of Indo-European origin, possibly with roots in central Asia. After migrating first to central Europe, a number of Indo-European tribes reached the top of the Italian peninsula and began moving southward around 1000 B.C., conquering the native peoples in their path.

The most important newcomers were the Latins, the group to which the Romans belonged. They settled on the volcanic plain of Latium, an area of about 700 square miles bounded on the north by the Tiber River. On the rocky but fertile soil, the settlers prospered with a wide variety of crops and began the slow process of growth.

Fortunately, Rome was granted centuries of relative freedom from the danger of foreign domination in which to accomplish the steady conquest of the Italian peninsula and to mold a national character. Seldom required to defend itself against a force more powerful than its own, Rome became accustomed to victories and acquired an immense self-confidence, the essence of which is captured in a few lines by the poet Propertius:

> . . . *Rome has marvels greater than all the others;*
>   *nature herself has made*
>   *our city great.*
> *This is a place of peace and not of bloodshed;*
>   *honor and fame were*
>   *granted us by fate.*
> *We've made our stand through faith no*
>   *less than fighting;*
> *even our wrath we learn to mitigate.*

Given assurance of this magnitude, it is possible to understand how these people could move from local triumphs to world domination, and affect the world so profoundly that their influence is still felt.

THE VIA APPIA, *first of the great Roman roads, was begun in 312 B.C. It reached southward 360 miles from Rome to Brundisium, an Adriatic port.*

THE WORLD CITY

The city of Rome spread from seven small hills on the Tiber to encompass an Empire of several million square miles. In the wake of the Roman legions came governors and civil servants, architects and merchants. They remade the world in Rome's image: in the teeming cities of the Near East and the rough Germanic provinces, citizens from all corners of the Empire walked down Roman streets. But Rome changed too. Its shops displayed Black Sea sturgeon and ostrich feathers from Africa; its Senate took in Spaniards and Greeks. Rome became the most cosmopolitan of cities, while the cities of Syria, North Africa and Gaul became lesser Romes, connected by a common bond of government and a great network of highways. Guidebooks listed 300 major roads throughout the Empire. In the words of a poet, Rome had "made one City, where once was a World."

HUB OF IMPERIAL POWER

Roman emperors made their capital a city of monuments. Massive public works, contrasting starkly with the crumbling tenements, were the outward signs of imperial power. Augustus boasted of restoring 82 temples. Vespasian built the Colosseum. Trajan constructed a towering column as a monument to his greatness—and also built his own forum.

The original Forum Romanum extended from the Curia (8) to the Temple of Venus and Roma (11). By the Second Century A.D. no fewer than six emperors had created nearby a series of Imperial Forums which stretched from the Forum of Trajan (6) to the Basilica of Maxentius (10). The city is shown in the model above at the height of its glory.

1. Temple of Aesculapius
2. Theater of Marcellus
3. Temple of Jupiter Capitolinus
4. Temple of Trajan
5. Baths of Constantine
6. Trajan's Forum
7. Temple of Mars the Avenger
8. Curia (Senate House)
9. Basilica Julia
10. Basilica of Maxentius
11. Temple of Venus and Roma
12. Temple of Jupiter Victor
13. Arch of Constantine
14. Colosseum
15. Temple of Claudius
16. Aqueduct of Nero
17. Palace of Septimius Severus
18. Circus Maximus

THE FIRST FORUM

As Rome was the center of the Empire, so the Forum Romanum, some of whose ruins are shown here, was the center of Rome. Oldest of the city's public squares, the Forum Romanum gradually grew into a complex of open spaces and government buildings, temples and shops. Its main concourse was closed to chariot traffic; senators, priests, businessmen, shoppers and hawkers daily thronged the area on foot. Here stood the Golden Milestone, from which all roads fanned out; here Romulus was said to be buried; here was the Senate, where Cicero spoke and Caesar was murdered. The Forum's monumental architecture was copied wherever Rome ruled, and cities from England to Egypt were centered on similar structures.

NEW PROPORTIONS OF GRANDEUR

Architecturally, the Romans were avid borrowers. They took over the Doric, Ionic and Corinthian columns of Greece, the arch of the Etruscans. But their primary interest was not so much to match the perfection of Greek proportions as to outdo the Greeks and Etruscans with great feats of engineering. They were tremendous, boastful builders.

Roman architects were the first to exploit concrete to achieve grandeur. Using this cheap, adaptable material they expanded the Etruscan arch into viaducts, aqueducts, triumphal arches and mammoth domes like that of the Pantheon *(opposite)*. For beauty's sake the concrete was veneered: with marble for great buildings; with brick, tile, pebbles, stucco or plaster for modest ones. The Pantheon dome, pride of the city, was covered with gilded bronze so that its gleam could be seen all over Rome.

MOUNTED EMPEROR, *this statue of Marcus Aurelius dominates Capitoline Hill. In style it is more heroic than Greek equestrian sculpture.*

A GRACEFUL TEMPLE *by the Tiber, although embellished with Greek columns, is shaped like the ancient round thatched huts which the Romans used as family dwellings in the time of Romulus.*

THE PANTHEON DOME, *largest and most daring of antiquity, caps a former temple. The only light for the interior, 142 feet in diameter, 142 feet high, comes through the opening in the dome's apex.*

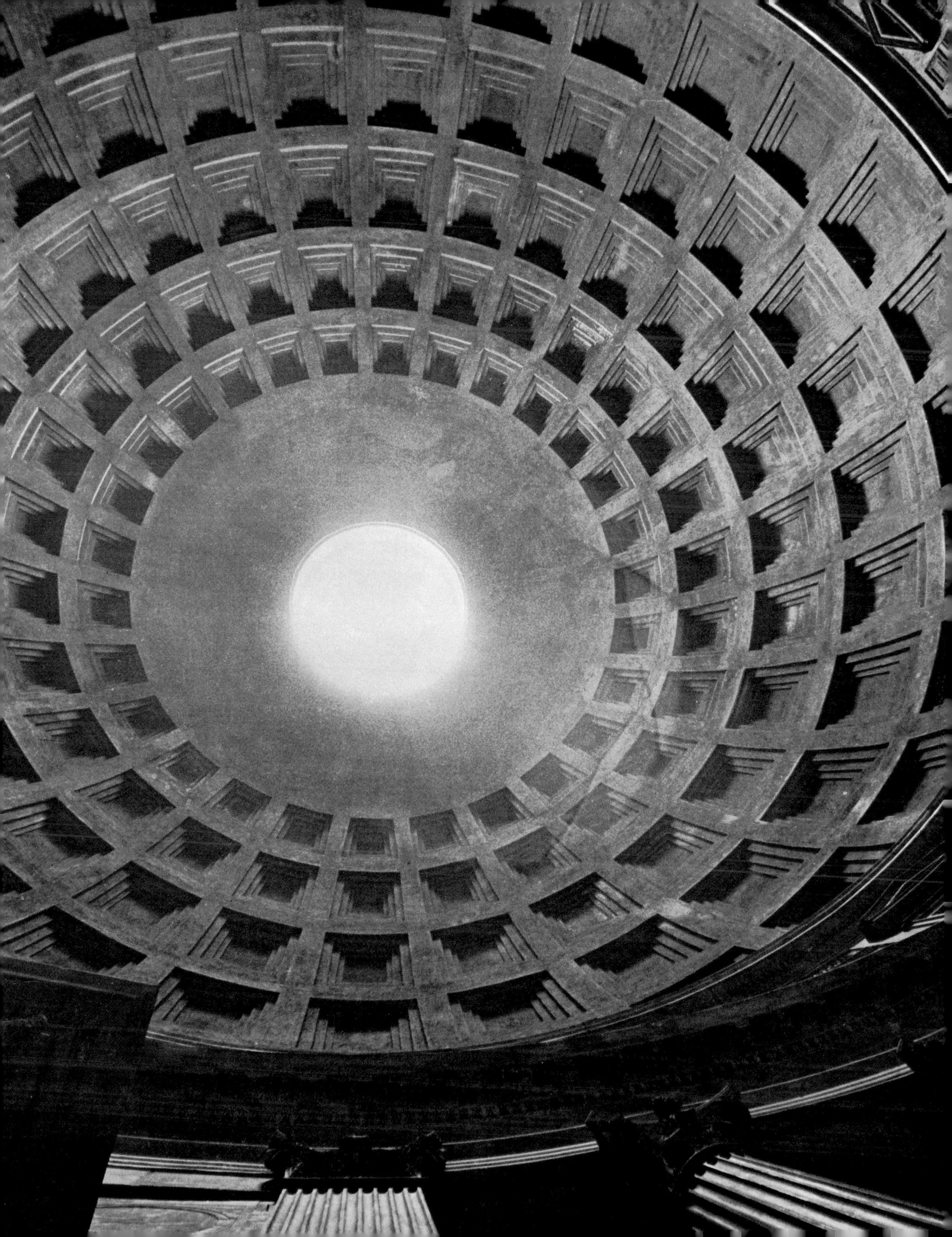

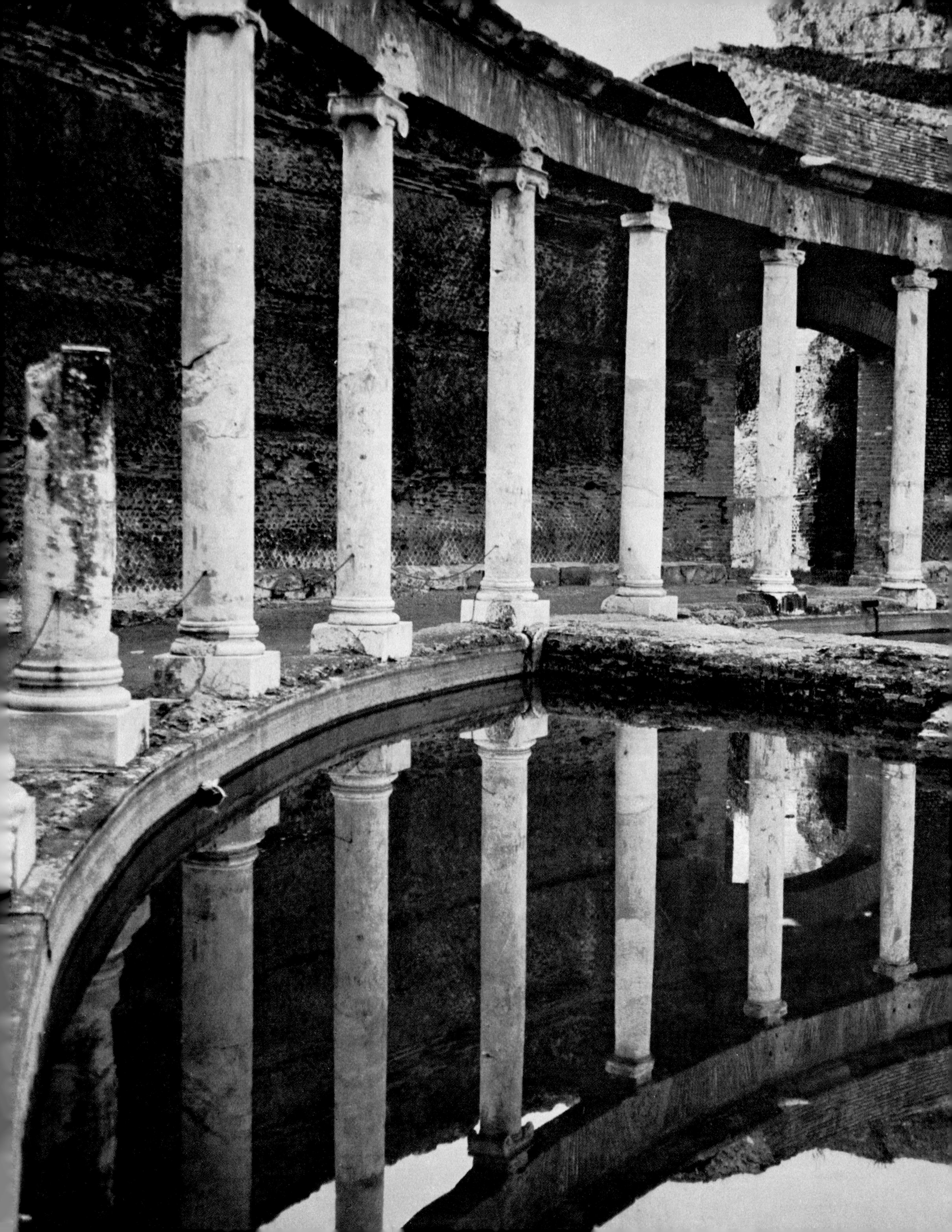

EASE AND SPLENDOR IN THE SUBURBS

In Rome, the satirist Juvenal suggested, no house could keep out the city's noise, day or night. Even the wealthy, he wrote, "can scarce afford to sleep." The rich sought quiet in country estates, or villas, outside Rome. These often became flourishing centers of patrician life. Senators brought works of art to their villas, dined off gold plates and entertained with lavish spectacles. The ruins of a sumptuous villa *(left)* built by the Emperor Hadrian can still be seen nestled in the hills near the town of Tivoli, some 17 miles from Rome: An esthete and assiduous emulator of Greek ways, Hadrian raised stately theaters, libraries and baths on his 150-acre estate. He landscaped the grounds with gardens, groves, pools and copies of famous Greek and Egyptian statues, and he simulated the Nile with a canal.

GIRL ATHLETES, *the winners of a local contest, are depicted in this mosaic from the Emperor Maximian's villa in Sicily. Such sports, and sportswear, were frowned upon by well-bred Roman girls.*

AN ISLAND RETREAT *within Hadrian's palatial villa is encircled by a pool and colonnaded pavilion. The Emperor retired here to meditate, isolating himself by closing a movable "swing bridge."*

A PROVINCIAL TEMPLE *with a Roman façade is carved from a rosy limestone hill in Petra, Jordan. Its interior is hewn out of caves in the living rock.*

A ROMAN RENEWAL IN THE EAST

In the provinces of the Near East (which the Romans called the "Orient"), ancient cities already had a layer of Greek culture. On this Rome superimposed imperial buildings, public works and circuses. In Antioch, capital of Syria and stopover for Roman generals touring the East, the main street was paved with marble and its arcades were lit up at night. Cities like Damascus and Palmyra expanded as mercantile centers, sending to Rome silks, spices and preserved fruits, bitumen from the Dead Sea and balsam from the groves of Jericho.

Romans at first used the word "Syrian" as synonymous with "scoundrel," but the Eastern provinces furnished Rome with a large share of its teachers, artists and doctors. The Roman attitude gradually changed. By the Second Century A.D., Orientals were taking their place in the Roman Senate.

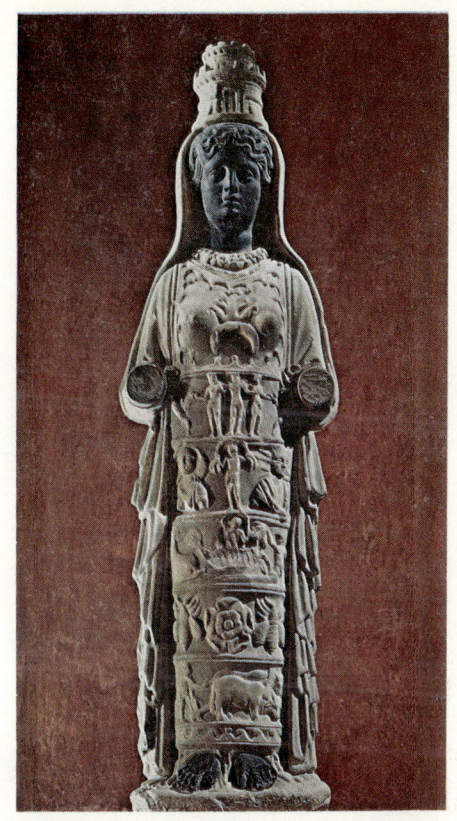

A GODDESS OF LOVE, *patron of an ancient cult in Aphrodisias, in southwest Turkey, continued to be worshiped when Romans ruled the East.*

A MUNICIPAL MARKET, *in the city of Smyrna, was designed and built by the Romans when the town's original marketplace was destroyed by an earthquake. The arches, now nearly 2,000 years old, formed the sunken first level of a massive three-story structure.*

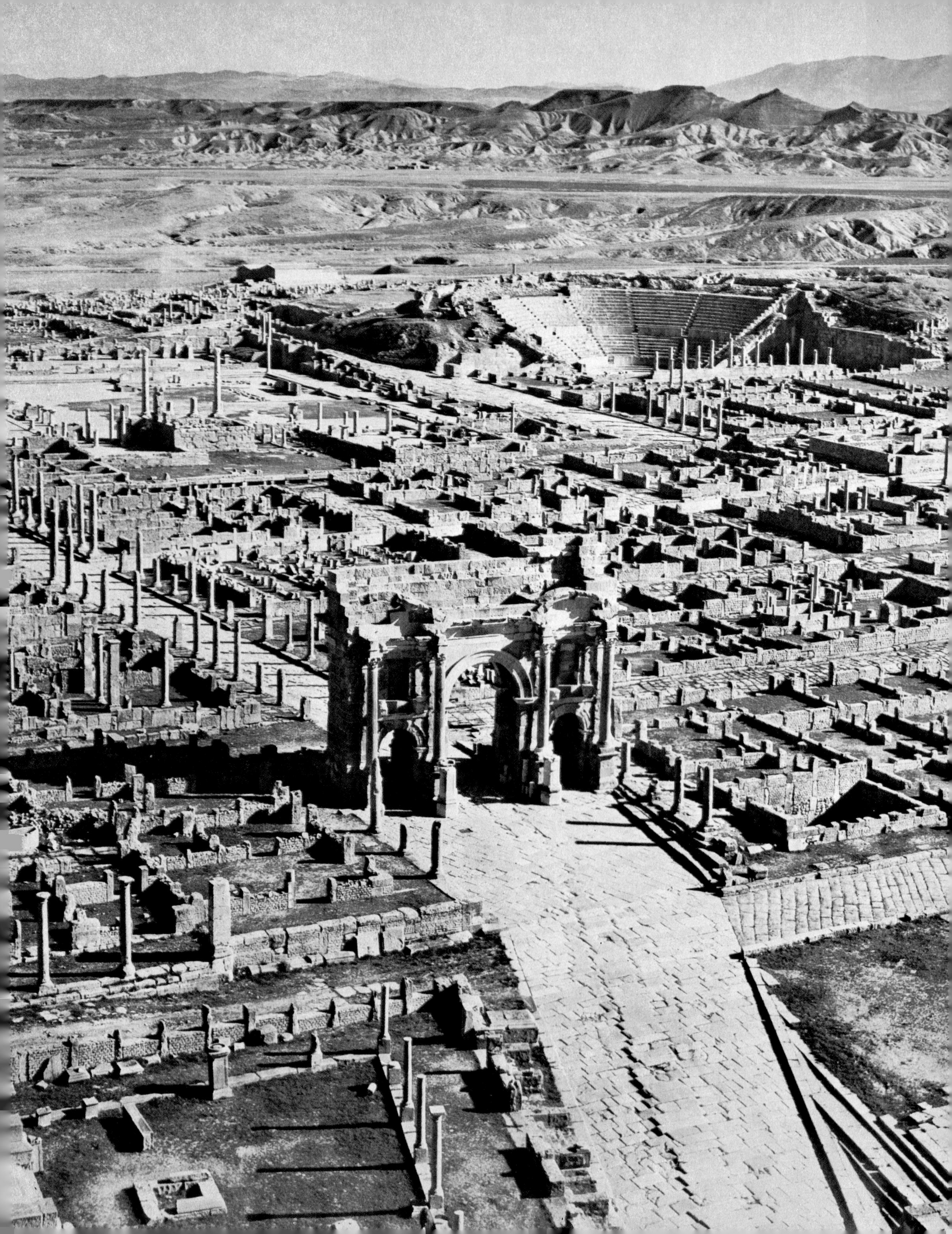

AFRICANS IN ITALY, *these pygmies are caricatured in a Pompeian wall painting. They are shown hunting crocodiles and hippopotamuses along the Nile.*

AN INFLUENCE FROM AFRICA

The fertile farmlands of North Africa and Egypt were the breadbasket of the Empire. Egypt yielded such a wealth of taxes, in grain and gold, that Roman emperors took a personal hand in its government. In North Africa 2,000 miles of coastland were irrigated with vast waterworks. Hundreds of new cities and towns were built and linked by a network of roads. Even Carthage, razed after the Punic Wars, was rebuilt.

While Rome put its imprint on Africa through architecture and government, Africa exerted its own influence. Romans in African settlements like Timgad, the ruins of which are shown at left, took up exotic provincial fashions. Women dyed their hair flame red and wore bright woolen gowns. In time Rome itself was affected: its buildings were decorated with multicolored African marble and with wall paintings (*above*) of remote, exotic scenes.

A ROME IN AFRICA, *the city of Timgad now stands deserted in the mountains of Algeria. Built in the Second Century at the intersection of six Roman roads, it had a triumphal arch, theater, basilica, forum and baths.*

ROMANIZING EUROPE

Spain and Gaul eventually became the most Roman of the provinces outside Italy. To the old, long-established cities of Spain, Rome added new towns like Saragossa, its name a Spanish rendering of "Caesar Augustus." Roads were built throughout Europe, and aqueducts as imposing as the one at Segovia *(right)* changed city skylines. Public works like these were used to put the unemployed to work.

Gaul was less urbanized than Spain but so Roman in its ways that part of the province was called "toga-clad" Gaul. Trade with Gaul grew so brisk that one import—the famous wine of southern Gaul—was restricted to protect Italian wine makers.

BARBARIANS IN GAUL *are shown bound with chains in a stone frieze once part of a triumphal arch. Captives often served in Rome's provincial militia.*

AN AQUEDUCT IN SPAIN, at Segovia, is still used as part of the city's waterworks. Half a mile long, the aqueduct's two-story arches form the final stretch of a 60-mile system the Romans built to bring water to the city from high mountain springs. The water flows in a channel along the top.

A CELTIC DEITY, Cernunnus, god of wealth, appears in a Gallic frieze between Apollo and Mercury bearing symbols of plenty in his lap and at his feet. Roman tolerance of local gods eased acceptance by provincials of Roman deities.

HADRIAN'S WALL in Britain, near the present Scottish border, marked the northern frontier of the Empire. Standing about 20 feet high and eight feet

SHIELD OF THE NORTHERN MARCH

Although the Romans first invaded Britain in 55 B.C., they were still putting down revolts in 61 A.D. Tacitus described the reception given one landing party: "On the shore stood the . . . dense array of armed warriors, while between the ranks dashed women, in black attire like Furies, with hair disheveled, waving brands. All around, the Druids . . . pouring forth dreadful imprecations, scared our soldiers." The trained Roman infantry defeated the Britons, but they still faced years of incessant warfare against other tribes, including Scots and Picts. These frontier savages harried the Romans until at last the Emperor Hadrian ordered the construction of an immense wall, a massive stonework that stretched for 73 miles, linking 14 forts and fortified at one-mile intervals with 100-man garrisons.

Thus the Roman Empire ended in the northern march, or boundary, facing the barbarian. Within the Empire's limits, over 50 million people enjoyed peace, and Roman customs endured for centuries.

thick, the wall faced a wild, barbarian land, and marked off one geographical extreme of an Empire which was won by force and held by strength.

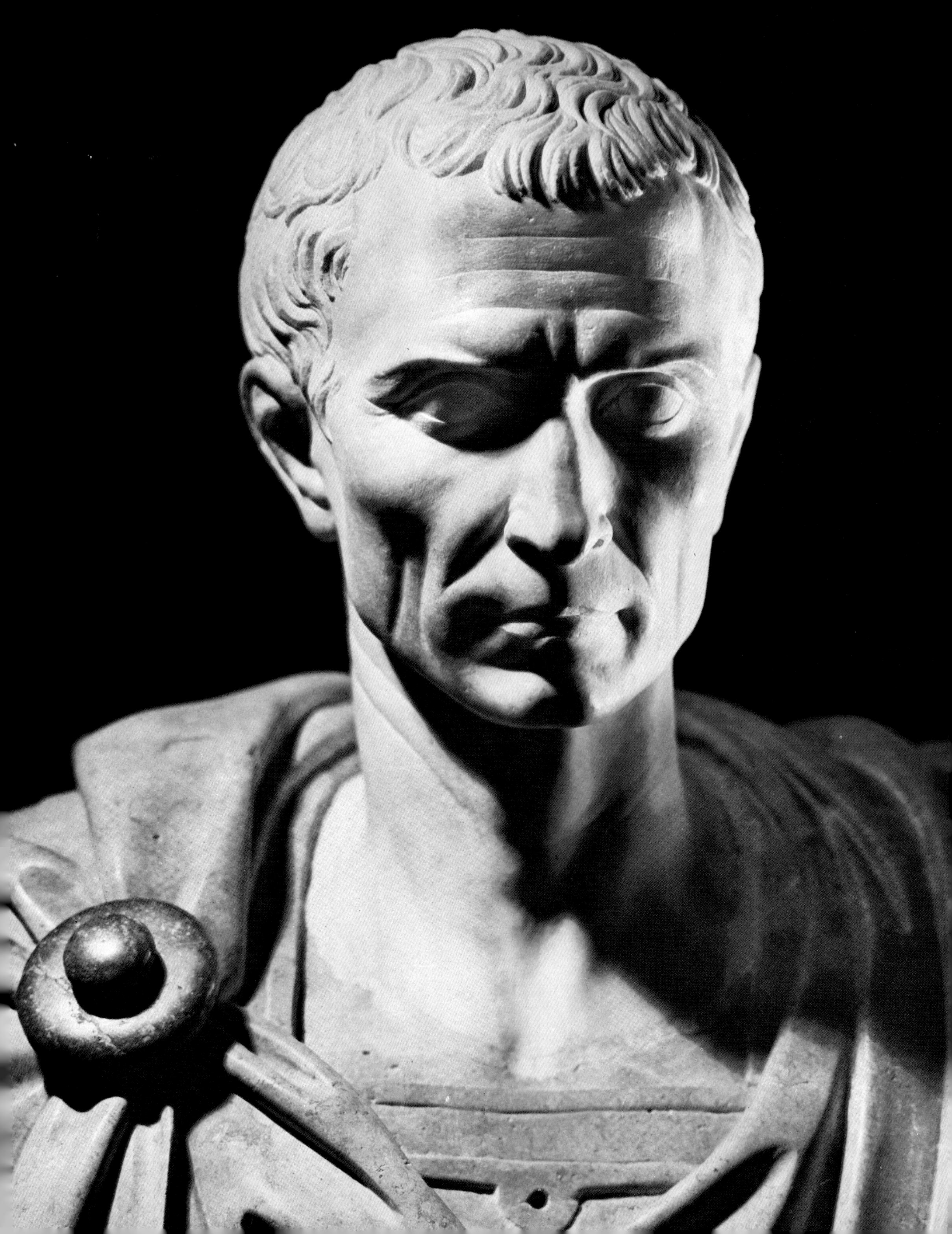

2
FROM VILLAGE TO EMPIRE

A BROODING CAESAR *is captured in marble in a bust carved six years before the dictator's assassination in 44 B.C. The unknown Roman sculptor took considerable license in treating his subject: Caesar was bald at the time.*

According to the Roman historian Livy, Rome became an empire because the gods had ordained it: "Go, proclaim to the Romans it is heaven's will that my Rome shall be the capital of the world," says Romulus, the city's legendary founder. The rude town on the banks of the Tiber did indeed fulfill this prediction, but the help of the gods had less to do with it than the valor and shrewdness of its mortal inhabitants. Over a period of 500 years a tough, dedicated people established a republic, conquered the Italian peninsula, and extended their dominion east and west to embrace most of the lands around the Mediterranean. After that they ruled an empire which lasted another 500 years.

The site of Rome was first occupied by prehistoric tribesmen, perhaps late in the second millennium before Christ, and they and their descendants remained largely undisturbed for some years. Around 800 B.C., a mysterious people, the Etruscans, landed on the Italian coast north of the Tiber and moved inland. They probably came from Asia Minor, but no one knows much more about them, partly because their language is not understood. They were to have an important role in the evolution of Rome.

From the evidence they left behind it is clear that the Etruscans were highly civilized, fond of music and dancing, adept at warfare and with some aptitude for government. They were merchants and traders, and they brought to the Romans their first contact with the bustling world of the eastern Mediterranean. By the Sixth Century B.C. the Etruscans dominated a large part of Italy, from the foothills of the Alps in the north to present-day Salerno in the south. Here they were halted by the presence of Greek colonists who had settled on the foot of the peninsula and in Sicily.

During this period Rome, perhaps stimulated by Etruscan example, grew from a tribal community to a town. Despite the hallowed legend which says that *Roma* derives from Romulus, the word seems to be Etruscan, and Roman legend also says that the city had three Etruscan kings. The last of them, Tarquin the Proud, was also the last king of Rome. The monarchy was brought down in 509 B.C. According to legend the immediate cause was the behavior of Tarquin's son, Sextus, who raped a kinsman's wife,

Lucretia, causing her to stab herself in shame. In the outcry that followed her death, Tarquin—whose power had been declining anyhow—was deposed and Rome became a republic.

The transition from one form of government to another seems to have been accomplished with relative ease, at least in the conduct of public affairs. Although the Romans had rebelled against their kings, they continued to accept the idea of supreme authority, which they called *imperium*. But now, instead of giving this power to a king who held it for life, the Romans placed it in the hands of two consuls who held it for one year. The *imperium* of the consuls was absolute, but either could veto the acts of the other, and neither could institute a change in the laws without the other's agreement.

Besides the two consuls the Government of the early Republic included a Senate and two assemblies, the *comitia curiata* and the *comitia centuriata*. From the beginning the Senate was technically an advisory council drawn from the *patres*, or "fathers," of the community—in other words, the patricians. The membership of the two assemblies was drawn from the entire citizenry of Rome. The *curiata* had a tribal foundation, the *centuriata* a military basis—but both were actually dominated by the patricians.

The history of the early Republic is the history of the struggle of the common people for a larger voice in the Government and for social equality. The two classes, patrician and plebeian, had become so sharply defined that they were practically separate communities; plebeians, for instance, could not marry into the patrician class and could not hold any important office. And yet plebeians were citizens, served in the Army, paid taxes, and were every bit as Roman in outlook and tradition as the patricians. The basic difference between them was one of religious status: certain religious rituals could be performed only by patricians. Since these rituals were prerequisites to holding high office, plebeians were effectively barred from advancement in the Government, and therefore in society.

The first breakthrough in the plebeians' struggle was the creation of the Tribunate of the Plebes early in the Fifth Century B.C. The tribunes—elected to office by the plebeian assembly, which consisted of all the plebes of Rome—served for a year and wielded unusual power. Only they could convoke the plebeian assembly. In the interests of their constituents they could block any measure proposed by a member of the Senate, or *comitia centuriata* —or indeed any act of any official—simply by calling out "*Veto!*" (I forbid). The person of a tribune was sacrosanct; anyone of any class doing him violence was liable to punishment by death. Following the establishment of the tribunate, a series of laws gave plebeians the right to intermarry with patricians, the right to hold the office of consul, and finally, in 287 B.C., the right to pass laws in the plebeian assembly without the consent of the Senate.

It was during this period of domestic discord that Rome began to extend its influence in Italy. Early Rome was like the farmer who wants not all the land in the world, but only what adjoins his boundaries. The Romans simply wanted to protect themselves, and they did so by neutralizing their neighbors—and then their new neighbors, and so on. In this fashion the Romans either made allies of, or subdued, first the nearby cities of the Latium plain, then the more distant Italic tribes and the Etruscans. By the beginning of the Fourth Century B.C., Rome was the leading city of central Italy.

But the Romans did not have matters all their own way. In 390 B.C. barbarian Gauls came down from the north and sacked the city. According to legend they did not leave until Rome had paid a ransom of 1,000 pounds of gold, and a half century passed before the city recovered. But when it did, the Romans once again took up their policy of neutraliz-

ITALY IN THE SIXTH CENTURY B.C.

THE EARLY ITALIANS were made up of many tribes, each with its own language and culture. The Ligurians were among the earliest settlers. Later came the Italic peoples—Umbrians, Latins and Samnites—probably from Central Europe. The Etruscans apparently arrived from Asia Minor in the Ninth Century B.C. Still later, Carthaginians and Greeks founded their colonies.

ing their frontiers, moving southward until finally they reached the Greek settlements at the foot of the Italian peninsula.

The Greeks were not a foe to be taken lightly. Although the settlements themselves were not powerful, they had powerful friends. One of the Greek colonies, involved in a dispute with a local tribe, sought the help of Rome. Another colony, fearing the Roman presence in the area, thereupon called for help from Greece in getting rid of the Romans. Rome, innocently involved, suddenly found itself engaged in a major war. Pyrrhus, mighty King of Epirus, arrived in Italy from the Greek mainland and defeated the Romans resoundingly near Heraclea. Rome lost 7,000 men, Pyrrhus 4,000. In a second battle the loss of life was equally great, and again Pyrrhus won. "Another such victory and I am lost," he is supposed to have said, giving rise to the expression "Pyrrhic victory" for battles won at too great cost. At last the Romans succeeded in defeating Pyrrhus, and this victory was decisive. He sailed home, leaving Rome, in effect, master of the whole Italian peninsula.

This victory gained Rome the status of a first-class power—and, inevitably, brought it into conflict with Carthage, the mistress of the western Mediterranean. Ultimately Rome would also have to deal with the three great Hellenistic kingdoms carved out of the world empire of Alexander the Great—the Seleucid Empire in Syria, the Ptolemaic Empire in Egypt, and Alexander's original Macedonian Empire. Rome found it impossible to live in a world of equals; it thought of the other four great empires as threats, and spent the next centuries attempting to neutralize them.

The first of three wars against Carthage—they were called Punic Wars, from the Latin word *Punicus*, for the Phoenicians, who were the original settlers of Carthage—began in 264 B.C., when Rome intervened in the affairs of a Carthaginian colony on Sicily. This war was fought mostly at sea, which put Rome at a great disadvantage. Carthage was a sea power, Rome was not, nor were the Romans especially skillful shipbuilders. But by a stroke of luck they found a stranded Carthaginian quinquereme, an oar-driven warship, and, with the help of Greek naval architects, made 100 copies of it in 60 days. To counter the enemy's seamanship, the Romans developed a naval tactic of their own. They could not outsail the Carthaginians but they could outfight them, and they perfected the technique of boarding a ship with a corvus, a kind of movable bridge. This enabled the Roman generals to put their soldiers on the enemy's decks for hand-to-hand combat. In 241 B.C. the Romans defeated the Carthaginians and drove them out of Sicily.

But the peace that followed, although it lasted 23 years, was actually only a truce. In 218 B.C. the Second Punic War broke out, instigated by Carthage. It was fought largely on land, and in it Roman troops were outmaneuvered and outfought by a brilliant Carthaginian general, Hannibal.

Hannibal attacked Italy from the north, bringing his troops and elephants over the Alps. This assault from an unexpected quarter caught the Romans off guard. Outwitting and routing one Roman force after another, the Carthaginians marched the length of the Italian peninsula. For almost 15 years, cut off from his lines of supply, Hannibal maintained himself through a combination of courage and ingenuity, harassing Rome on its own ground. But he never managed to defeat the Romans decisively. At last Rome counterattacked Carthage, and Hannibal hurried back to defend his homeland. He was defeated in 202 B.C. at the battle of Zama, near the Carthaginian capital.

Shortly after the Second Punic War, Rome found itself at war with two of the great powers in the East. One of them, Philip V of Macedon, had openly sided with Hannibal. In 200 B.C., Rome sent an Army against Philip on the pretext of coming to the aid of two small Greek states which he was threatening. After two years of skirmishing, Philip was defeated at the battle of Cynoscephalae and driven back to Macedon. But the Greek states, freed of Philip's domination, were not as free as they had expected to be; Rome attempted to exercise more control over them than they could happily accept. Observing this, Philip again stepped into the picture. He died before he could complete his new campaign, but his son, Perseus, carried on, only to be decisively beaten by Rome in 167 B.C.

During this same period, Rome also took on and neutralized a second powerful Eastern monarch, Antiochus III of Syria. Ambitious to extend his kingdom, Antiochus landed on the Greek mainland while the Romans were busy with Philip and allied himself with several anti-Roman Greek states. But the alliance and Antiochus' plans did not last long. Roman forces attacked and defeated Antiochus at the battle of Magnesia in 190 B.C., sending him in flight back to Syria.

With Carthage subdued, and Macedonia and Syria under control, Rome was now enormously powerful. In 168 B.C. it was able to prevent Antiochus IV (the son of its old enemy) from attacking Alexandria, simply by ordering him not to. Antiochus asked for time to consider his reply. At once the Roman envoy drew a circle around the Syrian ruler and told him to do his thinking and give his answer before he stepped outside. Antiochus capitulated, and withdrew.

Sometimes Rome exercised its power more violently, lashing out against those who questioned its authority and suppressing them ruthlessly. Thus, when Corinth and a confederation of other Greek cities refused to respect a Roman order, Rome first defeated the alliance, then sacked Corinth and burned it to the ground.

In the same year, 146 B.C., the Third Punic War

A BOARDING PARTY, *a Roman innovation in naval warfare, storms across a portable bridge to overwhelm Carthaginians. After the Romans maneuvered their man-of-war next to an enemy vessel, they slammed this bridge, called a corvus, onto the other deck. An iron spike at the far end of the corvus held the ships together.*

—which had begun when Carthage, in a dispute over a treaty infringement, refused to submit to Roman terms—ended in a similar but more drastic fashion. Rome not only leveled the city, but also plowed the site and sowed the furrows with salt, turning it into a wasteland. The Carthaginians were sold into slavery.

Paradoxically, while Rome's military activities had made the city rich, they also caused deep rifts in its social and political life. Wealthy Romans had become even wealthier, but the ordinary Roman farmer found it harder and harder to make a living. The political alignment now was between two new groups, *optimates* and *populares*. The *optimates*, made up for the most part of patricians and well-to-do plebeians, were conservative in political outlook; the *populares* were liberal, and represented the views of most of Rome's common people, although their number could and did include rich men with liberal sentiments. Complicating this political picture was a newly important social class, the equestrians, or knights.

Although the equestrians' name derived from an old military caste—men who could afford horses—by the First Century their importance hinged much more on their vote than on their position in the military establishment. Most of them were merchants, members of a large and politically ambivalent middle class whose views were sometimes liberal, sometimes conservative. The equestrians were courted by both *optimates* and *populares* and kept Roman political life in a state of ferment.

Although, in principle, public office had long been open to any man of talent, in practice Rome was still governed by its aristocracy. Government officials served without pay; consequently only the wealthy could afford to serve. Of the 108 consuls who governed Rome between 200 and 146 B.C., 100 came from wealthy Roman families that had traditionally supplied men for the position. Moreover, these men rose to high office through a fixed course of advancement which began with minor offices, and even these minor offices were barred to the common people. The bottom rung of this ladder was the post of quaestor, a petty official. Then a man became an aedile, a peace officer and supervisor of public works; then a praetor, or judge; and finally a consul.

After serving as a praetor or as a consul, a man was eligible to become a propraetor or a proconsul. In this capacity in the late Republic he could look forward to a profitable appointment as governor of a Roman province. Subject to little restraint from Rome and with almost unlimited power, a governor could and often did line his pockets. Caustic Romans said that during his first year a governor made enough to pay for the bribes that had got him the appointment; during his second year he made enough to bribe the jury that would eventually try him for malfeasance; and during the third year he made the fortune that would keep him in luxury for the rest of his life.

Graft, corruption, a quixotic foreign policy, economic excesses and economic depressions, all these combined to make the Roman political scene in the Second and First Centuries B.C. a tinderbox. Into this explosive situation stepped a succession of men, each determined to reorganize the Roman Government, and each with his own theory of the right way to do it.

The first of these reformers were the brothers Tiberius and Gaius Gracchus, who thought that the root of the trouble lay in the plight of the Roman farmer, once the backbone of the Republic and now a man without work or property. Tiberius got himself elected one of Rome's ten tribunes in 134 B.C. As one of his first acts of office he proposed reforms in the use of public farming and grazing lands. These huge tracts were normally monopolized by the aristocracy. Tiberius asked that some of the lands be assigned for use by the common people. The Senators, most of them large landholders, balked at the idea and convinced another, more sympathetic, tribune to veto it. Tiberius highhandedly overrode his fellow tribune. The angry Senate thereupon rigged a riot in which Tiberius and 300 of his followers were killed.

But Tiberius' ideas had too much popular support to be crushed so easily. In 124 B.C. his brother Gaius Gracchus was elected tribune. Gaius proposed land reforms even more sweeping than his brother's, and then further affronted the Senate with additional proposals—including the extension of Roman citizenship to other Italian cities, a right rarely granted. He also proposed that jurors, traditionally senators, be taken from the equestrian class. Fearful of Gaius, the Senate once again resorted to demagoguery: it provoked violence in the city, blamed Gaius, and declared him a public enemy. To avoid the disgrace of capture and public execution, he had himself killed by a servant.

For a time Rome's rebellious masses held their peace. Then, some 10 years later, a fresh Senatorial scandal aroused public indignation. An African subject-chieftain, Jugurtha, had illegally seized power in his own country, Numidia. Rome sent an Army to subdue him, but Jugurtha bribed the Roman general to make peace. The bribery became known, and Jugurtha was brought to Rome as a material witness. Once again he used bribery —this time to arrange, through friends in the Senate, to be excused from giving testimony. He left Rome sneering, "At Rome, all things are for sale."

In the popular outcry that followed, Gaius Marius, an equestrian who supported the *populares*, was elected consul. He attacked the nobles scathingly: *"They despise me for an upstart, I despise their worthlessness. They can taunt me with my social position, I them with their infamies. My own belief is that men are born equal and alike: nobility is achieved by bravery."*

Marius held the consulship six times between 107 and 100 B.C. During that period he managed to keep the domestic peace, but his principal contributions were military. He launched a campaign against Jugurtha, defeating him and bringing him back to Rome, where the African chieftain finally died in prison. Turning to Rome's northern frontier, Marius fended off a threatened invasion by Celtic and Germanic tribesmen. In the course of these operations, Marius changed the character of the Roman Army. Until that time its soldiers had been drawn from the ranks of Roman citizens. Marius permitted non-property holders to enlist and furnished them with weapons. Thus the Army became an organization of professionals, who made a career of military service and eventually came to give more allegiance to their commanders than to the Government in Rome.

Unfortunately, Marius could not control the more extreme of his supporters, and in 99 B.C. his political fortunes went into temporary eclipse. For almost a decade the Senatorial party regained control. But then, in 91 B.C., another spokesman for the *populares* rose to importance in the Government. Marcus Livius Drusus, elected tribune, put forward a number of thoughtful ideas for reform. One of them aroused the ire of both the *populares* and *optimates:* he proposed to extend Roman citizenship to all the cities of the Italian peninsula. Romans of every political stripe resisted this suggestion, and in the same year he took office, Drusus was assassinated. His death touched off the bloody two-year Social War, in which the cities of the Italian alliance tried to secede from Rome. The warfare ended only when Rome finally and belatedly granted citizenship to these allies.

But antagonisms between *optimates* and *populares* were far from resolved. Within a decade they flared up again, fanned partly by the rivalry between two men: Lucius Cornelius Sulla, an aristocrat, and Gaius Marius, the old leader of the *populares*. Again and again Sulla tried to curb civil disorder by strengthening the power of the Senate; again and again Marius resisted him. Elected consul in 88 B.C., Sulla had barely taken office when Marius tried to undermine his authority by having an Army command transferred from Sulla to himself. At the time, Sulla was in Naples preparing to leave for the East, where Mithridates, King of Pontus, was encroaching upon Roman territories and had reputedly killed 80,000 Italian colonials in one day. Instead of embarking, the furious Sulla led his army back to Rome—the first instance in Roman history of a Roman commander's leading his troops against the capital. As it turned out, the march was a quiet one. Marius fled to Africa and Sulla's forces entered the city almost without resistance.

Sulla remained in Rome long enough to take actions which he thought would prevent a recurrence of civil disorder: his enemies were condemned to death, and the power of the conservative Senate was strengthened. Then he set out again for the East. His campaign there was successful; Mithridates was defeated and Roman power in the East was restored. But Sulla's methods were brutal: he sacked Greek cities allied to Mithridates and plundered their temples. Of his assault on Athens Plutarch wrote, "there was no numbering the slain; the amount is to this day conjectured from the space of ground overflowed with blood."

During Sulla's absence from Rome, Marius had returned from Africa, seized control of the Government, and murdered many of Sulla's friends. Marius himself had died, but when Sulla returned in 83 B.C. he revenged himself on Marius' followers. He declared them enemies of the state and had them executed. In one instance he ordered 6,000 of them killed at once and confiscated their property. The slaughter, carried out within the Senate's hearing, horrified the Senators. But Sulla, Plutarch says, "with a calm and unconcerned expression . . . bade the senators pay attention to his speech and not busy themselves with what was going on outside: some naughty people were being admonished at his orders."

For the remainder of his political life Sulla was an absolute dictator. He gave the Senate more power and curtailed the power of the tribunes. He limited appointments to the judiciary to members of the Senate; at the same time he increased the Senate's size and packed it with his friends. He made it a mortal offense for a commander to lead his troops without permission outside the province to which they had been assigned, or to initiate wars without the Senate's approval.

In 79 B.C. Sulla voluntarily retired. One year later he died, and much of his totalitarian handiwork was soon undone. Despite the new laws designed to check the ambitions of powerful generals, Sulla's successor, after a brief period of Senatorial rule, was just such a general. Gnaeus Pompeius, called Pompey the Great, had in fact been one of Sulla's most trusted lieutenants. In 70 B.C., having won favor for his military exploits, he asked for, and got, permission to stand for consul even though he was underage and had not held the offices of quaestor, aedile or praetor. Once in office, Pompey quickly took steps to consolidate his popularity. He rescinded the most objectionable of Sulla's laws, restoring to the tribunes, for instance, much of their former authority. But he did not insist on re-election, and after one term of office he stepped down. Two years later, however, in 67 B.C., he was granted a three-year *imperium* to clear the pirates out of the Mediterranean. He accomplished the job in three months. He then turned to the East, where he defeated Mithridates of Pontus, who was again threatening Roman provinces.

While he was away from Rome, the city was again plunged into disorder, mostly through the machinations of an unscrupulous man named Catiline. The ambitious Catiline, thwarted three times in bids to become consul, plotted to take over the Government by force. His insurrection failed, and he was killed, but the extent of his support among the masses made it clear that they were deeply discontent with the existing state of affairs.

With the power of his army behind him, and a chaotic political condition at home, Pompey could have taken over the Government when he returned to Rome. Many people expected him to do so. Instead, following tradition, Pompey disbanded his army outside the city and waited for an official invitation to enter and be recognized for his feats. The Senate did grant him a "triumph," the equivalent of an official welcome, but refused to honor his deeds: it would not approve the agreements he had made with Eastern monarchs, and it refused to make any grants of land to his veterans.

Pompey thereupon formed a secret alliance with Caesar and Crassus, two other Romans who also had reason to be piqued with their treatment by the Senate. This unofficial coalition, based more on expediency than friendship, came to be called the First Triumvirate. Its three members did not plan to seize the Government, but simply, through their influence, to control the distribution of choice offices and military commands. Each thus achieved certain aims of his own: Pompey got recognition for his Eastern victories; Caesar was given command of Gaul, and Crassus was able to take the field against the Parthians. To make their pact more binding, Caesar gave his daughter Julia to Pompey in marriage. In 56 B.C., despite some friction between them, the three agreed to extend their arrangement.

Julia's death in 54 B.C. removed a link between Caesar and Pompey, and made the friction more acute. Then Crassus died in battle in 53 B.C., reducing the triangle to a two-man axis. From that time on, Pompey and Caesar were in open conflict. While Caesar, as proconsul of Gaul, was adding to his political stature with military victories north of the Alps, Pompey was consolidating his power at Rome. Soon the Senate and the *optimates* were Pompey's to command, while the *populares*, with Caesar's personal followers, were calling for Pompey's overthrow. In 49 B.C. Pompey made a decisive move: he persuaded the Senate to order Caesar to disband his army.

Caesar responded with his own bid for power. His qualifications for leadership were impressive. He was intellectually brilliant and physically imposing, a talented military commander, a skillful politician and a shrewd financier. As a quaestor in Spain he had amassed a great fortune; as a general in Gaul he had added all the lands west of the Rhine to Roman territory and had written his famous *Commentaries*. Now, ignoring the Senate's order and in open violation of the law, Caesar crossed the river Rubicon, the southern limit of his military command. It was clear that he meant to march on Rome.

With his army and most of the Senate, Pompey withdrew to Greece. From there he planned to mount a campaign against Caesar, using his control of the fleet to envelop Italy. But Caesar moved first. He attacked and defeated Pompey's adherents in Spain, and then in Greece, routing Pompey at the battle of Pharsalus in 48 B.C. Again Pompey fled, this time to Egypt, with Caesar still in pursuit. But Pompey's luck had run out. As he stepped from his ship in Egypt, he was stabbed to death by an agent of the boy-king Ptolemy, who was afraid to befriend Pompey and equally afraid to let him escape. His deed gained Ptolemy nothing. When Caesar arrived he was almost immediately beguiled by Ptolemy's co-ruler, his beautiful young

A TIME OF EMPIRE

The years during which Rome expanded from a provincial town to a world power were also a period of ambitious empire-building elsewhere, far beyond Rome's reach. In China, the short-lived but aggressive Ch'in Dynasty triumphed over neighboring states and formed the first Chinese Empire, covering a substantial portion of the modern nation. To consolidate his new territories and erect a bulwark against the marauding Huns of North Central Asia, the Ch'in ruler, Shih Huang Ti, himself a relentlessly cruel autocrat, extended the Great Wall *(above)* into a single fortified line stretching from the northwest frontier to the sea some 1,400 miles to the east. After his death, his dynasty gave way to the Han rulers who added further provinces to their Empire.

In India, after the invasion of Alexander brought a brief contact with the West, the Maurya emperors began in 322 B.C. to found a powerful kingdom. It reached its peak in the middle of the Third Century B.C. under King Asoka. After a fierce war, Asoka pushed his borders south to the Bay of Bengal. Then, converted to Buddhism, he repudiated violence and passed his years in the tranquil pursuit of peace.

sister, Cleopatra. Soon installed as Caesar's mistress, Cleopatra dominated Egypt after her brother's death in battle against the Romans.

Caesar returned to Rome more secure in his power than any Roman had ever been before. In defeating Pompey, whose support came from the Senate, Caesar had surpassed the Senate's authority and become in fact the sole ruler of Rome. On the whole he used his power well. He pardoned many of his old enemies, including Cicero, and reinstated them in the Government. He worked out the mechanics for a stronger, more efficient administrative system, undertook extensive colonization projects, provided work for the poor, tightened the laws against crime and usury (and also against certain kinds of ostentation such as the wearing of pearls and the building of elaborate mausoleums). He planned a highway across Italy and gave Rome, and Western civilization, the Julian calendar, the immediate forerunner of the calendar in use today.

Despite these good works and acts of clemency, however, many Romans were filled with foreboding. It was clear that Caesar meant to make his power absolute, and a conspiracy formed against him. On the Ides of March, 44 B.C., Caesar was stabbed to death in the Senate by the conspirators.

After Caesar's death, Rome lived through the turmoil of another struggle for power. This time the combatants were the Senate and two of Caesar's heirs: one was Octavian, his grandnephew and legal heir, the other was Mark Antony, Caesar's co-consul. Despite Octavian's right to Caesar's papers, Antony seized them and claimed his mantle of authority. The Senate threw its support behind Octavian, who seemed more tractable. This mildness, however, was a pose. Actually Octavian wanted the consulship, and when the Senate refused to give it to him, he occupied the city with his army and forced his election to the office. Then he formed an alliance with Antony and another of Caesar's top lieutenants, Lepidus. As the Second Triumvirate, these three divided and ruled the Empire, Antony taking command of the East, Octavian of the West, and Lepidus of Africa; all three shared control of the Italian homeland.

The first order of business of the new rulers was the capture and punishment of the men who had killed Caesar. Then they turned to disposing of their own personal enemies, real and imagined, making deals with each other when they could not agree. "They traded their own relatives and friends for liquidation," commented the historian Appian, ". . . proscribing some for enmity or mere friction, some because they were friends of enemies or enemies of friends." (Among those Antony insisted on killing was Cicero.) Not unexpectedly, the uneasy coalition soon began to turn on itself. In 36 B.C. Octavian ousted Lepidus and took over the African provinces, at the same time usurping sole control of Italy. Then Antony, completely captivated by the lovely Cleopatra, rejected his legal wife, Octavian's sister, and married Cleopatra. The two men were now entirely alienated: Octavian reviled his brother-in-law, contrasting Antony's profligacy with his own virtue.

In 32 B.C. Octavian produced a document that he claimed was Antony's will, and read it to the Senate: it bequeathed all of Rome's Eastern territories to Cleopatra. The angry Senate promptly gave Octavian permission to annul Antony's powers and declare war on Cleopatra. Next year, at the battle of Actium, the Roman fleet defeated the Egyptians, and Antony and Cleopatra fled back to Egypt. There, in despair, they killed themselves.

Actium ended the civil war that had plagued Rome for a century. It also ended the Republic, although Octavian kept insisting that he had restored it. In fact, Rome's dominions had grown too vast to be managed by anything but a strong central authority. Octavian was to provide that authority.

IN A DEADLY CONTEST *recorded on a bas-relief, a lion and a lioness lunge at a gladiator. One gladiator has fallen; a third spears the lion from behind.*

ROMAN HOLIDAYS WITHOUT END

During festivals, huge crowds would converge on Rome's great amphitheater and many circuses to attend a day of games. In the vast Colosseum, up to 50,000 people could watch gladiators fight wild beasts or other gladiators. In the even larger Circus Maximus, some 260,000 gathered to cheer daredevil charioteers as they raced around a perilously tight track. "Such a throng flocked to all these shows," wrote Suetonius, "that many strangers had to lodge in tents pitched . . . along the roads, and the press was often such that many were crushed to death."

These brutal spectacles were usually staged by the Government, and one of their chief purposes was to divert the menacing hordes of Roman unemployed, who at times numbered as many as 150,000. According to various dour commentators, these idle Romans were interested only in two things: bread from the public dole, and circuses. Eventually, as emperors continued to proclaim festive occasions, more than half the days of the year became holidays. Though Roman intellectuals were shocked by the carnage, the poor found the spectacles an outlet for passions that might otherwise have been turned against the state.

THE HUNT FOR VICTIMS

Great numbers of wild beasts fought and died in Roman arenas. The slaughter was often immense: 5,000 animals were slain in a single day. To supply the arenas, hunters spread through the provinces rounding up lions, tigers, panthers, bulls, hippopotamuses, rhinoceroses and elephants.

As shown in the mosaic above, from North Africa, the hunts were spectacles in their own right. In the mosaic, Roman colonials direct the pursuit on horseback, while beaters chase the animals on foot. Beforehand, the area of a hunt was closed off with huge nets. Then the mounted hunters rode down their prey, using trained dogs, javelins, stones and long sticks tipped with bright red feathers. At last the beaters, protected by shields and brandishing long, flaming torches, trapped the cornered, panicky beasts and packed them in crates (shown in the mosaic) for the long journey to Rome.

So many creatures were captured in this fashion that whole species were threatened: the hippopotamus was wiped out in Nubia; the lion in Mesopotamia; the elephant in North Africa. Harassed colonial governors struggled to keep up with the demand. Cicero, who served for a time as Governor of Cilicia (now part of Turkey), finally protested when he received an order for more panthers. It was not the animals he was worried about; the hunters were complaining, he wrote, that "they are the only creatures in my province that are persecuted."

AMPHITHEATER AT ARLES, *in Gaul, seated 26,000. Arenas were built everywhere in the Empire, for governors found the splendor and violence of games an effective way to impress their provincials.*

TOURNAMENT OF BEASTS

In amphitheaters like the one above, Romans could see, according to Pliny the Younger, that "the love of glory and the desire to win inhabited the bodies of even slaves and criminals." The crowds delighted to see odd spectacles—domesticated panthers pulling chariots in harness, or elephants kneeling before the emperor's box to write Latin in the sand with their trunks; bears wrestling buffalo, or bulls battling rhinoceroses. The impresarios who staged these spectacles were always thinking up unequal matches. An army of archers might meet a pack of panthers, or a gladiator might be forced to fight for his life against a lion *(right)*.

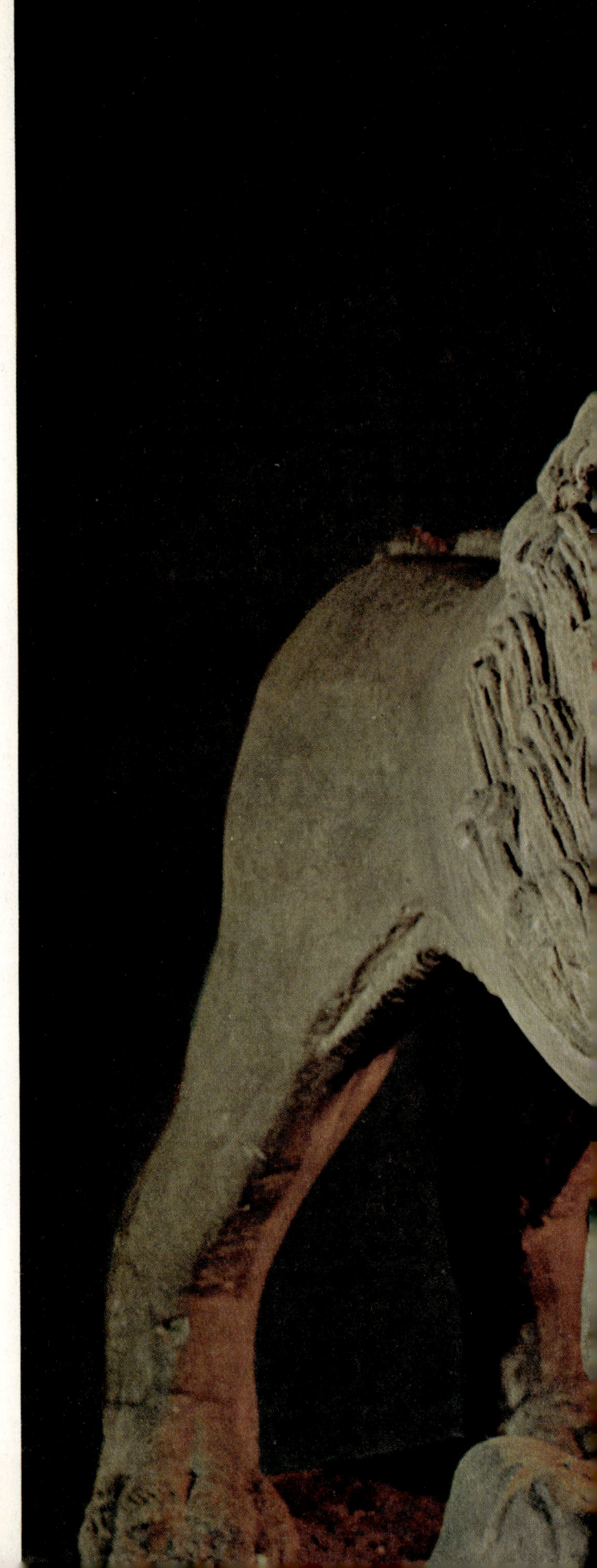

A TRIUMPHANT LION, *brought to a pitch of madness by starvation, prepares to devour a fallen gladiator. In such matches a fighter usually was equipped with short sword, shield and arm guard.*

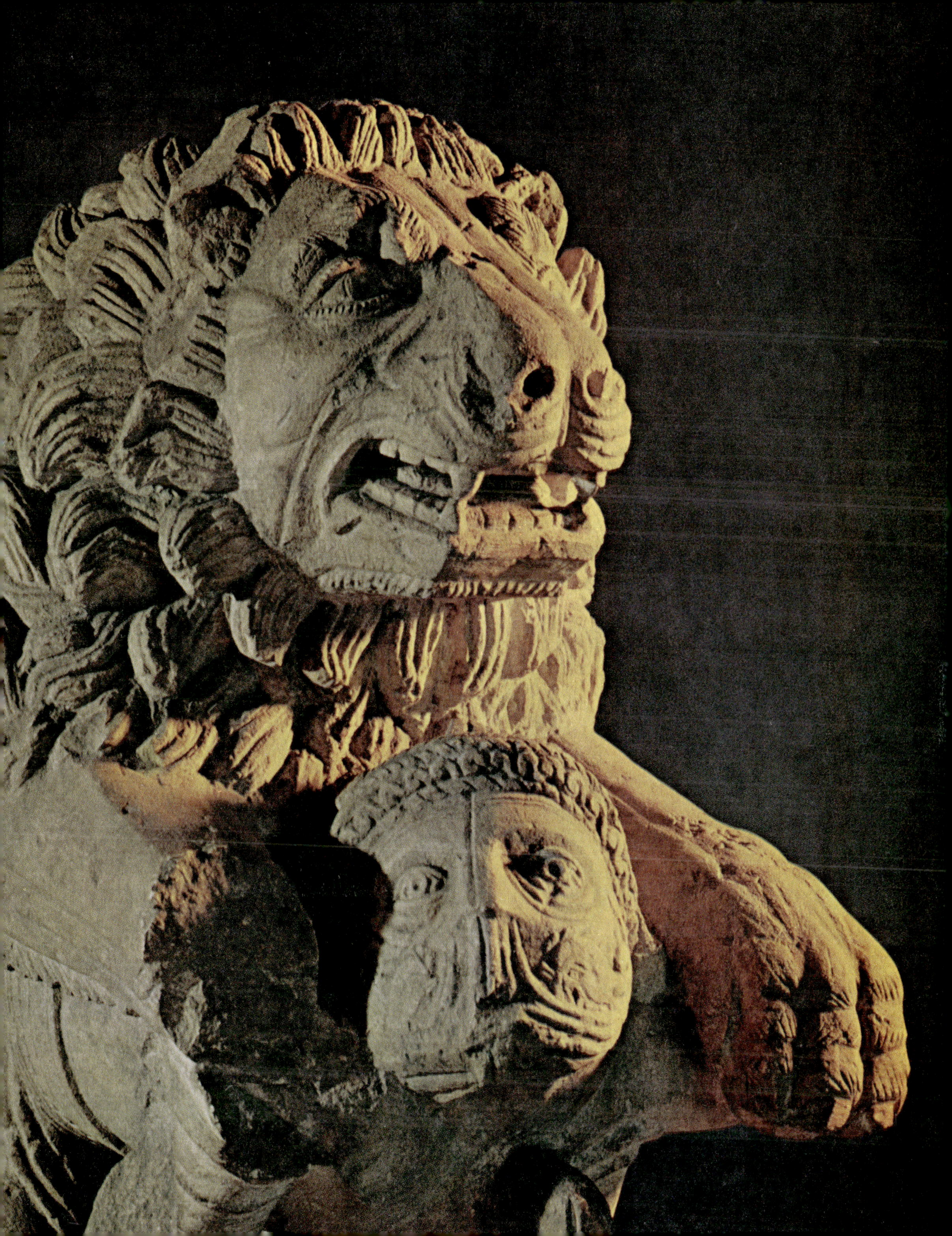

BIZARRE "GAMES" FOR GLADIATORS

"Hail Emperor, those who are about to die salute you." With this solemn address, the gladiators scheduled to fight filed past the imperial box. Most of them were prisoners of war, slaves or criminals sent through stern training schools. The night before, they had been feted at a lavish banquet, where fans came to eye favorites and gamblers to estimate odds. Now, in the stands, peddlers hawked cold drinks, buns and sausages.

The more unusual the contest, the better the Romans liked it. Gladiators often fought with mismatched weapons. Negroes, a rare sight in Rome, were matched with each other. A dwarf might be pitted against a woman. A superb fighter became a popular idol, and might even win his freedom. But if a gladiator who had made a poor showing fell, the crowd shouted "Cut his throat!" and the emperor turned thumbs down—sealing the loser's fate.

A BATTLE OF BEASTS *features a whipper who forces a naked victim to separate a chained bear and a bull. The whipper holds another victim by the hair in preparation for the next event.*

A BATTLE OF GLADIATORS *is accompanied by a band of musicians, shown in this mosaic (at far left) playing such instruments as the bronze horn and water organ. The gladiators, some in simple breechcloths, others in armor, fight with short swords, daggers, spears and harpoonlike tridents. A badly wounded gladiator (center) fights on with a short sword after dropping his trident.*

ECHOES IN A CHILD'S WORLD

Youths were quick to mimic games and sports that fascinated their elders. Just as adult hunters snared bulls and rhinoceroses, spear-carrying youngsters hunted hares *(opposite)*. The craze for chariot racing also spread to the children. Youngsters drove about the courtyards of their fathers' villas in carts drawn by sheep, goats and dogs. The smallest boys, said Horace, could be seen "harnessing mice to a little cart." A mosaic panel from the child's room of a Sicilian villa *(below)* shows wood pigeons in harness; in other panels, chariots were pulled by flamingos and geese. Youths, complained Tacitus, preferred these sports to studies: "Really I think that the . . . passion for gladiators and horses [is] all but conceived in the mother's womb. . . . Few indeed are to be found who talk of any other subjects in their homes, and whenever we enter a classroom, what else is the conversation of the youths?"

THE END OF THE HUNT *is portrayed in this decoration for a child's room. The round object above the hare may be the trap the boys used to catch the animal. Other panels show children clubbing a peacock, spearing a goat, and fighting off a buzzard and a big rooster.*

THE CEREMONY OF VICTORY *is celebrated in a mosaic showing a child in his toy chariot. Harnessed to it are wood pigeons. Now faded, they were once tinted green, the color often worn by horses representing the emperor. Another child offers a victor's palm.*

AT THE CIRCUS

Chariots wheel around a stylized track in this Gallic mosaic depicting the main event at a Roman circus. The track's official *agitator* (driver), at bottom right, whips the horses on as the *sparsor* (sprinkler), at top left, throws water on the chariots' smoking wheels. Two lone horsemen, probably pacesetters, accompany the chariots around the track. Two competitors have spilled at the turns. The *spina*—literally, "backbone"—in the center, consisting of two rectangular basins, contains ceremonial figures used for marking laps: seven bronze dolphins on the outer bars, with water pouring from their mouths, and seven wooden eggs on the inner bars. With each lap, an official would reverse a dolphin and take one egg down. Obelisks mark the ends of the *spina*; at the center, officials hold the winner's palm and wreath of victory. A Roman circus also had acrobats, clowns, brass bands and gala processions.

55

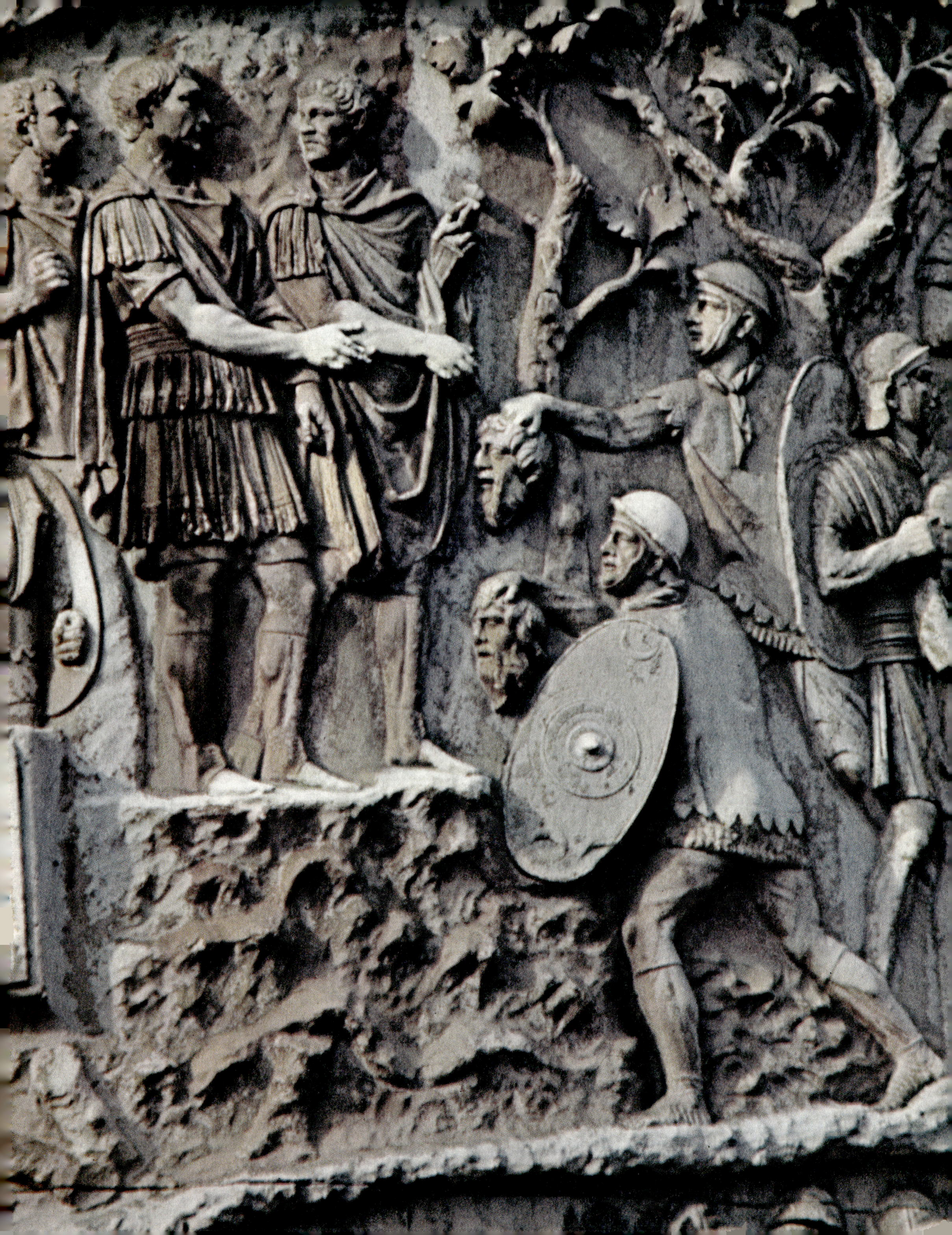

3
THE PAX ROMANA

Rome had been torn by civil war for almost a century when Octavian, Julius Caesar's heir, at last emerged as undisputed head of the Government. Having disposed of his co-consul, Mark Antony, and repossessed the Eastern provinces that Antony controlled, Octavian returned to the capital. In 27 B.C., in a carefully staged meeting, he entered the Senate and announced that the Republic had been restored. Then, in a show of humility, he offered to resign. Instead of accepting his offer, the Senate, knowing it could not really oppose him, made him *princeps*, or "first citizen," and bestowed upon him various offices of state. Octavian himself took the title "Augustus," or "revered one."

Thus was the Roman Empire formally established, although Augustus carefully refrained from calling himself emperor. The irony of this performance was not lost on men like Tacitus, who had idealized the old Republic. Augustus, wrote Tacitus, "was wholly unopposed, for the boldest spirits had fallen in battle, or in the proscription, while the remaining nobles . . . preferred the safety of the present to the dangerous past." Yet Augustus was not mocking the ancient institutions; he was merely being pragmatic. The fact was that the Republic had broken down: the provinces were mismanaged, the armies undisciplined, the Senate incompetent and corrupt. Rome had grown into an empire and needed an emperor to manage its affairs. Augustus knew it, but he also knew that Romans would never give up the time-honored traditions of the Republic. He met these conflicting demands by preserving the forms of the old institutions while reserving the real powers of state to himself. He created a new edifice under cover of restoring the old.

The powers which the Senate granted Augustus gave his regime a basis of constitutionality. For a time he was officially consul, then proconsul, and finally the Senate granted him the additional powers of tribune. Holding the authority of several offices at once, he was able to serve as head of the state and governor of the important provinces, and to exercise veto power over the Senate as well, all under the cloak of legality. The fact is that Augustus did not really rule by virtue of any office. His authority was derived from the prestige that was associated with his title of *princeps*. Under this title three cen-

GRUESOME BOOTY, *severed Dacian heads are given to Emperor Trajan (left) in this detail from the column in Rome which bears his name. Completed in 114 A.D., the column is ornately carved with scenes of war and peace.*

STANDARD-BEARERS   STATUE OF JUPITER   SPOILS OF WAR   PIPERS

A TRIUMPHAL PROCESSION, *winding its way toward the Forum, celebrates the Emperor Trajan's victory over the Dacians. The scenes shown on these and the following two pages are based on reliefs carved on the Arch of Trajan. Such colorful processions, honoring a successful general's return from a foreign war, were led by standard-bearers holding unit emblems, and by a reclining statue of the god Jupiter. The triumphant general, far back in the line (P. 61), was borne in a golden chariot drawn by four horses. Before him marched the evidence of his exploits: prisoners, a litter heaped with spoils, white bulls for the sacrificial altar, and various attendants, or lictors. Behind him came every order of the Roman hierarchy, from magistrate to soldier.*

turies of emperors were to rule Rome—sometimes wisely, as Augustus did, sometimes despotically, as in the cases of Nero and Domitian.

Once the foundations of his government had been established, Augustus turned to the task of administering it. Like several of his predecessors, he found the old offices of the Republic distinguished but inadequate. Julius Caesar had tried to cope with the problems of a burgeoning empire and the need for more public servants by proposing to expand the size of the Senate. The additional members would have come from among Caesar's supporters in the Roman middle class and from high-ranking provincial families. But the Senate had resisted this change in its historic character.

Augustus took a different tack. He left the historic offices of government untouched and continued to appoint Senators to head them. But he turned over the everyday business of government to an imperial "household" that was in embryo a true civil service. For its membership Augustus drew largely upon the lower levels of Roman society.

Under Augustus, talented freedmen and even slaves began to hold routine administrative posts in the imperial household. Although their titles might be insignificant, their functions were often important. The secretary of accounts and finance was really the secretary of the imperial treasury, and the secretaries for correspondence and petitions were in effect secretaries of state. The imperial household also included the palace cook and butler. Thus staff positions had connotations of personal service, and because of this, upper-class Romans would not take household posts; they considered such work beneath their dignity. Not until the reign of the Emperor Vespasian, almost a century after Augustus, did Roman Senators deign to become part of the imperial household. By that time the household had become a vast and very influential bureaucracy.

With a competent civil service to carry out his edicts and programs, Augustus was free to turn his attention to improving the state in other ways. In the epitaph he prepared for himself, called the *res gestae*, or "achievements," he could boast that he had beautified the city with magnificent buildings (Suetonius says Augustus claimed to have found Rome brick and left it marble); encouraged religion by building temples and shrines; strengthened morality by imposing on Rome a variety of strict laws governing personal behavior; and established a peace which endured throughout his long reign.

Augustus' civil service kept him in such close touch with the affairs of the Empire that he was

SACRIFICIAL BULLS   PRISONERS AND GUARDS   HORN PLAYERS

able before his death to give a complete accounting of his stewardship. It summarized, says Suetonius, "the conditions of the whole empire; how many soldiers there were in active service . . . how much money there was in the public treasury . . . and what revenues were in arrears. [Augustus] added, besides, the names of the freedmen and slaves from whom the details could be demanded." In later years, the civil service expanded even more. An inscription recording the death of a slave named Musicus, who served Augustus' successor Tiberius as a minor functionary in a province in Gaul, reveals that Musicus himself had a staff: a businessman, a purchasing agent, three secretaries, a doctor, a man and woman in charge of silver, a valet, two chamberlains, two footmen, two cooks, and one girl named Secunda, whose duties go unrecorded.

This was the retinue of an imperial slave, at the bottom of the bureaucracy. At the top there were freedmen who in time became so powerful they could sneer at the Senate. In one of his letters Pliny notes that during the reign of Claudius the Senate voted to reward the freedman Pallas with a gift of 15 million sesterces for his services as the Emperor's secretary of finance. The arrogant freedman refused the gift, saying that this was "the only way he could show more contempt." Later, when the same Pallas was dismissed by the Emperor Nero, he made it a condition of his resigning that he not be questioned for any of his past acts, and that his accounts with the state be considered balanced.

Augustus died in 14 A.D. Although there was no constitutional formula for the choice of his successor—this was a difficulty that would plague the principate to its end—Augustus had solved the problem simply. He had designated his stepson Tiberius to be his successor, conferring upon him in advance the powers which would guarantee his acceptance as the next *princeps*.

It quickly became clear that not all *principes* were the equal of Augustus. Tiberius dissipated much of the prestige which his stepfather had accumulated. Morose, suspicious and unpopular, and almost 55 years old at the time of his succession, he quickly gained a reputation as a depraved and brutal ruler who disposed of anyone he so much as suspected of treachery. "Not a day passed without an execution," Suetonius wrote, "not even days that were sacred and holy, for he put some to death even on New Year's day. Many were accused and condemned with their children and even by their children. The relatives of victims were forbidden to mourn for them. . . . The word of no informer was doubted."

Nevertheless, Tiberius seems to have been an efficient administrator. One writer, Velleius Paterculus, described his reign as one in which "strife has been banished from the Forum, canvassing for office from the Campus Martius, discord from the senate house . . . the magistrates have regained their authority . . . the courts their dignity . . . and all have either been imbued with the wish to do right or have been forced to do so." Tiberius, it seems obvious, respected the accomplishments of Augustus and tried to emulate him; the very idea of *princeps* had begun to take on a life of its own, above and beyond the character of the man who served in the office at any particular moment.

Tiberius spent the last 11 years of his reign at Capri, scandalizing Romans with his debauchery and terrorizing them by leaving the Government in charge of a powerful and unscrupulous lieutenant,

CAPTIVE CHIEFTAINS   PRISONERS AND THEIR WEAPONS   CHAINED PRISONERS

Sejanus. "The people were so glad of his death," Suetonius wrote of Tiberius, "that at the first news of it some ran about shouting 'Tiberius to the Tiber' while others prayed to Mother Earth . . . to allow the dead man no abode except among the damned."

Tiberius was succeeded by his grandnephew Caligula. The new Emperor was at first hailed as a popular hero. He pardoned political offenders, banished informers, reduced taxes and sponsored lavish games. But Caligula soon carried the limitless powers of the *princeps* beyond all bounds. He claimed the right to be addressed as a god and proposed that his horse be elected consul; he outfitted the animal for the office by giving it a marble stall and purple blankets. When the treasury was exhausted by his extravagance, he forced rich men to bequeath their wealth to the state, on pain of death and the confiscation of their property. His cruelty and caprice bordered on madness and outraged all of Rome—including, at last, even some members of his own household troops, the Praetorian Guard.

In 41 A.D. a group of officers in the guard assassinated Caligula and hastily buried the body, leaving Rome not only without an emperor, but without even an appointee. Caligula had been only 30 and had not named a successor. While the Senate debated the problem, the Praetorian Guard decided to pick its own emperor. Roaming through the palace, members of the guard found Claudius, the 50-year-old uncle of Caligula, cowering behind a curtain, and promptly made him Emperor. The Senate, still vacillating, was forced to accept him.

Claudius, paralytic and ungainly, was said by some people to be a fool; his grandfather Augustus, while acknowledging that the boy had brains, had been ashamed to have Claudius sit with him in public. Yet in spite of appearances Claudius proved to be a sensible, steady ruler. During his regime the civil service was expanded and made more efficient, and new powers were extended to imperial governors abroad. This seeming paradox between the weakness of the man and the strength of his government has suggested to some modern interpreters that Claudius promoted his doltish reputation as a form of protective coloring, to lull the Praetorians and possible rival claimants.

The Empire which Claudius governed was a restless one. Provincial cities were becoming industrial centers as important as Rome, and were demanding a larger role in the Roman Government. The pattern was not new, but the pace had stepped up, creating internal stresses which led Claudius to abandon some of the old Augustan policies of geographical and political containment. Augustus had urged that the Empire be kept within the boundaries of the Danube, the Rhine and the Euphrates; Claudius found it expedient to include Britain, which had become a haven for Celtic tribes fleeing from Roman Gaul.

Augustus had seldom extended Roman citizenship to provincials; he had felt that Roman citizens should have Italian ancestry. Claudius returned to Julius Caesar's more liberal policy of permitting some highly placed provincials to be citizens of Rome. In 48 A.D. he went still further: he admitted Gallic chieftains to membership in the Senate.

Once this course was charted, there was no turning back. Roman citizenship was now theoretically available to any qualified person in the Empire. The satirist Petronius invented a convincing tale of an Asian king who became a slave in Rome so

LICTORS   TRIUMPHANT GENERAL   SENATORS AND MAGISTRATES   SOLDIERS

that he might, upon gaining his freedom, become a Roman and advance in the world. Pliny notes that one official who supervised Rome's grain supply was "descended on his father's side from a tribe that went about in skins." The great Seneca himself was a Spaniard, and his wife came from southern Gaul.

By the time of Claudius' death in 54 A.D., the word "Latin" no longer had a geographical meaning. More and more provincial cities held the "Latin right," a prerogative which bestowed Roman citizenship on their top officials, although not on the people at large. The Latin right was much sought after, since it gave cities, through their officials, a certain status in dealing with Rome. The Latin right was soon extended to cities in the western Alps; before long it was further extended to all the cities that Rome controlled in Spain.

Claudius was killed by a dose of poison administered by his fourth wife, Agrippina. Before serving him the fatal dish of mushrooms, she had persuaded him to adopt her son by an earlier marriage, a youth named Nero, and to give Nero precedence over Claudius' own son, Britannicus, as heir to the scepter.

Nero became Emperor at the age of 16. He had been in office scarcely a year when he poisoned Britannicus. Later he decided that his mother too should be dispatched. First he tried poison, only to discover that Agrippina, apparently alarmed by the fate of Britannicus, had foresightedly built up an immunity to the poison by taking small amounts at a time. When the poison did not work, Nero arranged for the ceiling over Agrippina's bed to collapse. When this failed, too, he sent her cruising in a ship so constructed that it fell apart at sea. But Agrippina swam ashore. Finally Nero took direct action: he accused her of plotting against the Emperor and had her assassinated.

A great fire swept Rome in 64; Nero was suspected of starting it, especially when he used it later as an excuse to rebuild Rome to his own glory. "Whether [the fire was] the result of accident or of the emperor's guile is uncertain," wrote Tacitus, "as authors have given both versions. . . . It started first in that part of the Circus which adjoins the Palatine . . . where, amid the shops containing inflammable wares, the conflagration broke out, instantly gathered strength, and, driven by the wind, swept down the length of the Circus. . . . The blaze in its fury ran first through the lower portions of the city, rose to the hills, then again devastated the lower portions." The fire continued to spread for more than six days.

Nero, away at Antium at the time, did not return until his own palace was threatened. Then, notes Tacitus, "he threw open the Campus Martius, the public structures . . . and even his own gardens, and put up temporary structures to receive the destitute multitude. The necessities of life were brought up from Ostia and neighboring towns, and the price of grain was reduced. . . . These acts, though popular, were of no effect, because a rumor had spread about that, at the very time when the city was in flames, the Emperor had mounted his private stage and sung of the destruction of Troy, comparing present misfortunes with the calamities of the past."

Nero had always fancied himself an artist and insisted on giving public performances, in which he sang and played the lyre. Roman traditionalists were outraged: it was a scandal for a nobleman to be seen on the stage. Nero, unabashed, made at-

61

tendance compulsory. "While he was singing," Suetonius wrote, "no one was allowed to leave the theater even for the most urgent reasons. And so it is said that some women gave birth to children there, while . . . [others in the audience] feigned death and were carried out as if for burial."

Nero's excesses created wide discontent. In 65 A.D. a Senate-inspired conspiracy against him was discovered and crushed; Seneca was among the prominent Romans implicated and forced to take their own lives. At the same time Nero was faced by local disorders in Armenia, Britain and Judaea, and finally, in 68 A.D., by rebellion within the Army itself. Roman commanders in Gaul, Africa and Spain tried to seize power in their respective provinces. Confronted by mounting resistance, Nero at last fled the city. He was thereupon condemned to death *in absentia* by the Senate. At this, he took his own life. His last words were: "What an artist the world is losing!"

The death of Nero touched off a period of virtual anarchy known as the Year of the Four Emperors. As Tacitus noted: "The secret of Empire was out: emperors could be made elsewhere than in Rome." The first of the four new emperors was Galba, one of the military commanders who had rebelled against Nero's rule. He took office with the support of the Praetorian Guard, but the Guard, dissatisfied with his stinginess, soon murdered him and handed the office to Otho, Governor of a province in southwest Spain. Then soldiers stationed outside Rome decided to play the same game. The legions on the Rhine, acclaiming their general Vitellius as Emperor, marched on Rome and defeated the forces of Otho near Cremona. Otho committed suicide, leaving Vitellius in control—whereupon the legions on the Danube, supporting still another general, Vespasian, marched on Rome and killed Vitellius.

The ravages of war once again spread over Italy. In the fighting that brought Vespasian to power, the city of Cremona fell to his forces. "Forty thousand armed men now burst into the city," Tacitus writes, "together with sutlers and camp followers. . . . Ravishing was mixed up with slaughter, and slaughter followed upon outrage. Old men and women, well stricken in years and of no value for plunder, were maltreated by way of sport. Grownup maidens and comely youths that came in the way were violently torn to pieces by the ravishers, who ended by falling in murderous conflict with each other. Men carrying off for themselves money or offerings of solid gold from the temples, were hewn down by others stronger than themselves. . . . In an army so varied in character and tongue . . . every man had his own cupidity . . . nothing was unlawful."

Vespasian, whose cause had provoked these acts, was actually many miles away in the East, completing the campaign to suppress the Judaean insurrection of 66-70. His men proclaimed him Emperor in an apparently spontaneous demonstration. As Tacitus reports it: "One day, as Vespasian emerged from his bedchamber, a few soldiers standing by in the usual formation . . . saluted him as emperor; then others ran up, calling him Caesar and Augustus and heaping on him all the titles of the principate. [Soon] all Syria had sworn the same allegiance. . . . All the provinces washed by the sea as far as Asia . . . and all the territory extending inland to Pontus and Armenia, took the oath." To consolidate his position, Vespasian seized Egypt, thus cutting off the grain supply on which Rome depended. Then, after the death of Vitellius, he proceeded to Rome and asked that his imperial authority be officially confirmed by the Senate.

Vespasian, like Augustus, recognized the value of a constitutional base for his reign. Glad to have an end to the year-long confusion, the Senate decreed "that he shall have the right . . . to conclude treaties with whomever he wishes . . . to convene the Senate . . . to extend and advance the boundaries . . . to transact and do whatever he deems to serve the interests of the state and the dignity of all things divine, human, public and private." Ever since Nero's death, the Army had been openly in control of the Roman Government. Now, with Vespasian's installation under civil law, the Government was—in form, at least—returned to the hands of the Senate and civil authority.

With Vespasian, whose family name was Flavius, began the Flavian dynasty and a new era of peace. Vespasian was a wise ruler, and during his reign Romans became encouraged to think that the Empire was, in the end, more important than the man who ruled it. In 70 A.D., according to Tacitus, a Roman general, Petilius Cerialis, observed in an address before a group of ex-revolutionary Gauls: "From praiseworthy emperors you derive equal advantage though you dwell far away, while the cruel ones are most formidable to those near them. Endure the extravagance and rapacity of your masters just as you bear barren seasons and excessive rains and other natural disasters. . . . The good fortune and order of eight centuries has consolidated this mighty fabric of empire, and it cannot be pulled asunder without destroying those who sunder it."

Vespasian, pursuing Claudius' policies of extending citizenship to the provinces, gave Latin status to cities throughout Spain. He also carried these policies a step further by granting citizenship to all provincials who served in his armies. To stabilize the spreading Empire, he tightened discipline in the provincial governments and in the Army, strengthened the frontiers in Britain, Germany and the Near East through a system of new roads and forts, and established colonies of veterans in backward areas.

Vespasian also sought to restore the bankrupt treasury by cutting expenses and introducing new taxes. But, according to Suetonius, he took care not to be too severe in enforcing his economies: "To a mechanical engineer who promised to transport some heavy columns to the Capitol at small expense, he gave no mean reward for his invention, but refused to make use of it, saying that he should not be forced to take from the poor . . . the work that fed them."

The imperial household, as before, saw to the details of government, carrying the business of the principate into every province. Through this huge civil service, as much as through his armies, Vespasian's presence was felt everywhere. The inscription on a milestone along a road near Smyrna, in Asia Minor, reads: "The Emperor Caesar Vespasian Augustus, pontifex maximus, holding the tribunician power for the sixth year, acclaimed imperator thirteen times, father of his country, consul six times, designated consul for a seventh time, censor, saw to the repair of the roads."

Using the prestige of his office, Vespasian led Rome out of what Tacitus called "a period rich in disasters." In doing so he performed what was, perhaps, his greatest service: he restored good relations between *princeps* and Senate. On that slender constitutional prop rested the peace begun by Augustus. This peace had at first been taken as no more than another lull in the chronic wars which had plagued the world from the beginning of Greek and Roman times. Slowly, as it stretched out beyond the first Emperor's lifetime, it had come to be recognized as a peace not of Augustus the man, but of his system of government, a *pax Romana* rather than a *pax* of Augustus.

Under Vespasian and his successors, the Senate changed somewhat in character. The high posts of the imperial household, now recognized as too important to be limited to freedmen, were being taken over by equestrians, and the Senate began to function as an upper body of civil servants. Through its members' accumulated experience in posts of

THE MEN WHO RULED THE EMPIRE

THE ROLL OF EMPERORS *spans more than 500 years of Roman history. All of those listed below bore the title; a dozen of the most famous are portrayed in the borders of the chart. The list has been simplified by excluding certain usurpers, claimants and co-emperors of relatively little importance. The length of the emperors' reigns varied enormously. The Golden Age of Augustus lasted 41 years, and Theodosius II served for 42 years; but in the troubled years 68-69, Galba, Otho and Vitellius averaged less than six months on the throne. By the end of the Fourth Century, during the reign of Honorius, the Empire had been permanently divided, with separate rulers for the West, in Rome, and for the East (E), in Constantinople.*

Augustus	27 B.C.-14 A.D.	Aurelian	270-275
Tiberius	14-37	Tacitus	275-276
Caligula	37-41	Florian	276
Claudius	41-54	Probus	276-282
Nero	54-68	Carus	282-283
Galba	68-69	Carinus	283-285
Otho	69	Diocletian	284-305
Vitellius	69	Maximian	286-305
Vespasian	69-79	Constantine, Licinius	307-324
Titus	79-81	Constantine	324-337
Domitian	81-96	Julian the Apostate	360-363
Nerva	96-98	Valentinian I	364-375
Trajan	98-117	Valens	364-378
Hadrian	117-138	Theodosius I	378-395
Antoninus Pius	138-161	Honorius	395-423
Marcus Aurelius	161-180	Arcadius (E)	395-408
Lucius Verus	161-169	Theodosius II (E)	408-450
Commodus	180-192	Valentinian III	425-455
Pertinax	193	Marcian (E)	450-457
Didius Julianus	193	Maximus	455
Septimius Severus	193-211	Avitus	455-456
Caracalla	211-217	Leo I (E)	457-474
Geta	211-212	Majorian	457-461
Macrinus	217-218	Severus	461-465
Elagabalus	218-222	Anthemius	467-472
Severus Alexander	222-235	Olybrius	472
Maximinus	235-238	Glycerius	473-474
Gordians I, II, III	238-244	Nepos	474-475
Philip the Arab	244-249	Zeno (E)	474-491
Decius	249-251	Romulus Augustulus	475-476
Valerian	253-260	Anastatius (E)	491-518
Gallienus	253-268	Justin I (E)	518-527
Claudius Gothicus	268-270	Justinian (E)	527-565

authority throughout the Empire, the chamber also became a repository for administrative advice. When the Flavian dynasty foundered, it was this change in the Senate's role which enabled it to take on the task of naming an emperor.

Vespasian was succeeded in 79 A.D. by his son Titus, who reigned for only two years. With Titus' death, Vespasian's second son, Domitian, inherited the mantle of empire at the age of 29. He was a man beset by suspicion and fear, and for 15 years he terrorized Rome. Domitian ferreted out suspected opponents in the Army and Senate and had them executed. His informers were so diligent, it was said, that men forgot the use of their tongues. He was killed at last by a member of his own household. After his death, the Senate ordered Domitian's name removed from all public places and refused to give him a state burial. Then, for the first time in Rome's history, the Senate designated its own choice as Emperor, a respectable old lawyer named Nerva.

With Nerva began the era of the "five good emperors." While his own reign was short, he left as his legacy a rational approach to the problem of imperial succession: he adopted a qualified candidate and trained him for the job. The result was a long period of stability. Indeed, Trajan, Hadrian, Antoninus Pius and Marcus Aurelius, who followed Nerva in succession, were among the greatest men ever to govern Rome. In time, the plan of succession instituted by Nerva would break down; perhaps it was too much to expect that in disposing of the power of the principate men would always be guided by reason. During the reign of the good emperors, however, the Empire reached its height.

Nerva's immediate successor, Trajan, was a comparatively unknown but promising Spanish commander. Under him the boundaries of the Empire were pushed to their outermost extent. Trajan moved beyond the Danube into Dacia and, at the end of his reign, led an expedition into Armenia and Mesopotamia.

Trajan also made changes in the Government, especially in the internal administration of provincial cities. Heretofore the emperor had administered the provinces through a Roman governor who operated at the provincial level. Local self-development and civic affairs were left to native magistrates and town or city councils. But abuses and extravagances at the local level led Trajan to send out curators to supervise municipal governments, either as advisors or as administrators charged with specific duties. This was the beginning of a bureaucratic expansion which would go on into the Fourth Century.

The Empire under Trajan enjoyed unparalleled prosperity, the provinces flourishing no less than Rome. One index of this prosperity was the increase in public and private philanthropy throughout the Empire. Philanthropy was an old Roman tradition, inherent in the relation of a patron to his freedmen. But it became, in many instances, a matter of civic pride. The Younger Pliny, for example, discovering that children in his native town of Como had to go to school in Milan because Como had no teacher for them, put up a third of the expense of hiring an instructor, stipulating that his fellow townsmen must raise the rest. During his lifetime Pliny also gave 30,000 sesterces a year from rentals on his lands for the support of Como's lower-class children; in addition, he built the city a municipal library and provided for its upkeep. On his death, he left the town a great sum of money for the support of 100 freedmen who had been his slaves, adding that after their death the income should be used to provide an annual banquet for the people. Throughout the Empire, cities were growing rich and foundations were being established to do for other communities what Pliny had done for Como.

Philanthropy was also a Government concern.

THE EMPIRE AT ITS HEIGHT

THE ROMAN WORLD at the death of Trajan in 117 A.D. stretched from the shores of the Caspian Sea in the east to Spain's Atlantic coast in the west; from Britain in the north to Egypt in the south. In all, Rome's 43 provinces occupied some two million square miles. Some 50,000 miles of roads (gray lines) served to bind these scattered provinces to Rome. Although the roads were originally built to allow rapid military movements throughout the provinces, they soon became busy arteries of commerce and travel. The Romans also built many hundreds of miles of fortifications along the exposed borders of Dacia, Raetia, Syria, Germania and the African frontiers, thus helping to insure a peace within the Empire which was to last for more than a hundred years.

THE ROMAN EMPIRE, 117 A.D.

Grain was given free to the poor: there was no charge for the circuses or the theaters. In one of the most remarkable philanthropies of all, Trajan took the equivalent of the imperial budget for a single year and with it established a system of low-cost farm loans, the interest from which was used to support orphans and the children of the poor. Although girls were granted somewhat less than boys, and illegitimate children received still less, all got some degree of public support. This program, known as the *alimenta*, was expanded by Trajan's successors and continued to operate for almost 200 years.

Following Nerva's precept, Trajan adopted a Spanish kinsman, the brilliant general Hadrian, as his heir. Thus, when Trajan died in 117 A.D., the continuity of the principate was assured. Hadrian departed somewhat from Trajan's policies. He felt that the Empire had been overextended, and he gave up Trajan's foothold in Armenia and Mesopotamia. He also thought it best to withdraw a bit in northern Britain, where Rome had just lost a whole legion in border warfare. It was Hadrian who built the famous wall separating the Roman-held south of Britain from the unconquered north.

Hadrian traveled widely within his Empire, visiting almost all the provinces, taking a personal interest in their far-flung administrations, raising new buildings for them and attempting to ease their heavy tax burden. Perhaps his most noteworthy act on their behalf was the standardization of Roman law, making all legal procedures the same throughout the Empire. The Roman world was becoming a genuine commonwealth, rather than a central Government ruling over scattered overseas dominions.

The changing status of cities reflected this increasing unity. From Republican times and throughout the first part of the Empire, Rome had governed provincial peoples by giving their established towns the status of city, administered on the Roman model. Beyond this, so long as the taxes were collected and public order maintained, the provincials were left to govern themselves. For convenience, in isolated, backward areas Roman administrators sometimes combined several small towns or granted the status of city to a scattered tribe.

Slowly, in province after province, more and more cities appeared, and the older, more developed ones made application for closer association with Rome. Towns were granted the Latin right, making their magistrates Roman citizens, and in time were recognized as *municipia*, or municipalities, all of whose people were accepted as citizens of Rome.

Utica, an old Phoenician colony in Africa, underwent such an evolution. Julius Caesar had granted it the Latin right in 44 B.C., and Augustus later made it a municipium. Under Hadrian, the town applied for a further change of status, requesting the designation of *colonia*, or colony. This would theoretically give it the same status as a town founded by emigrants from Italy. Although there was no legal or financial benefit to this designation, it was rich in prestige: to be a *colonia* was to be as Roman as Rome itself. By Hadrian's time, municipia throughout the Empire were eager to be called colonies, to adopt the Roman heritage as well as the citizenship. Rome had never tried to impose its own culture on the provinces, but the grants were freely made.

The last of the five good emperors, Antoninus Pius and Marcus Aurelius, presided over the most majestic days of the Empire. During Antoninus' reign, Aristides, a visiting professor from Asia Minor, delivered an oration on what he considered to be Rome's greatest accomplishment: "I mean your magnificent citizenship with its grand conception . . . there is nothing like it in the records of all mankind. Dividing into two groups all those in your Empire, [which covers] the entire civilized world, you have everywhere appointed to your citizenship, and even to kinship with you, the better part of the world's talent, courage and leadership. And the rest you have recognized as a league under your hegemony."

Under Marcus Aurelius, whose reign lasted from 161 to 180 A.D., the sense of unity, the reconciliation of peoples, was remarkable. Greek writers could say with sincerity that "an attack on Rome is an attack on us," and Greek scholars studied Roman law at a great law school established by Rome in distant Syria. Provincial families, having risen generation by generation into the higher ranks of Roman society, were sending their members to serve in the Roman Senate.

Yet at the same time there were ominous signs of change. In the last years of Marcus Aurelius' reign, Rome's borders on the Rhine, the Danube and the Euphrates were all endangered at once. Although it would be another 200 years before those borders were breached in any strength, Marcus Aurelius' time was increasingly taken up with military matters. He was often at the frontiers, moving from camp to camp, personally leading his armies (and, between battles, finding time to write down his enduring *Meditations*). The military campaigns eventually put a severe strain on the treasury and on civilian manpower. With so many men called up for military service, provinces along the borders began to turn to barbarian peoples for help on their farm lands—leading, ironically, to the appearance of barbarian settlements within Rome's borders. And, as a final portent of trouble, plague spread through the Empire, demoralizing the people and undermining the economy.

At its very height, Rome faced some of its severest tests. "Our history now plunges," wrote the Roman historian Cassius Dio, "from a kingdom of gold to one of iron and rust."

THE CRUCIAL VICTORY of Augustus—his defeat of Antony at Actium—is commemorated in this carved gem. It shows the Emperor as Neptune, god of the sea, to whom he attributed this naval triumph.

AUGUSTUS, FIRST EMPEROR

The 41-year reign of Gaius Julius Caesar Octavianus, first and greatest of Rome's many emperors, was long remembered as a golden age. Romans called him Augustus, meaning "the revered," and provincials hailed him as a god. Augustus was above all a consummate politician. He was a man of calculated modesty who gave the appearance of simplicity, but, as Suetonius noted, wore shoes that were "high-soled, to make him look taller than he really was." Julius Caesar's adopted son, Augustus fought his way to power by eliminating the leaders of the old Republic, most notably Mark Antony. He "won over the soldiers with gifts," said Tacitus, "the populace with cheap grain, and all men with the sweets of repose . . . while he concentrated in himself the functions of the Senate, the magistrates, and the laws." Once Augustus was in power, he reorganized Roman government so brilliantly that it served less able—even demented—emperors for centuries to come.

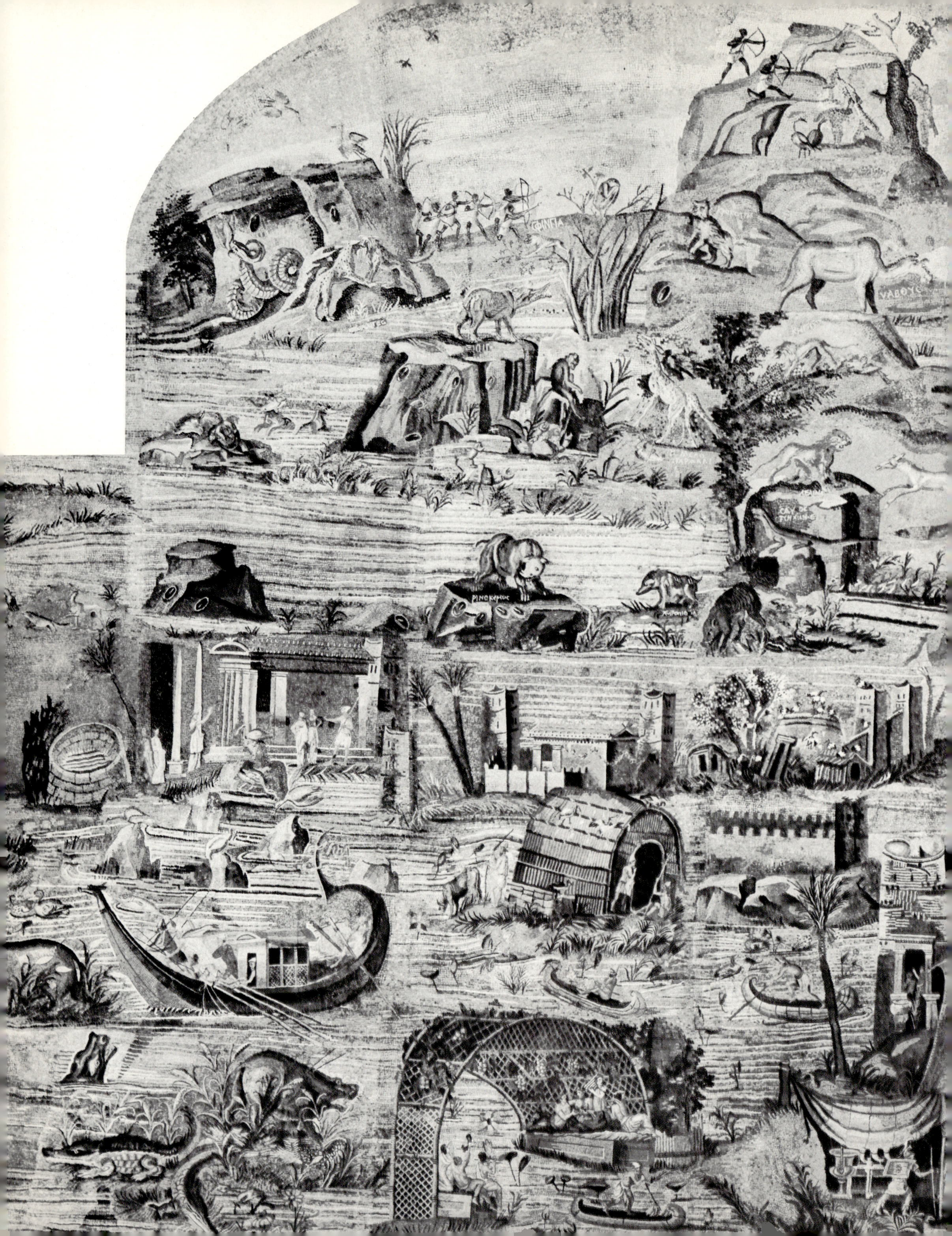

EGYPT'S SPOILS AND SPLENDORS

The Empire which Augustus ruled was a vast collection of subject kingdoms and provinces. Its crowning jewel was Egypt, a prize that Augustus won by defeating Mark Antony. Although he left the government of other provinces to the Senate, Augustus treated Egypt as though it were his private estate. He even barred Senators from setting foot there without his permission.

Of all the remote regions of the Empire, Egypt seemed to Romans the most exotic, as is apparent from the mosaic at left, which is from Palestrina, a small town outside Rome. It depicts the province on the Nile as a strange land of fabulous animals, amorous living and gorgeous temples. The upper half of the picture abounds in strange and wonderful creatures, both real and mythological. The lower half pictures an extravagant storybook life. In a great awninged building *(bottom right)*, soldiers eat and drink with women; above and to the right is a small shrine where worshipers play tambourinelike drums; there is more wine-bibbing in a latticed arbor *(bottom left)*. Throughout the mosaic ply Nile river-boats with curved prows, and canoes, one of them (under the arbor) bearing lotus blossoms.

But Egypt was more than merely an eastern paradise of finery and feasts. It was also one of the financial mainstays of the Roman Empire. Its great harvests and ample revenues helped Augustus to subsidize Roman business and underwrite Government expenditure. He made little distinction between the revenues from Egypt and his personal wealth—which, as a side benefit, made it possible for him to claim that he was paying state expenses out of his own pocket. "Whenever the payments of the revenues were in arrears," he wrote solemnly, "I paid into the treasury from my own patrimony the taxes, whether due in grain or money, sometimes of 100,000 persons, sometimes of more."

THE FORUM ROMANUM *at its height, 150 years after Augustus' reign, is shown above in a monumental reconstruction made as a movie set in Spain.*

Augustus' rebuilding program inspired similar efforts by later emperors.

THE SEAL OF AUGUSTUS, *in the form of a sphinx, was stamped on official dispatches and private letters. Augustus also had signet rings bearing a head of Alexander the Great, and his own likeness.*

THE STATE TRANSFORMED

Augustus left no aspect of Roman life untouched. Among other things, in his four decades of rule he changed the face of the city with temples, basilicas, baths and a huge new aqueduct. But buildings were only the outward symbol of his changes. He brought Rome an age of peace, and to ensure internal stability he imposed regulations covering areas as disparate as marriage and the marketplace.

The greatest change was in the structure of the Roman state. He left the people only a minimal political role and was intolerant of public opposition. He controlled the armies, he was pre-eminent in the Senate, he managed state enterprises with an iron hand, and he made the most of his great power of patronage. This was dictatorship. But Augustus was clever enough to drape it in the toga of tradition— by restoring the Republic in form though not in practice. "I refused every office," he wrote, "which was contrary to the customs of our ancestors." However, he had, as the Third Century historian Cassius Dio put it, "absolute power in all matters, for life."

GODS AND GOVERNMENT

As a priest, with a toga covering his head, Augustus is shown in the marble relief above leading Romans in sacrifices to their ancient gods. This was part of his great campaign to restore the "old Roman virtues" among his people. In keeping with this aim, his own life was remarkably austere. Suetonius reported that "he always slept on a low and plainly furnished bed" and "wore common clothes." He encouraged Vergil to write the *Aeneid* as poetic propaganda, venerating the heroes of the Roman past. Horace, for his part, supplied odes on Simplicity, on Purity and on the Vanity of Riches. As overseer of laws and morals, Augustus even exiled both his daughter and his granddaughter on charges of immorality.

IMPERIAL PROTOTYPE

The Roman Senate deified Augustus *(right)* after his death; shrines to him were built throughout the Empire. For during his reign, as Horace wrote, "the fame and majesty of our empire . . . spread from the sun's bed in the west to the east." Augustus had said that his purpose was to "establish the state firm and secure," and to be "the author of the best possible government." So well did he achieve this end that his administrative system remained the central bastion of the state through the reign of his successor, the dour Tiberius, and of later rulers—good Emperors like Hadrian and Trajan, capricious ones like Caligula and Nero, and despots like Commodus. His highest honor was, to use his own words, that "the Roman people with one consent greeted me as father of my country."

AUGUSTUS AND ROMA, *a goddess who personified Rome, were honored in shrines throughout the provinces. In this cameo, like the one on the opposite page, Augustus holds the imperial scepter.*

THE GOD AUGUSTUS, *wearing a tiara (top center), is shown as father of an imperial line. His heirs include the Emperors Tiberius (bottom center) and Caligula, shown as a child (left).*

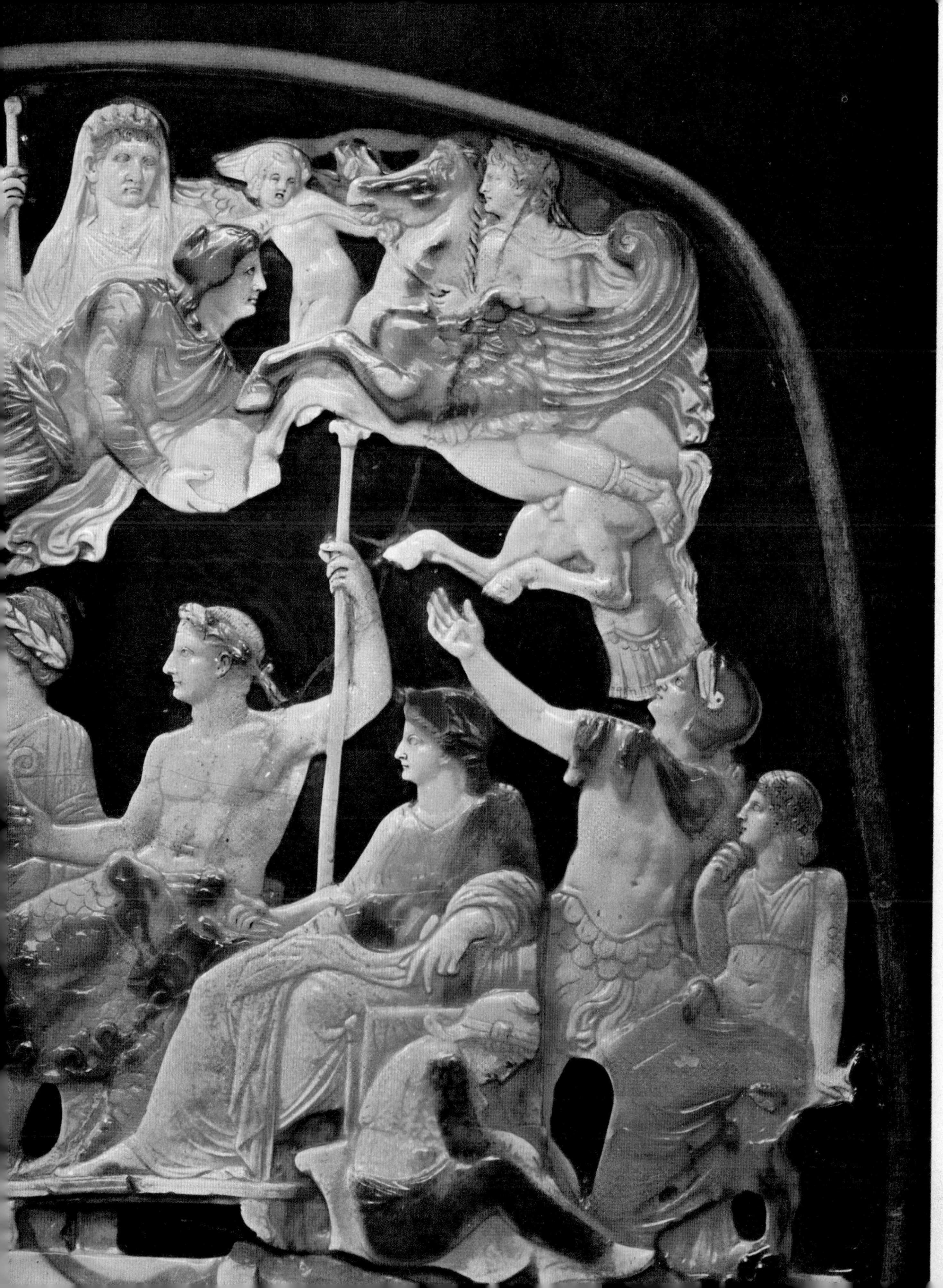

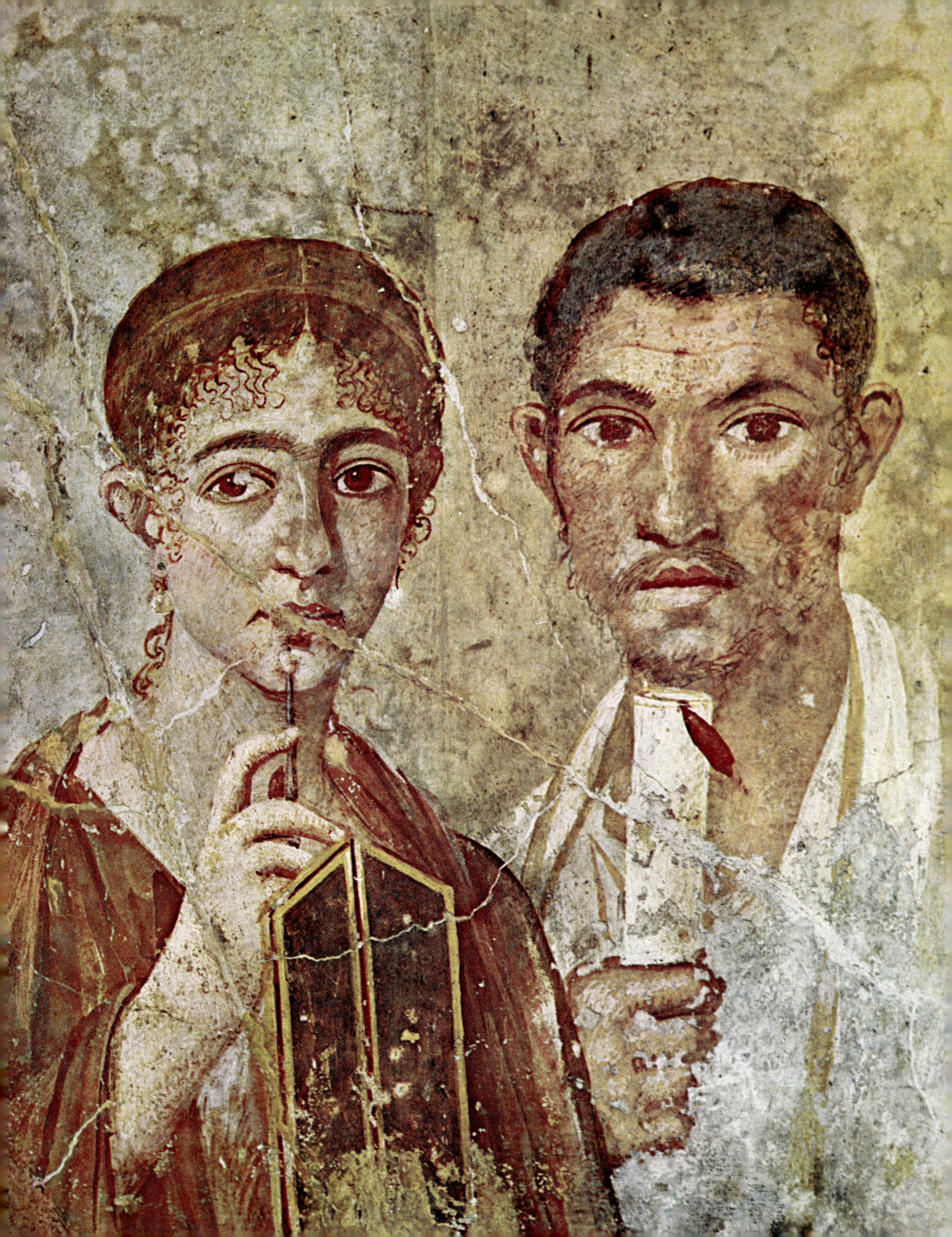

4
THE RITUAL OF DAILY LIFE

From his first hour of life, when he was laid at his father's feet for ceremonial acceptance, the Roman lived in a world of order and ritual. He was, above all else, a traditionalist, a man who acknowledged change only grudgingly, and in domestic and social life hardly at all. Thus, while Rome itself was changing from a small city-state into a vast empire, its people maintained the old ceremonies and customs almost unaltered.

The First Century A.D.—the mid-point in the history of ancient Rome and the time of the Empire's robust infancy—offers a good vantage point from which to observe how the Roman lived and the forces that shaped his actions and his values. At least it is possible to observe how one class of Romans lived: it is characteristic of ancient history that almost all of the information available on social life relates to the upper classes, from which most of the writers on social life came.

Although all Roman citizens were equal before the law, there were sharp social stratifications among them. A Roman's education, marriage, military service, career—even the decorations on his clothes—reflected his social status. Class lines were sometimes blurred or redrawn through the centuries, but the barriers always remained. By the First Century, three distinct divisions of society had developed among free Romans. Comprising the upper class were the hereditary office holders, the *nobiles*—the old patricians, plus a few influential plebeians. Next were the equestrians—or more properly, knights—who were mainly businessmen. The plebeians—along with the freedmen, liberated slaves who did not have the full rights of citizenship—made up the largest part of the population.

In both the social and the legal sense, the family was the basic unit in Rome; the Romans attached great importance to kinship. In the early Republic the head of the house, or *pater familias*, had possessed legal control amounting to virtual ownership over his household; centuries later his authoritarian powers were still recognized, although rarely used. For example, he maintained the legal right to punish any member of his household with death—but by the First Century A.D. he would have been shocked at the thought of doing so. By that time, family councils were beginning to re-

A NEAPOLITAN COUPLE, *dressed in holiday best, gazes intently at the First Century A.D. artist who painted what may be their wedding portrait. Some scholars suggest that the husband's scroll means he was a learned man.*

FASHIONS IN HAIRDOS *went through as many cycles in the Roman Empire as they do in modern times. "I cannot keep track of fashion," complained Ovid. "Every day, so it seems, brings in a different style." Roman women were adept in the use of curling irons, hairnets, dyes, switches and hairpins. In addition, dark-haired Latin ladies occasionally clipped the blonde tresses of German slave girls and made them into wigs, an aid to beauty not readily available to modern women.*

place the *pater familias* as the chief source of authority; these councils ultimately achieved such standing in custom that the father's legal power to punish became archaic. There were three forms of marriage service, two of which made the wife a legal chattel of her spouse—but that did not keep the wives from exercising a profound influence, even control, over their husbands. It is also worth noting that in this family-oriented society the stigma of illegitimacy was social rather than moral: the unacknowledged child owed loyalty to no family and so had no rightful place in the society.

A man's name proudly established his family affiliations. In such a familiar triple name as Marcus Tullius Cicero, for example, the important identification was given by the middle name or *nomen*, Tullius, which referred to the *gens* or clan from which the man sprang. The *cognomen*, Cicero, specified the branch of the Tullius clan to which he belonged. The *praenomen*, Marcus, identified the individual. In formal documents or speeches, Marcus Tullius Cicero would be addressed by the full triple name; in less formal circumstances only the *nomen* Tullius would be used. Intimates, even slaves, would call him Marcus. An unmarried woman usually had only two names—the feminine form of her father's *nomen* combined with a *cognomen* like *Maior*, *Minor* or *Tertia* to indicate her chronological rank among the girls of the family. Thus, the second daughter of Nero Claudius Drusus would be known as Claudia Secunda. When she married, a form of her husband's *cognomen* was added to her name.

Marriage, according to the Roman jurist Modestinus, was "a union of man and woman, a partnership of all life, a sharing of rights human and divine." Parents arranged the matches with a keen eye for status and material advantages. Friends often served as matchmakers. There is in existence a charming letter from Pliny to a friend who had asked the writer to find a husband for his niece. Pliny was pleased to be asked, for he had known the girl's father—and he had just the fellow for her. This was a young man of good family and unblemished character. "He has great energy as well as application, joined with a high degree of modesty," Pliny wrote. ". . . He has the look of a gentleman, fresh-colored and blooming, and a natural handsomeness in his whole build together with a certain senatorial grace." Furthermore, the young man had already served in a series of important political offices—and was rich, besides. He obviously was an excellent prospect.

Once the match had been made, the betrothal was formalized in a ritual. At this ceremony the dowry was stipulated, and the bride-to-be, usually 14 or 15, received gifts and a pledge of marriage from her fiancé. Symbolic of this pledge was a metal ring worn on the third finger of her hand, from which a nerve was believed to lead directly to the heart.

Of the three different forms of marriage in vogue at the time of the early Empire, the most formal, used only by patricians, was the *confarreatio*. Under this contract, the woman's person and property were surrendered to her husband. For women who demanded greater freedom from their husbands, there were other, less rigid forms of marriage. In the *coemptio*, the groom symbolically "bought" the bride from herself. In the *usus*, somewhat similar to modern common-law marriages, the couple would agree to live as man and wife without any religious ceremony. After a year they were considered legally married. In such an alliance the woman might actually retain rights to property she owned —provided she absented herself from her husband's bed and board for three nights every year.

Weddings—especially the *confarreatio* form— were rich in ceremonial. The date was selected with care: many days of the year, including all of March and May and half of June, were considered unlucky. On the eve of the big day, the bride dedicated her childhood dress and toys to the household gods of her father. On the day of her wedding she attired herself in a special tunic, fastened about her waist by a woolen girdle in a "Hercules knot," which only the groom might untie. Over this she wore a saffron cloak and a veil of flaming orange. Her hair was arranged in an elaborate six-plaited coiffure, topped by a crown of flowers.

The wedding was conducted by two priests. The couple sat side by side on stools covered with a single sheepskin, and shared a sacred wheat cake and clasped hands as a sign of union while the marriage contract was read, witnessed and sealed.

Following an important wedding, the assembled guests feasted until nightfall. As the festivities ended they were offered pieces of a wedding cake made of meal steeped in new wine and then baked on bay leaves. Then the bridal party proceeded to the home of the bridegroom, accompanied by flutists and boys who chanted the *epithalamium*, a cheerful and often ribald song. Nuts, symbolizing fertility, were distributed to children along the way.

At the bridegroom's house, the bride anointed the door with oil and hung woolen ribbons on the door posts. She was then lifted over the threshold (though not by the bridegroom); the purpose of this ritual was to prevent her from stumbling, which would have been a bad omen. The bridegroom presented her with a lighted torch and a filled vessel, the symbols of fire and water, essential for maintaining the Roman home. She lit a fire on the hearth, then tossed the torch to the company, which scrambled for it as a lucky memento, a custom that survives in the bridesmaids' scramble for the bride's bouquet.

Childbirth was the occasion for another series of rituals. The newborn infant was bathed by a nurse and then carried to the father and placed at his feet; he took the child in his arms, thereby accepting responsibility for its upbringing. This tradition stemmed from an earlier era when an unwanted child, usually a girl or deformed boy, was often left by the roadside to die, unless saved by passersby. On the ninth day after birth, the infant was ceremonially named and given a few symbolic trinkets, the most important of which was a *bulla*, or locket, which was a charm to avert the "evil eye." Girls wore the *bulla* until marriage, boys until they reached manhood; sometimes a man would don it again in later life for some special occasion such as a triumphal procession.

In the early days of Rome, it had been the parents' duty to raise, care for and teach their children, but over the centuries these obligations had been generally turned over to others, mostly educated Greeks. A well-to-do Roman of the Empire usually hired a Greek governess to care for his young children; a Greek slave called a *paedagogus* was his offspring's first personal companion and mentor in matters of etiquette.

Except for the earliest years, there was no co-education in Rome: boys were given one kind of education, girls another. This is not to imply that Roman women were less learned than their husbands; on the contrary, they had more time for education, and they made the most of it. Many contemporary commentators considered Roman women far better informed than the men; they were also likely to be ostentatious about their knowledge. Juvenal, exasperated by Rome's many "learned women" and their displays of grammatical proficiency and erudition, urged a friend: "Let not the wife of your bosom possess a style of her own . . . Let her not know all history; let there be some things in her reading which she does not understand."

Perhaps one reason why the women were so well taught is that once they reached their teens they did not get a formal education, but were given individual instruction in the homes instead. Both boys and girls of well-to-do families attended elementary classes, presided over by a *litterator*, who taught reading, writing and arithmetic. At 12 or 13, the girls returned home for special tutoring. The boys moved on to classes conducted by the *grammaticus*, who taught Greek and Latin grammar, history, geography and astronomy, using great works of literature as textbooks.

When the young Roman had completed this secondary education at about 16, he was ready for the ceremony that marked his coming of age. Surrounded by his father and family friends, the boy went to the forum, there to exchange his red-bordered toga for the plain *toga virilis*, the dress of a man. He was also given a man's haircut and his first shave. After this came a feast of liberation. The boy was now enrolled in his clan and became a Roman citizen as well.

His education continued, however. He might now proceed to the *rhetor*, who taught composition and oratory at the equivalent of college level.

The entire process of education and its goals were summed up by the North African writer Apuleius, author of the novel *The Golden Ass:* "The *litterator* . . . begins to polish the roughness of our mind. Then comes the *grammaticus* who adorns us with varied knowledge. Finally it is the *rhetor's* turn who puts in our hands the weapon of eloquence."

The quality of these schools was not always of the best. Tacitus viewed the institutions of the *rhetors* in particular with dismay. The students were immature, he complained, and the teachers not much better. As for the themes that were presented, Tacitus fairly spluttered as he listed some examples: "The Reward of Tyrannicide," "The Ravished Maid's Alternatives," "A Remedy for the Plague," "The Incestuous Mother."

The completion of formal schooling did not necessarily conclude the education process. For those Romans who could afford it, travel to the centers of ancient Greek civilization—especially Athens—provided the equivalent of postgraduate study.

For the rest of their lives, educated Romans continued to broaden their knowledge by extensive reading. Rome had a lively trade in books; Martial, describing a problem that has bedeviled authors for centuries, tells how he advised a would-be borrower to go and buy his book at a stall. Most of the bookshops were located in a part of the city called the Argiletum. Signs on the columns of the buildings gave the titles and prices of new books; writers gathered at the shops to compare literary gossip; people sidled up to read for nothing the books they could not afford to buy. Many Romans had private libraries, and there was even a brisk trade in rare books.

Of the several public libraries in Rome in the First Century, the two established by Augustus were the most magnificent and perhaps the best stocked, with separate sections for Greek and Latin books. The books, written in columns on rolls of papyrus, were stacked on shelves with identifying tags. A bucketlike container held together the separate rolls required for lengthy works. By the Fourth Century, there were no fewer than 29 public libraries in the city.

Although learning was respected, it bore little relationship to success in one's career. Indeed, aside from politics and the law, the army or farming, there were few approved professions for Roman gentlemen. If a senator, for example, wanted to make money in a business venture, he had to hire an agent to take care of all the details and management. Major commercial ventures, including finance and insurance, were in the hands of the equestrian, or knightly, order. Shopkeeping and the crafts were left to the lower classes.

In addition to the ties of family and class, all Romans except slaves were bound in another relationship that has no modern counterpart. This was the patron-client association, which required large numbers of Romans above the plebeian class to assume an obligation for the well-being of certain of their inferiors.

The practice had existed during the early days of the Republic as a mutual assistance arrangement between patricians and needy but useful followers. Under this relationship the rich patron offered his client such benefits as protection in lawsuits and perhaps a contribution to his daughter's dowry. In return the patron received the client's political support, plus another manifestation of gratitude that was less practical but equally valuable to a Roman: an open show of loyalty and respect whenever the two met.

By the time of the Empire the system had become an institution; according to some accounts every Roman but the emperor himself owed obeisance to someone higher, every Roman but the plebeian owed assistance to someone lower. While this may be an exaggeration, the fact remains that the patron-client relationship was a major influence in the lives of thousands of Romans. The nature of the protection had broadened, too. The assistance provided by a patron to his clients was now of a highly practical nature. It might be food; more often it was money. For a man out of work this daily dole might be the only source of income. Every morning between 7 and 9 the streets of Rome were filled with bustling clients, hurrying off to the homes of their patrons to pay their respects and collect their payments. Having collected, a man might then hurry home to be available in turn to his own clients. A poor man might contrive to attach himself to a number of patrons; his morning would be spent traveling from one to another on a round of collections. Wherever he went he took care to observe the proper forms: in addressing his patron the client was not to call him by name but must refer to him as *dominus*—master. A slip in etiquette might cost him the day's dole.

The patron-client relationship was inextricably involved with matters of politics and economics. Generals were patrons of the people they conquered; influential men from the provinces often represented their town's interests in Rome; wealthy amateurs patronized artists and writers. The patron-client tie formed the basis of many social clubs and provided the vain man with a retinue to follow him through the streets.

Women were excluded from this relationship as they were from many other social institutions. By modern standards the Roman woman was a homebody, though far more liberated than the women of ancient Greece. By the end of the First Century women of highest rank rarely practiced such old domestic arts as cooking, spinning and weaving; when they did it was usually for show. The Roman wife was mainly a supervisor. Every household with any pretensions to comfort had at least two or three slaves to do the chores, and wealthy families might own hundreds of them. Even the humble poet Horace, who was the son of a freedman, had 10 slaves.

The burden of slavery was a matter of degree. The slave's lot improved somewhat as Rome progressed from republic to empire, but certain classes of slaves continued to lead lives of misery. Those who worked on construction or dug in the mines had it the worst. They were often fed a bare subsistence diet, were worked until they were too sick or too old, and were then abandoned. Urban slaves usually fared somewhat better. After wars like the Gallic or Judaean, which resulted in large hauls of prisoners, even skilled slaves sometimes became a glut on the market. In ordinary times, however, a fine craftsman, an entertainer or a skilled Eastern cook with a repertory of exotic dishes fetched a high price at auction. So specialized did slavery become that a man who wanted to build a house or stage a show to entertain his friends would have to contract with the owner of a troupe of slave construction workers or actors.

Some household slaves became beloved friends of their owners; an example is Cicero's famed Tiro, whom he eventually freed. Others, by paying their owners a royalty, were allowed to carry on their own businesses. Though technically a chattel without property or privileges, a slave could enjoy a form of marriage with a woman slave and even accumulate a fund called a *peculium*, with which he might eventually buy his own freedom or that of a favorite child. Once he became a freedman he, too, could own slaves.

The small upper class, sitting on top of a slave society many times as large, lived in constant fear of an uprising. All Rome remembered the famous slave revolt in the First Century B.C., led by a gladiator slave named Spartacus (who has since become one of Soviet Russia's heroes). Spartacus commanded a raging army of 70,000 slaves who terrified Rome for three years. In the end, internal jealousy broke up his army. The Romans put down the rebellion and, in a grisly warning against future outbreaks, crucified 6,000 slaves and lined the 130-mile road from Rome to Capua with their crosses. During the years that followed, drastic laws were passed providing that all the slaves in a household, even when they numbered in the hundreds, might be killed if one of them murdered his master. The threat seemed to work; there are no further serious slave outbreaks on record.

The formal living room of a Roman home was the atrium. This room had an opening in the roof that dated back to earlier Roman days, when dwellings had only one room and a ceiling vent was needed to let light and air in and smoke from the hearth out. In later years the atrium became a large reception area; the roof opening remained, but the hearth was replaced by a pool to collect rainwater.

Through a similar process, the *tablinum*, originally a lean-to shed behind the atrium, became a study or a small dining room. Once the *tablinum* had opened onto a simple vegetable garden. Now it provided access to a tastefully landscaped enclosed court on which most of the bedrooms faced. This court, the *peristylium*, which was lined with columns, was a favorite gathering place for Roman families in good weather. It often contained fountains and statues. Sometimes there was a stone dining table as well. In the rearmost part of the house were the kitchens, work rooms and slave quarters.

The look of a house within, not the appearance from outside, was what mattered to the Romans. No windows opened onto the street, and many Romans added to the incomes from rental properties by building small shops and apartments into otherwise unused exterior walls. Within his own living space, a householder decorated his floors with patterned mosaics and his walls with paintings, frequently scenes from Greek mythology. Furniture was sparse—bed, chairs, tables, candelabras, chests—and simple in design, but it was often richly decorated with ivory or gold.

In wealthy homes, there was also a *triclinium*, or formal dining room. The dinner party was the main event of Roman social life, and it adhered closely to a traditional form. In the *triclinium* were usually three couches, each capacious enough to hold three reclining guests. When the Roman planned a small party, he composed his guest list so as to have between three and nine people dining, including members of the family. "Not less than the Graces nor more than the Muses," was the formula he went by.

A luxurious party began in the early afternoon and ran well into the evening. The guests assembled, removed their shoes and took their places on the couches, reclining on their left elbows before movable tables. The room was often decorated with flowers: blossoms were credited with absorbing the fumes from the lamp lights and with neutralizing the intoxicating properties of wine as well.

Romans ate three-course meals. First came the *gustus*, an appetizer course that might include salads, shellfish, eggs and honey wine. Then the *cena*, or dinner proper, was served. The hosts went to great lengths to achieve exotic novelty. Juvenal describes one such meal: "The huge lobster, garnished with asparagus . . . a mullet from Corsica . . . the finest lamprey the Straits of Sicily can purvey . . . a goose's liver, a capon as big as a house, a boar piping hot . . . truffles and . . . apples."

GOURMETS OF ANTIQUITY

THE ROMAN BANQUET *included everything from the raw fish and crustaceans shown in the mosaic above, to the exotic specialties listed on the menu below, taken from the famous cookbook by Apicius. The affair usually lasted through the night. Entertainment was provided by dancers, musicians, acrobats and poets.*

APPETIZERS

Jellyfish and eggs
Sow's udders stuffed with salted sea urchins
Patina of brains cooked with milk and eggs
Boiled tree fungi with peppered fish-fat sauce
Sea urchins with spices, honey,
oil and egg sauce

MAIN COURSE

Fallow deer roasted with onion sauce, rue,
Jericho dates, raisins, oil and honey
Boiled ostrich with sweet sauce
Turtle dove boiled in its feathers
Roast parrot
Dormice stuffed with pork and pine kernels
Ham boiled with figs and bay leaves, rubbed
with honey, baked in pastry crust
Flamingo boiled with dates

DESSERT

Fricassee of roses with pastry
Stoned dates stuffed with nuts and pine
kernels, fried in honey
Hot African sweet-wine cakes
with honey

During such sumptuous feasts the guests were beguiled by professional entertainers. Then came a "second table" of desserts, with cakes, fruits, nuts, and wine mixed with water. Each guest had his own servant beside him to see to his comfort, to wash his hands between courses, to help him put his shoes on and to light his way home. It was considered good manners for the departing guest to take home tidbits.

No such luxury was seen at the tables of the poorer Romans, where the traditional staples were bread, olives and grapes, with honey for sweetening. Most Romans of the lower classes ate little meat; in fact, soldiers on a campaign once complained because they were issued a meat ration when their grain supplies ran out. What meat they did eat was usually mutton or pork. Romans liked fruits, and generals returning from foreign service took special pride in introducing new species from distant lands.

Romans ate little or no breakfast. The early Romans took their chief meal, the *cena*, at midday; eventually a late afternoon *cena* became fashionable, and with it the *prandium*, or lunch, consisting simply of leftovers from the previous night's meal.

For formal dress all Roman citizens wore togas, which encased them in dignity and about 10 square yards of undyed wool. Senatorial togas bore a broad purple stripe; equestrians were entitled to a narrower stripe of the same rich color. Under their togas, Romans wore a tunic—a woolen shirt extending to the calf—that also served as a nightshirt. When working, or when lounging informally, a man wore only a tunic; in cold weather he might wear several under his toga. Emperor Augustus, a man susceptible to cold, wore as many as four tunics and also wrapped long strips of wool around his legs. Only outdoor laborers wore hats, but everybody wore strap sandals. In bad weather or for formal occasions most Romans used heavier shoes which somewhat resembled modern footwear.

Women wore a long *stola*, or exterior tunic, belted at the waist, over the inner tunic. A rectangular cloak was worn outdoors. Roman ladies carried parasols and fans. They also used mirrors and combs, and their coiffures, from the First Century onward, became increasingly elaborate.

The Roman at leisure might gamble with dice at home or play simple games, but usually he demanded spectator entertainment—circuses, plays, beast-baiting and gladiatorial combats. Such spectacles were frequent and long-lasting, often running from dawn to dusk. Admission was free. There were no team sports.

Public bathing was practically another form of entertainment. Beginning in the Second Century B.C., bathing establishments became more and more elaborate, providing not only baths but games, lectures, musical performances, calisthenics, and places to lounge and gossip. Seneca, who once lodged over a public bath, has left a vivid description of its sights and sounds:

> *When your strenuous gentleman, for example, is exercising himself by flourishing leaden weights; when he is working hard or else pretending to be working hard, I can hear him grunt, and when he releases his imprisoned breath, I can hear him panting in wheezy and high-pitched tones. Or perhaps I notice some lazy fellow, content with a cheap rubdown, and hear the crack of the pummelling hands on his shoulders, varying in sound as the hand is laid on flat or hollow. . . . Add to this the arresting of an occasional roisterer or pickpocket, the racket of the man who always likes to hear his own voice in the bathroom, or the enthusiast who plunges into the swimming tank with*

A CITY WITHIN A CITY

ELABORATE PUBLIC BATHS constructed by the Emperor Caracalla were a center of Roman social life and one of the great engineering triumphs of the Third Century A.D. Sprawling over some 33 acres on Rome's outskirts, the baths were a vast complex of business and entertainment establishments. At the center of everything were the baths themselves —a "frigidarium" (cold bath), several "tepidaria" (warm baths) and a "calidarium" (steam bath); most bathers passed through them in that order. Aqueducts fed thousands of gallons of mountain water into the system. Water for the "tepidaria" and "calidarium" was heated by wood-burning furnaces connected to a network of steam pipes beneath the floors. The cutaway illustration below and the ground plan accompanying it are based on the impressive ruins still standing at the site.

1. Libraries
2. Gymnasia
3. Sports stadium
4. Shops and offices
5. *Frigidarium*
6. *Tepidaria*
7. *Calidarium*

unconscionable noise and splashing. . . . Then the cakeseller with his varied cries, the sausagemen, the confectioner, and all the vendors of food hawking their wares, each with his own distinctive intonation.

Among the best preserved and most magnificent of the public baths were those built by the Emperor Caracalla. Large sections of this Roman showplace, which accommodated 1,600 bathers a day, still survive. A spacious central building gave access to various dressing, bathing, club and game rooms. Underground furnaces heated the water and poured steaming hot air into spaces between the outer and inner walls. The grounds were decorated with gardens, colonnaded walks and statuary.

The baths were but one expression of the Romans' love of grandeur, of imposing buildings and impressive public areas. Of all the monumental works in the great metropolis, nothing matched the majestic vastness of the open forums, where all of Rome met for business or pleasure. "I need no ivory temple for my delight," wrote the poet Propertius; "enough that I can see the Roman Forum." The original Forum Romanum, built over a filled-in swamp at the foot of the Palatine Hill, was the seat of the city's business and government, a place to shop, meet friends, exchange gossip and watch public ceremonies.

Along with the grandeur of the city, Romans had to accept many limitations. For one thing, a townsman had to carry a map of the capital in his head: most of the residential streets were unnamed and all houses were unnumbered. Any stranger in town quickly found that a guide was an absolute necessity. There were few sidewalks. The streets were narrow and crowded and—in an era when the easiest way to dispose of trash was to throw it out the window—frequently dangerous.

A walk through Rome at night was a grim adventure. There was no street lighting. Chariots, tradesmen's carts and other heavy traffic, barred from the streets by day, jammed them by night. Prostitutes prowled the avenues. Crime was rampant. Wise Romans stayed home after sunset.

Travel outside the city, by day or by night, was almost equally difficult. The well-to-do traveled by carriage, accompanied by a large retinue of slaves and servants. Rather than stop in the hostelries—which offered little comfort and much dirt, and tended to be robber hangouts—the Roman traveler preferred to sleep in his carriage, or in a tent pitched by the roadside—or, even better, with a friend, if he could find one on his route. There was a whole social system of *hospitium*, or "guest-friendship," that was like lodge membership: men who were bound by the tie of *hospitium* felt obliged to afford one another protection and hospitality on the road.

Because of their strong sense of family and tradition, the Romans were especially attentive to ceremonies surrounding death and burial. When a man died, professional undertakers prepared his body for burial or cremation, and dressed it in a toga adorned with the insignia of whatever offices he might have held in life. The body, reclining on a funeral bed, was borne to the burial place, followed by a slow procession of family, professional mourners and actors wearing the death masks of distinguished ancestors. Music accompanied the ritual. The poor were buried in common pits, the wealthy in ornate roadside tombs. Some Romans formed clubs and built joint burial places that came to hold hundreds of urns in tiers of niches.

From birth to death, the life of the Roman was determined by position and regulated by traditions, many of which survive today. The persistence of these rituals the ancient Roman would find only a fitting and proper tribute to his civilization, which set such store by them.

AN ASSAULT TOWER *is rolled toward the wall of Avaricum, where the Romans staged one of their greatest sieges.*

MASTERS OF WAR

"He who desires peace should prepare for war." This maxim by the military writer Vegetius was a keystone of Roman foreign policy, and Rome's standing Army remained unequaled for centuries. In building their military machine the Romans borrowed weapons and tactics wherever they could find them—from the Macedonians, the Carthaginians, the Spanish. But the real strength of the Army lay in its men. Romans were bred to warfare. The aristocracy produced such brilliant generals as Julius Caesar and Pompey. The common people contributed fearless infantry. Roman warriors fought, said Josephus, a Jewish historian who lived through a Roman siege, as if their weapons were permanently attached to them.

89

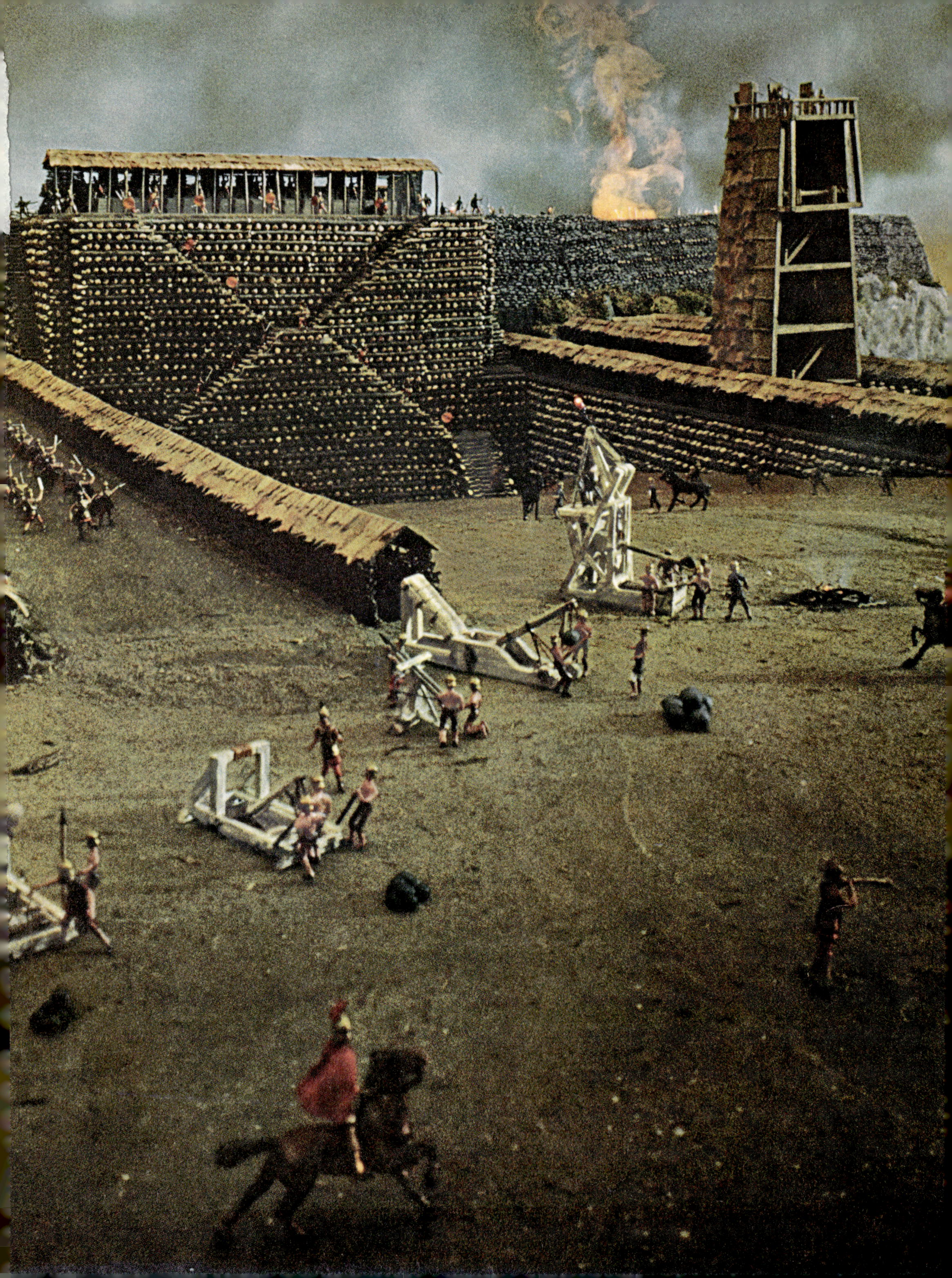

ROMAN SUPREMACY IN THE SIEGE

The Romans were experts at the ancient art of siege warfare. They demonstrated their mastery on many occasions, notably in the siege of the old Gallic town of Avaricum in 52 B.C., which brought Julius Caesar a dramatic triumph over the Gauls. When the Gauls holed up in the fortress-town, Caesar built a great siegework—a broad terrace and two ramps—against its massive, heavily defended wall. Then his legionaries rolled two assault towers up the ramps and fought across the wall, as shown at left and on the following pages.

The whole siegework and much of the supporting weaponry had to be constructed on the spot. The soldiers carried their own saws, pickaxes and other tools; in addition each legion had its specialists—masons, smiths, carpenters. Trees were felled for timber, leaving the terrain studded with stumps (left). Most of the construction was done under hastily built sheds erected to protect the soldiers from the barrage of arrows, javelins, stones, logs, molten pitch and firebrands hurled by the defenders.

The Gauls also took more direct measures to nullify the Roman efforts. As the towers grew higher, the besieged forces raised their own towers and attempted to destroy the Roman works. Caesar kept his men at the task day and night, for 25 days. When at last the Romans were ready, the terrace stood 77 feet high, and the towers rose some 20 feet over the top of the wall. Drawbridges were let down, and hundreds of Roman soldiers poured into the town.

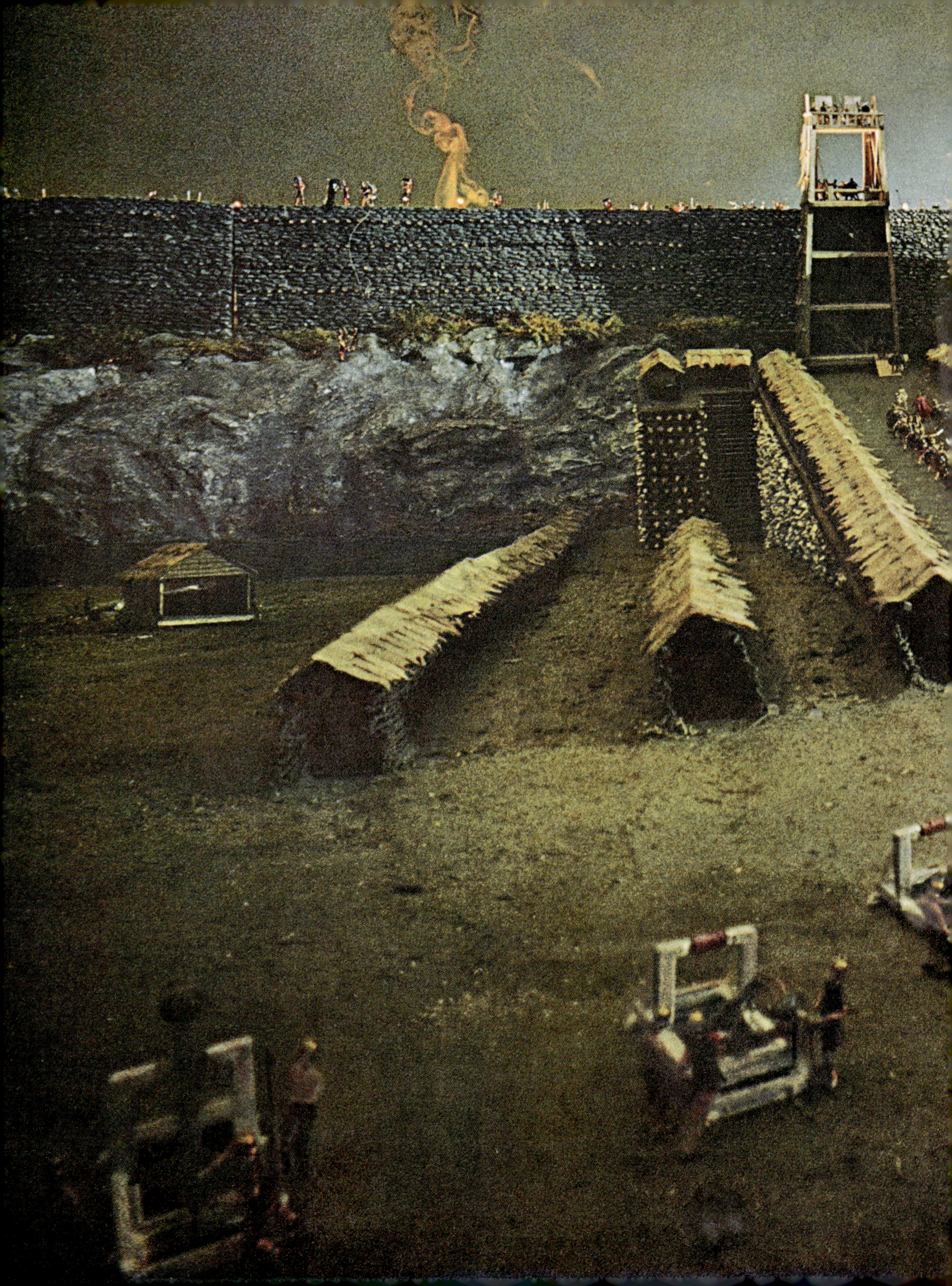

THE ROMAN BATTLE PLAN *in the Siege of Avaricum is shown in this specially constructed model. On limestone cliffs at the foot of the town wall (far left), a detachment of Roman soldiers attempts to pry stones loose, while the Gauls above bombard them and try to catch their tools in a noose. To their right, between two long sheds used to protect workmen, a group of soldiers marches toward an assault tower whose drawbridge has been lowered onto the wall. The broad siege terrace at top center, built of logs, supports a gallery from which archers, slingers, javelin hurlers and other troops fire down on defending Gauls. Reinforcements rush up the steps of the terrace to replace the wounded. The second assault tower, on the right, is still being pushed into place by men and teams of horses. Arrayed on the field at center are Roman war machines, hurling missiles at and over the wall. Flaming projectiles have set fires within the town. Watching the action in the right foreground is Caesar, mounted on a white charger. A trumpeter at his left transmits his orders to the troops.*

A FIRE THROWER, *this large ballista could fling 12-foot flaming darts 2,000 feet or more. Soldiers turn windlasses to add tension to the firing ropes.*

THE FEARSOME ARSENAL OF ROMAN WAR MACHINES

A MOBILE CATAPULT, this onager hurled heavy rocks or bags of small stones—the Roman equivalent of shrapnel. A larger version of the onager is shown below.

A LETHAL CROSSBOW, this weapon fired long darts tipped with burning rags. It could shoot its projectiles in rapid succession—and strike home with very great accuracy.

HEAVY ARTILLERY came in various sizes. A small ballista (left) had a range of about 1,400 feet; a large onager (right) could lob a 60-pound missile a distance of half a mile.

THE ASSAULT ON THE RAMPARTS

APPROACHING THE WALL, *a detachment of Roman soldiers moves up behind the assault tower as it is slowly rolled into place. The men on top of the tower rain missiles on the hard-pressed Gauls.*

THE FINAL ATTACK *comes as Romans charge over a drawbridge which has been dropped from their assault tower. Amid the melee, at the lower left, a Roman standard-bearer raises his golden eagle.*

96

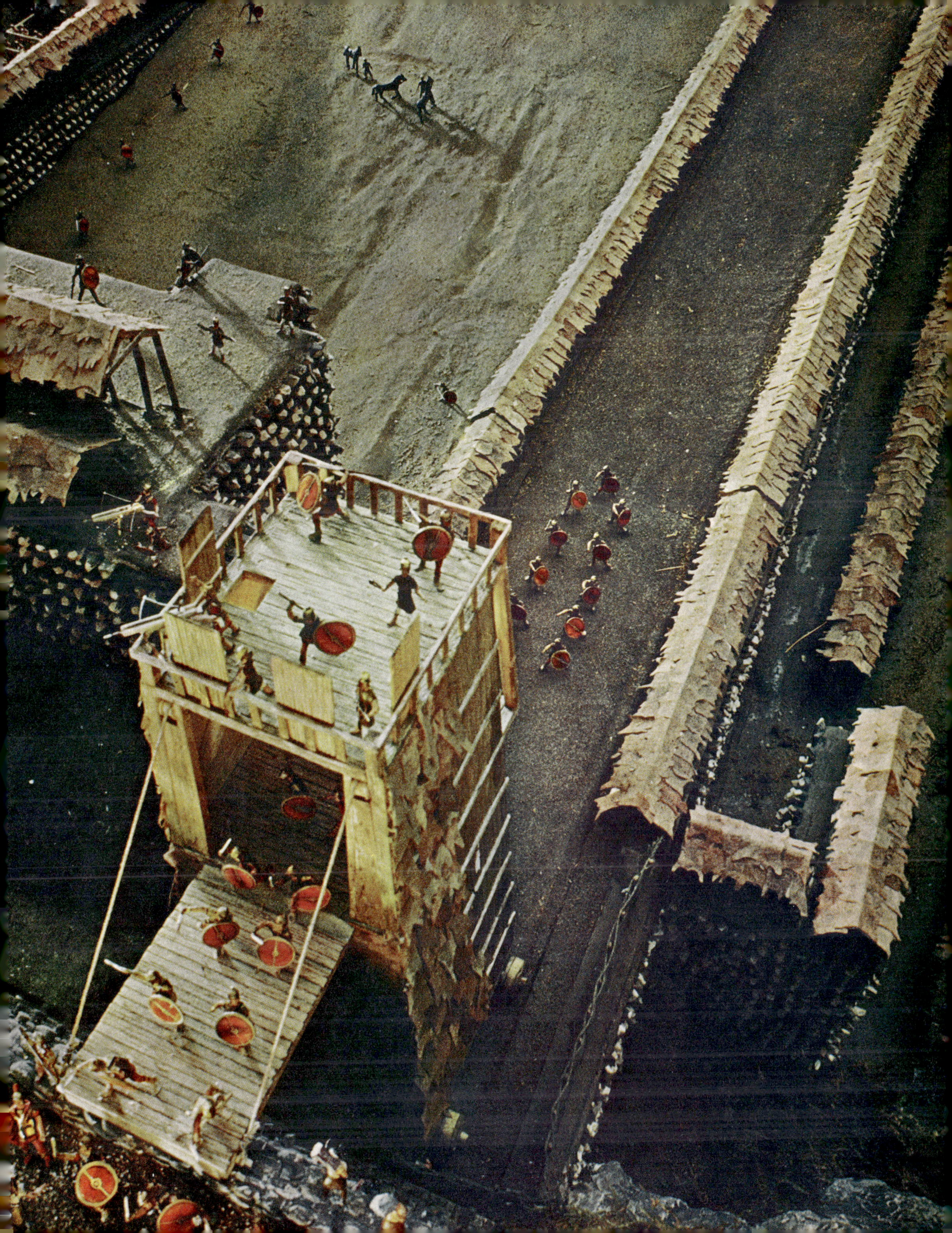

A SKIRMISH AT DAWN *between Roman and Macedonian scouting parties sets the battle in motion. By chance the two armies had camped on opposite sides of a hill.*

A DECISIVE TRIUMPH IN THE FIELD

The Romans excelled not only at sieges but at outmaneuvering their enemies in the field. Their formations and tactics alike were flexible—and in 197 B.C., against a Macedonian phalanx at Cynoscephalae, they demonstrated that this combination of mobility and adaptability was almost unbeatable. When the battle shown on these pages was over, the rigid phalanx had been routed, and the Romans had broken Macedonia's hold on Greece.

The Macedonian phalanx was an awesome sight. When one Roman general saw "the formidable appearance of a front thus bristling with arms," wrote Plutarch, "he was seized with amazement and alarm." At Cynoscephalae the Macedonians stood shield to shield 16-deep. At first those Romans shown at lower left in loose formation were thrown back by the phalanx. Meanwhile troops of the Roman right wing moved up to head off Macedonian reinforcements. From the top of a ridge *(opposite)*, a mounted tribune now looked back and saw his countrymen hard pressed. He turned with a small force to attack the Macedonian rear. The ensuing battle is depicted on the following pages. The soldiers shown here represent a larger force: there were about 26,000 men on each side.

A WALL OF MEN *armed with long spears faces the flexible Roman battle line (left). The Romans, with their short swords, could not break the enemy formation.*

THE TIDE TURNS *as a tribune (right) decides to attack the enemy rear. "Opportunity in war," said Vegetius, "is more often to be depended upon than courage."*

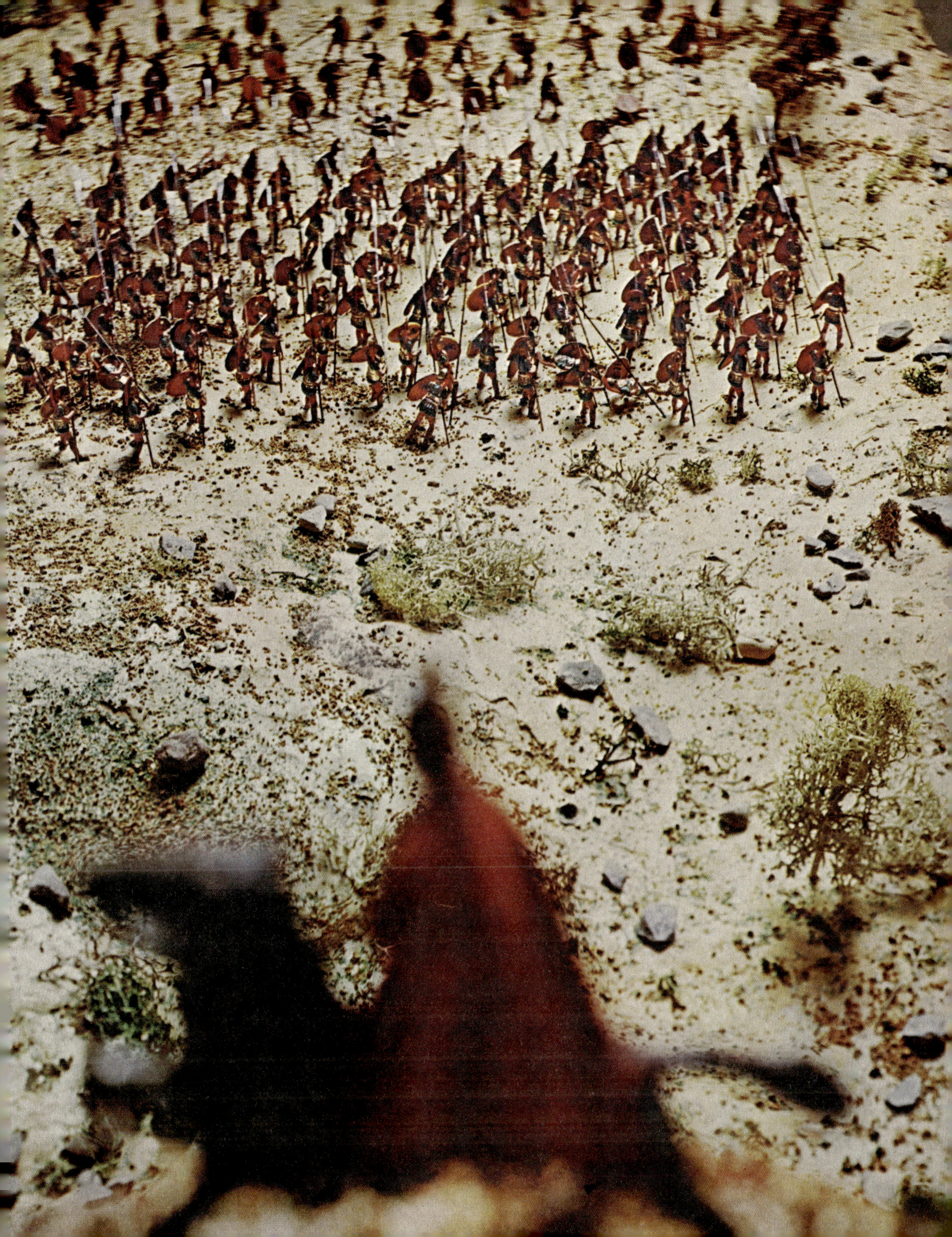

FLANKING A PHALANX

The mobility of the Romans at Cynoscephalae, indicated by colored lines in the battle scene above, enabled them to outflank and rout the massive Macedonian phalanx, which seemed impregnable from the front. The thrust of the phalanx at first threatened the Roman line at left. The Roman right, led by war elephants, moved uphill to defeat a second phalanx *(blue lines)*. It was a Roman leader *(red line)* on the right who, seeing the Roman left in trouble, turned a unit on the first phalanx and attacked it in the rear *(orange lines)*. The Macedonians, holding 21-foot spears and heavy shields, could not wheel about to face the new threat. The Romans cut them to pieces: 8,000 Macedonians died; only 700 Romans.

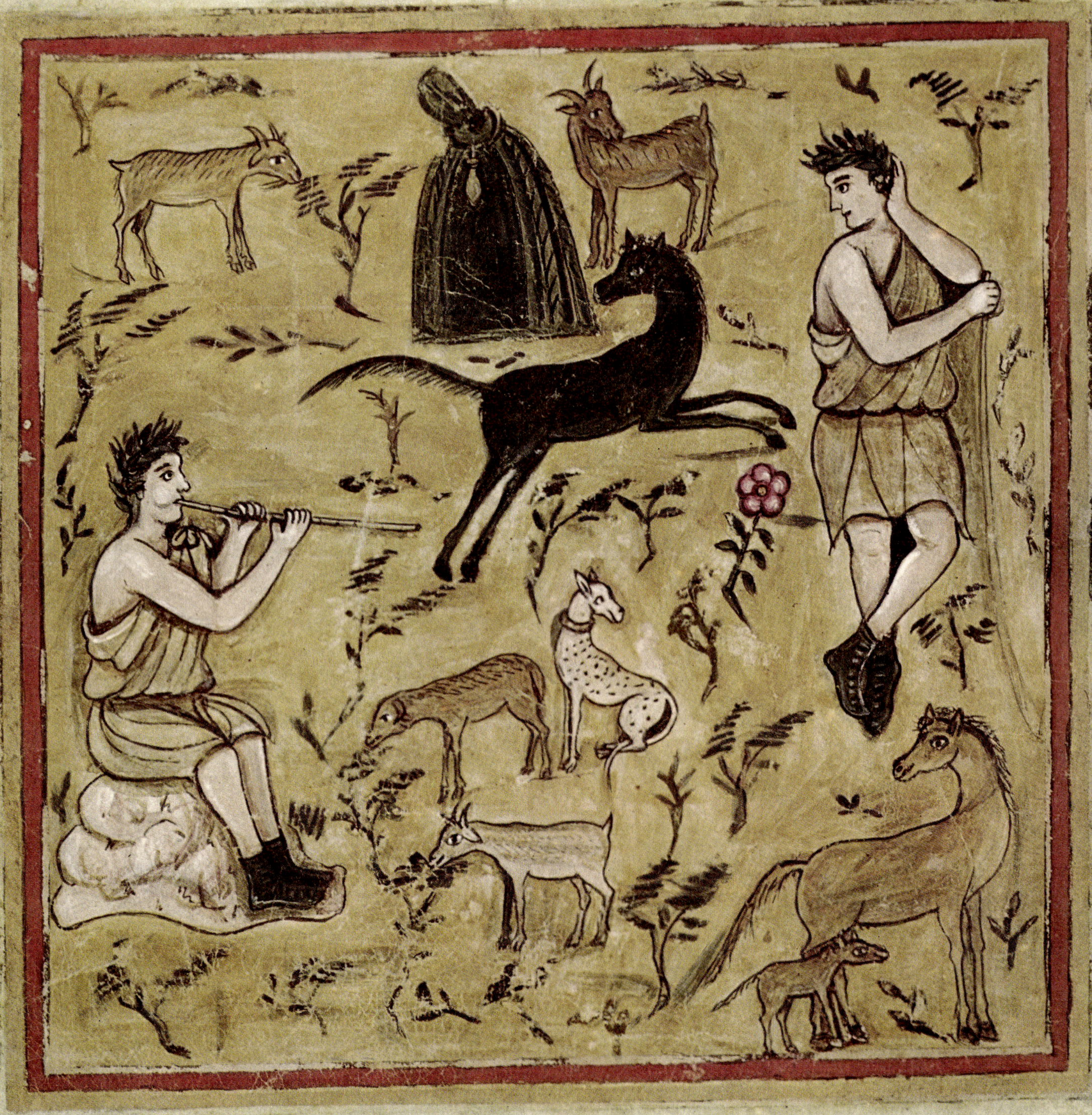

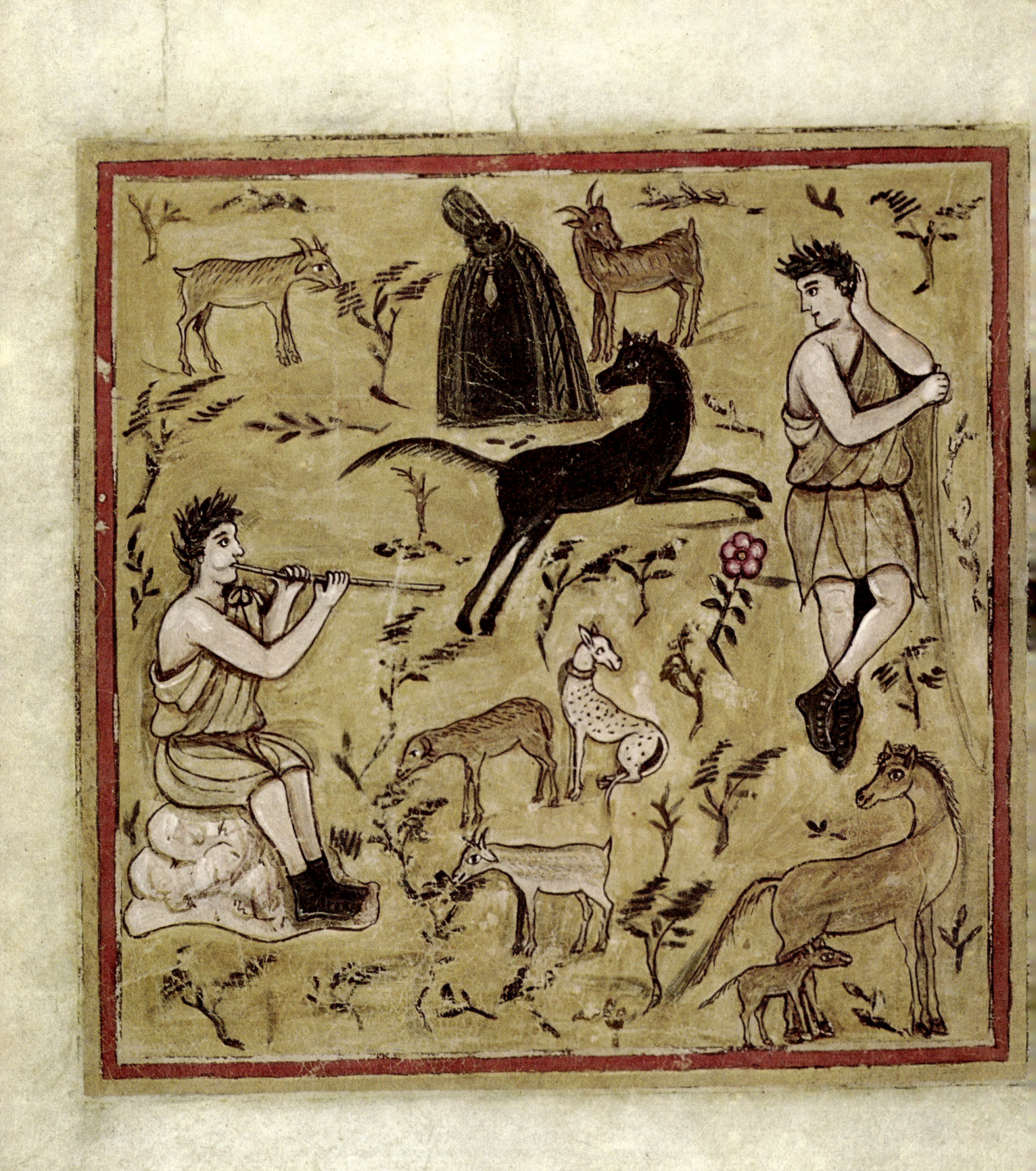

5
POETS AND PROPAGANDISTS

A BUCOLIC SCENE *from Vergil's "Georgics," antiquity's handbook of animal husbandry and farming methods, is offered in this crude but charming illustration of shepherds and barnyard creatures from an ancient manuscript.*

Whenever a Roman gentleman of the early Republic needed to put his thoughts into literary form, he looked to the Greeks for a model; in fact, educated Romans never ceased to be influenced by Greek literature. But by the end of the Third Century B.C., Roman writers were developing a literary style of their own and ultimately they produced a superb literature, one of the best the world has ever known. Especially in the areas that seemed to suit them best—instructional poetry, history and satire—the Romans were brilliant innovators and they left Europe a legacy it drew upon for centuries.

Not surprisingly, the earliest writer to use the Latin language for the literary arts was a Greek, an ex-slave turned playwright, Livius Andronicus. Livius translated the *Odyssey* and several Greek dramas into Latin and composed one hymn of his own. He also produced the plays he translated and even acted in them. He was followed by Naevius, one of the most original of the early Latin writers, author of a historical epic and several plays.

Soon afterward, four poets emerged who began for the first time to explore the real potentialities of the Latin language. One of them, Ennius, rested his chief claim to fame on his success at adapting the sonorous Greek hexameter into Latin in his great historical work the *Annals*. (He also believed himself distinguished in another respect: he thought that the soul of Homer, having passed through several other bodies, currently resided in his.) Equally substantial was the contribution of the poet Lucilius. Lucilius wrote the first true satires; his poems were colloquial, topical verses ridiculing the weaknesses of society.

The other two poets of this early period were both comic playwrights, and both of them owed something to the spirited comedies of the Greek dramatist Menander. Plautus, the earlier of the two, was an actor who wrote rollicking musical comedies for the Roman man-in-the-street, a rather unimaginative fellow who liked his plots simple and his humor broad. His plays abound in seductions, mistaken identities, tyrannical fathers, shrewish wives—in short, in all the stock characters and situations of farce. Terence, the other playwright, had a much quieter, more subtle humor. Originally a Carthaginian slave, educated and freed by his master, Terence became the favorite playwright of Rome's aristocrats and was famous for his polished style, his warmth and his maxims, many of which have endured over the centuries (e.g., "A word to the wise is sufficient," and "While there's life, there's hope").

While Latin poetry was making these impressive strides, Latin prose was developing along more functional lines—notably in the Senate and in the courts, where men were learning to use the language as a magnificent tool. The greatest of these prose craftsmen was Cicero. If a single writer had to be chosen as representative of all that is good in Roman literature, that man would be Cicero. His ringing speeches are the finest specimens of Roman oratory that have come down to us. His essays are models of lucidity and the masterful use of language. His abundant letters offer fascinating insights into Roman politics of the First Century B.C.—and also into the character of a complex man.

About 60 of Cicero's hundred or so speeches survive, including the four impassioned diatribes he delivered in 63 B.C. against Catiline, in his efforts to block that unprincipled man in his conspiracy to overthrow the Government. But Cicero's essays on oratory, political theory, ethics, philosophy—and even on such personal concerns as the prospect of growing old—have proved to be an even more precious bequest. In the charming essay "Concerning Old Age" he observes:

> *Just as apples when they are green are with difficulty plucked from the tree, but when ripe and mellow fall of themselves, so with the young, death comes as a result of force, while with the old it is the result of ripeness. To me, indeed, the thought of this "ripeness" for death is so pleasant, that the nearer I approach death the more I feel like one who is in sight of land at last and is about to anchor in his home port after a long voyage.*

As for his letters, these are remarkable in another way: Cicero wrote nearly 800 of them, sometimes as many as three a day to the same person. They are wise, witty, humorous, ambitious, egocentric, artful, patriotic—in short, the written mirror of a far from simple man. In public life Cicero shifted from one position to another on minor issues, fitting his response to the currents of public opinion. But on major issues he steadfastly held to his own beliefs. After Julius Caesar's death in 44 B.C., Cicero threw himself into the nearly hopeless fight against Caesar's successor Mark Antony in the hope of restoring the form of government to which he was profoundly attached, a republic ruled by the old senatorial aristocracy. The following year Antony, his triumph assured, ordered Cicero's death. For a while the old orator—he was 63 by then—took refuge in the countryside. Then, shunned by his former friends, he decided to take ship and quit Italy. After boarding the boat, for reasons we shall never know, Cicero changed his mind. He returned to shore, and, sitting on his litter, calmly awaited his murderers and the sword blow that sent his head rolling in the sand.

The only one of Cicero's contemporaries to approach him in fame as a prose writer was Julius Caesar, Rome's brilliant military commander. The two were lifelong political opponents, but each greatly admired the other's literary style. "You have gained a triumph to be preferred to that of the greatest generals," said Caesar to Cicero, "for it is a nobler thing to enlarge the boundaries of human intelligence than those of the Roman Empire." This was praise indeed, for Caesar had his own claim to greatness in both fields. His two *Commentaries* —on his campaigns in Gaul and the civil wars in Rome—were written as routine military reports from a commander to his superiors in the Government. But they are couched in language of such clarity and force that even Cicero was moved to

A WRITER'S TOOLS *might include an inkwell and papyrus scrolls or less expensive wax tablets and stylus. The tablets could also be bound, as shown here, and they could be erased with the flat end of the stylus. Papyrus was made of the pith of a water plant; ink was a mixture of soot, resin, wine dregs and cuttlefish secretions.*

A BRONZE INKWELL

A BOOK OF WAX TABLETS

TWO KINDS OF STYLUS

PAPYRUS SCROLLS IN A CANISTER

comment; they were, he said, "naked and straightforward and graceful, stripped of all finery as of a garment. . . . In history nothing is more agreeable than simple and lucid brevity."

While Cicero and Caesar were trading compliments for producing some of the most memorable examples of Latin prose, two other writers were creating the first Latin poetry to dwell upon intensely personal concerns. Although they had this in common, in other respects Lucretius and Catullus could hardly have been more dissimilar. Lucretius was a philosopher, somber and full of grandeur; Catullus was a romantic, all sensitivity and restrained passion. A candid advocate of love for love's sake, Catullus poured out his heart in lyrical verse to a mistress whom he addressed as Lesbia (her real name was Clodia; she was the wife of a Roman nobleman and some 10 years Catullus' senior).

> *No woman, if she is honest, can say that she's been blessed with greater love, my Lesbia, than I have given you;*
> *nor has any man held to a contract made with more fidelity*
> *than I have shown, my dear, in loving you.*

Lucretius' only surviving work, *On the Nature of Things*, is a lengthy poem (six books) of evangelical intensity, expounding the central belief of the Epicurean philosophy: that the world is composed of random arrangements of atoms, without any divine plan, and therefore that there is no reason to fear any god. In the end Lucretius' most lasting contribution was not his poetic message but his masterful use of language, which had a profound effect upon his immediate successor, Vergil. With two other writers, Horace and Livy, Vergil ushered in the most dazzling half century of Roman literature.

The peace of Augustus freed Rome for the first time in a century from the climate of uncertainty fostered by shifting factional alignments. To Roman writers, this enlightened state seemed a legitimate object of admiration, and Augustus, himself a man of education and taste, saw uses for their feelings and talents. One of his friends was Maecenas, a wealthy patron of the arts, and among Maecenas' protégés were Vergil and Horace. Maecenas seems to have encouraged the poets to write on matters that he thought would be pleasing or useful to Augustus. These two, together with Livy, who wrote prose, produced works designed to fill Romans with patriotic pride and to reinstill in them the old Roman morality. In the process, all three also managed to produce enduring literature.

Vergil, the first of the Augustan poets, was the son of a farmer; his early pastoral poems, called the *Eclogues*, or *Bucolics*, reflect his deep love of the Italian soil. By the age of 33, he was famous—a situation not always pleasing to him. Shy and ill at ease in society, he visited Rome as infrequently as possible and avoided public appearances. At Maecenas' suggestion, and in line with Augustus' wish to make farming seem a more attractive occupation, Vergil produced the *Georgics*, four books of the most technically perfect verse he ever wrote:

> But neither flowering groves
> Of Media's realm, nor Ganges proud,
> Nor Lydian fountains flowing thick with gold,
> Can match their glories with Italia . . . .
> Hail, O Saturn's land,
> Mother of all good fruits and harvests fair,
> Mother of men!

Vergil was by no means a fast writer. He took seven years to complete the *Georgics*, finishing, on the average, less than a line a day. Vergil himself is quoted as having said that he "licked them into shape like a she-bear its cub." He worked 10 years on the *Aeneid*, the epic song of Rome's founding, and he never finished it. On his way home from a trip to Greece, Vergil fell ill and died. Perhaps he had had a premonition of this; in any event, before embarking he begged his friends to burn the uncompleted manuscript if anything should happen to him. But Augustus would not hear of its destruction, and ordered the poem published in its unfinished state.

Although the *Aeneid* fitted neatly into Augustus' policies, Vergil himself was deeply committed to its message—the destined glory of Rome—and was eager to communicate it. In the first six of its 12 books, the *Aeneid* relates the adventure-filled journey of Aeneas and his band of Trojans from Troy to Italy; in the last six it describes the Trojan conquest of Latium and the founding of the Roman nation. But the story is simply an instrument on which to sound the glorious notes of Rome's splendor. Thus Vergil at one point has Aeneas descend into the underworld and there meet the unborn heroes of Rome's future—among whom is Augustus:

> This is he whom again and again you have heard in
>   the promise
> Of prophecy, Caesar Augustus, son of a god.
> He shall found once again an era of gold in the land
> Of Latium, throughout the fields that Saturn once
>   ruled.

The only other work approaching the influence of the *Aeneid* in expressing the ideals of Rome is the voluminous history of Livy. Less than a quarter of it survives, but this fragment is enough to assure Livy at least second place as a propagator of Roman patriotism. Livy recounts the history of Rome from its founding in 753 B.C. up to the death of Drusus, in 9 B.C., during his German campaign. It is a brilliant recounting, but not always an accurate one. While he admitted some decline in the values of his own times, he interpreted Roman failings generously, and, when he had to admit to superior qualities in a non-Roman, he managed to salvage something for Rome in the telling. He concedes, for example, that Hannibal was a great general, but places the praise on the lips of Hannibal's conqueror, Scipio Africanus—adding generosity to the rest of Scipio's noble qualities.

The writer who was closest to Maecenas was Horace, who combined qualities that have made him beloved by all men in all nations throughout history. Horace's verse has neither the grandeur of Vergil's nor its majestic meter, but he too praised Roman traditions and the Augustan virtues. A man of simple yet elegant tastes, he preferred to deal with everyday things—a dish too highly seasoned with garlic, a persistent bore, a cure for hangovers (fried shrimp and African snails). His tone is genial and conversational, but it masks a matchless skill of description and a surgically sharp gift for satire. "Tell them the truth with a smile," was his motto. Here are his instructions on how to punish a man who has killed his father:

> *Whenever a man uses his ungodly hands*
> *   to strangle his poor old father,*
> *make him eat garlic: it's deadlier than hemlock.*
> *   Farmers' guts must be like iron.*

His finest work is often considered to be his four books of *Odes*, perfect examples of lyric form, written in no less than 19 different metrical patterns, and covering an almost infinite variety of themes—love, friendship, advice to the young:

> *Better to live, Licinius, not always*
> *   rushing into deep water, and not, when fear*
> *of storms makes you shiver, pushing too close to*
> *   the dangerous coast.*

While the praises of Augustan Rome were being sung by poets of the stature of Vergil and Horace, other poets eluded the Augustan net and, in fact, defied it. These were the singers of love songs—Gallus, Tibullus, Propertius and Ovid—who cared little for affairs of state but dedicated themselves to the exploration of their own sensibilities.

Of the four, the most prolific and appealing was the witty Ovid. No other Roman poet used verse as such a natural idiom, no other wrote poetry simply to entertain. Strangely enough, this poet of the frivolous was educated for a career in politics, but Ovid opposed his father's wishes and instead turned his attention to romance and poetry, in that order. For Ovid, one inspired the other: "When I was from Cupid's passions free, my Muse was mute and wrote no elegy." In his three early books of *Amores*, Ovid tells of his love for an imaginary mistress named Corinna. In his *Heroides*, a series of letters in verse supposedly written by famous women of legend to their absent husbands or lovers, he gently lampoons some of the foremost figures of Greek and Roman literature—including even the sacrosanct Aeneas—by pointing out their human frailties as seen by the women they loved. But Ovid's masterpiece is his *Metamorphoses*, a retelling, in some 12,000 lines of verse, of virtually every story of classical mythology. It is a wonderful play of fantasy and gaiety that begins with the dawn of creation and ends with the final metamorphosis of Julius Caesar into a star.

Ovid's early work, *The Art of Love*, was considered a bad influence on Roman society by Augustus, because of its immorality, and in 8 A.D., when the poet was in his fifties, Augustus suddenly ordered him to be exiled. Almost simultaneously, Julia, Augustus' granddaughter, was also banished. People believed, although it has never been confirmed, that the poet and the princess were somehow involved in a scandal too flagrant to be ignored.

Placed aboard ship and dispatched to the bleak city of Tomi on the Black Sea, Ovid spent nearly 10 weary years lamenting his loneliness for his native land. He sent two books of verse back to Rome, the *Tristia* and *Epistles from Pontus*, hoping for forgiveness; it never came. Eventually his bones were returned to Rome but by that time, with Augustus himself dead, the Golden Age of Roman literature —an extraordinary epoch—was over.

The last important period in Roman literature lasted 124 years, from the reign of Tiberius to that of Hadrian. It was characterized by writing that was far more concerned with style than with content. Writers of this period doted on the unusual phrase, the apothegm, the calculated witticism. By its very artificiality, this writing encouraged mediocrity. The poet Seneca illustrates the age at both its best and its worst. His reputation as one of the most significant figures in Latin literature is assured less by the quality of his work than by its influence on the playwrights of Elizabethan England who were attracted by its grand passion and violent deaths. Shakespeare's tragedies owe a great deal to the tortured, ghoulish tragedies of Seneca. In *Agamemnon*, Clytemnestra emotes with a theatricality that is typical of Seneca's style:

> *Too dire my grief to wait time's healing hand.*
> *My very soul is scorched with flaming pains:*
> *I feel the goads of fear and jealous rage,*
> *The throbbing pulse of hate, the pangs of love.*

Writing was only one of Seneca's activities. He was also a lawyer, a vinegrower, a moneylender; in fact, he was a millionaire many times over. An influential public figure, he served the Emperor Nero in key posts in the Government. Seneca also was deeply immersed in Stoic philosophy, as is revealed in his many essays on philosophical subjects, called *Dialogues*, and his volumes of *Moral Letters*. His personal adherence to Stoicism enabled him to die with a theatrical disdain for death worthy of the heroes in his dramas. When Nero accused him of complicity in a plot against the throne and ordered him to commit suicide, Seneca opened his veins, and, lying in a warm bath, let his life ebb away.

Aside from Seneca, this literary period is remembered largely for its excellent satire. Its three foremost satirists were Petronius, Martial and Juvenal. Petronius was Nero's advisor on artistic matters, and by Tacitus' account a bit of a fop. The *Satyricon*, generally credited to him, is a rambling picaresque novel, which survives only in fragments and is a curious mixture of realism, pornography and refined criticism of literature and art. Its best-known segment, the Dinner of Trimalchio, is a hilarious and devastating account of the attempts of a wealthy ex-slave to achieve elegance. In the process, he commits every conceivable breach of good taste: he sets his table with spoons of precious metal weighing half a pound apiece, entertains his guests with table talk about his own elaborately planned funeral, and during the meal offers them wine to wash their hands with instead of water.

While Petronius used prose to satirize society, Martial and Juvenal used poetry. Unlike Petronius, who moved in wealthy court circles, both were poor men and both wrote with the candor of the outsider. In Martial's hands the epigram, originally a short inscription for a tomb or a work of art, became a polished and barbed poem:

> *Maronilla, Gemellus doth adore thee*
> *With instant prayers and vows doth oft implore thee,*
> *And many a lover's gift he lays before thee;*
> *Since neither beauty, grace, nor charm attend thee*
> *What makes him seek thee so, and thus commend*
>   *thee?*
> *A churchyard cough that promises to end thee.*

Where Martial was tart and detached, Juvenal was indignant—obsessed by the immorality of Roman society and intolerant of human stupidity in general. He attacked with both rapier and bludgeon, and his satire was a triumph of scornful ridicule:

What should I do in Rome? I am no good at lying.
If a book's bad, I can't praise it, or go around
 ordering copies.
I don't know the stars; I can't hire out as an
 assassin
When some young man wants his father knocked off
 for a price. . . .

The lurid picture that Juvenal drew of Rome between the reigns of Domitian and Hadrian may have been somewhat distorted, for the same age also produced learned, civilized men like Pliny the Elder. Pliny was a remarkable scholar, the editor of an astonishing *Natural History* that ran to 37 volumes and embraced everything that he could learn about men and beasts, stones and stars, medicines and magic. So conscientious was his research that he died of asphyxiation after attempting to observe the eruption of Mt. Vesuvius from too close a vantage point.

The last important writers of the Silver Age were the historians Tacitus and Suetonius. Little is known about Tacitus except through his works; in them is combined a power of language surpassing Seneca's and an intense concern with morality. In his major historical works—the *Annals*, which cover the period from the death of Augustus to Nero; and the *Histories*, spanning the period from Nero's death to the death of Domitian—Tacitus idealizes the Republic and indicts the imperial regime. He details, in sensational fashion, the enormities of many of the figures who held or coveted imperial power: many of the emperors emerge as monsters, Tiberius as a morose lecher, Claudius as the weak

THE QUOTABLE ROMANS

A STOREHOUSE OF MAXIMS, *the literature of the Romans has provided succeeding generations with capsule wisdom for every occasion. Some of these aphorisms are shown below, along with a mosaic warning thieves to "beware of the dog."*

I fear the Greeks even when bringing gifts.
Love conquers all.
Arms and the man I sing.   VERGIL

It is quality rather than quantity that matters.
Not lost, but gone forever.
It is a rough road that leads to the
     heights of greatness.   SENECA

My heart was in my mouth.
Not worth his salt.   PETRONIUS

No sooner said than done.   QUINTUS ENNIUS

There are some remedies worse than the disease.
Many receive advice, few profit by it.
No one knows until he tries.   PUBLIUS SYRUS

There is no place more delightful
     than home.   CICERO

Over head and heels.
Forever, brother, hail and farewell.   CATULLUS

More brawn than brain.   CORNELIUS NEPOS

109

tool of his wife, Nero as a cultured degenerate.

Suetonius, Tacitus' junior by 14 years, was a secretary to Hadrian and had access to official records for his *Lives of the Caesars*, a collection of biographies of the rulers from Julius Caesar to Domitian. But his gossipy accounts paid more attention to personal idiosyncrasies and backstairs intrigue than to policies and programs. Nevertheless, the book is an important source of all sorts of information, including personal details about the emperors; only from Suetonius is it possible to learn, for example, that the Emperor Augustus wore long underwear.

During the Second Century A.D., the quality of Roman literature dropped sharply, but one man, Apuleius, is worthy of mention. His book *The Golden Ass* is a curious mixture of philosophy, religion, adventure, love and obscenity. Its style combines archaisms with juicy vernacular tidbits. This was an engaging work; after it, Latin literature, with rare exceptions, degenerated into dullness.

But Rome still had one last burst of vitality to contribute to the literature of the Western world. The impetus came from Christianity, and from its adherents' passionate eloquence in defense of their faith. There was Tertullian, a convert to Christianity who defended his new religion against the Roman persecutors so impetuously and dramatically that some of his sentences have become proverbial: "We multiply every time we are mowed down by you; the blood of Christians is seed." And there was the Spaniard Prudentius, the first great poet among the Christians. Writing 200 years after Tertullian, when the faith of the Christians had gained official sanction, Prudentius attempted to transform the stories of the early martyrs into a new body of Roman legend. But he was occasionally carried away by his fervor: a tortured Christian utters six tirades against the heathens after his tongue has been cut out; and St. Lawrence, being roasted alive, is made to say: "Turn me over; I'm done on this side."

During the Fourth Century, working in a very different spirit, the ascetic scholar St. Jerome translated the Bible into Latin. This translation, known as the Vulgate Bible, became the standard text in Roman Catholic services in most of the world. At about the same time, St. Augustine was writing his moving *Confessions*—the final masterpiece of Roman literature. Augustine describes his love of God in prose that is virtually lyric poetry:

"But what do I love when I love Thee? . . . I love a kind of light, and melody, and fragrance, and meat, and embracement when I love my God, the light, melody, fragrance, meat, embracement of my inner man: where there shineth unto my soul what space cannot contain, and there soundeth what time beareth not away, and there smelleth what breathing disperseth not, and there tasteth what eating diminisheth not, and there clingeth what satiety divorceth not. This is it which I love when I love my God."

In his *City of God*, Augustine argues that there is a divine city superior to earthly cities; the earthly cities are doomed to perish, but the City of God is immortal.

Earthly Rome, its seat of empire removed to Constantinople and its proud forums sacked by barbarian invaders, was dying even as Augustine wrote. With it went Roman literature. And yet death was not the end. In later centuries Latin's daughter tongues—French, Spanish and Italian—would produce literature to equal in range and originality that of the great Romans. It was Salvian, a Fifth Century priest from Marseilles, describing the commonwealth's last years, who perhaps best epitomized the decline of Latin literature: "It dies and yet it smiles."

A PAINTED GARDEN *which is part of a large mural in Pompeii depicts a heron and thrush amid oleander bushes and flowering trees.*

HOMAGE TO ITALY

"Out of this heart my song, however slender, offers my country all its humble praise. . . ." This simple couplet from a poem by Sextus Propertius epitomizes the ardent attachment of Roman poets and painters to their land. While the poets —Vergil and Horace, Ovid and Propertius—were celebrating in verse the splendor of the Italian countryside, painters now forgotten covered Roman walls with scenes drawn from nature *(above)*. They decorated villas, basilicas, inns and even modest homes, using skills taught them by Greek artists. On the following pages appears a selection from these tributes to the Italian land, together with photographs of the scenes that might have inspired both the paintings and the poems.

A LEGEND OF LOVE

Greek myths supplied themes for many Roman paintings and for such poems as Ovid's *Metamorphoses*. To these tales the Romans often added naturalistic touches: for example, figures of gods appeared with Roman faces and in Roman settings *(right)*. Ovid was the idol of young poets, and his love poems were avidly read by girls and young women. Remarking on Ovid's appeal, Seneca said, "He filled the age with his quotations."

> "...Chain'd to a rock she stood; young Perseus stay'd
> His rapid flight, to view the beauteous maid.
> So sweet her frame, so exquisitely fine,
> She seem'd a statue by a hand divine,
> Had not the wind her waving tresses show'd,
> And down her cheeks the melting sorrows flow'd.
> Her faultless form the hero's bosom fires;
> The more he looks, the more he still admires...
> The beauteous bride moves on, now loos'd from chains,
> The cause, and sweet reward of all the hero's pains..."
> —OVID

ANDROMEDA ENCHAINED, soon to be rescued by Perseus, is seen in a painting (right) uncovered at Pompeii. The artist's rock resembles the famous "Sirens' Rock" near the Sicilian coast, shown in the photograph at left.

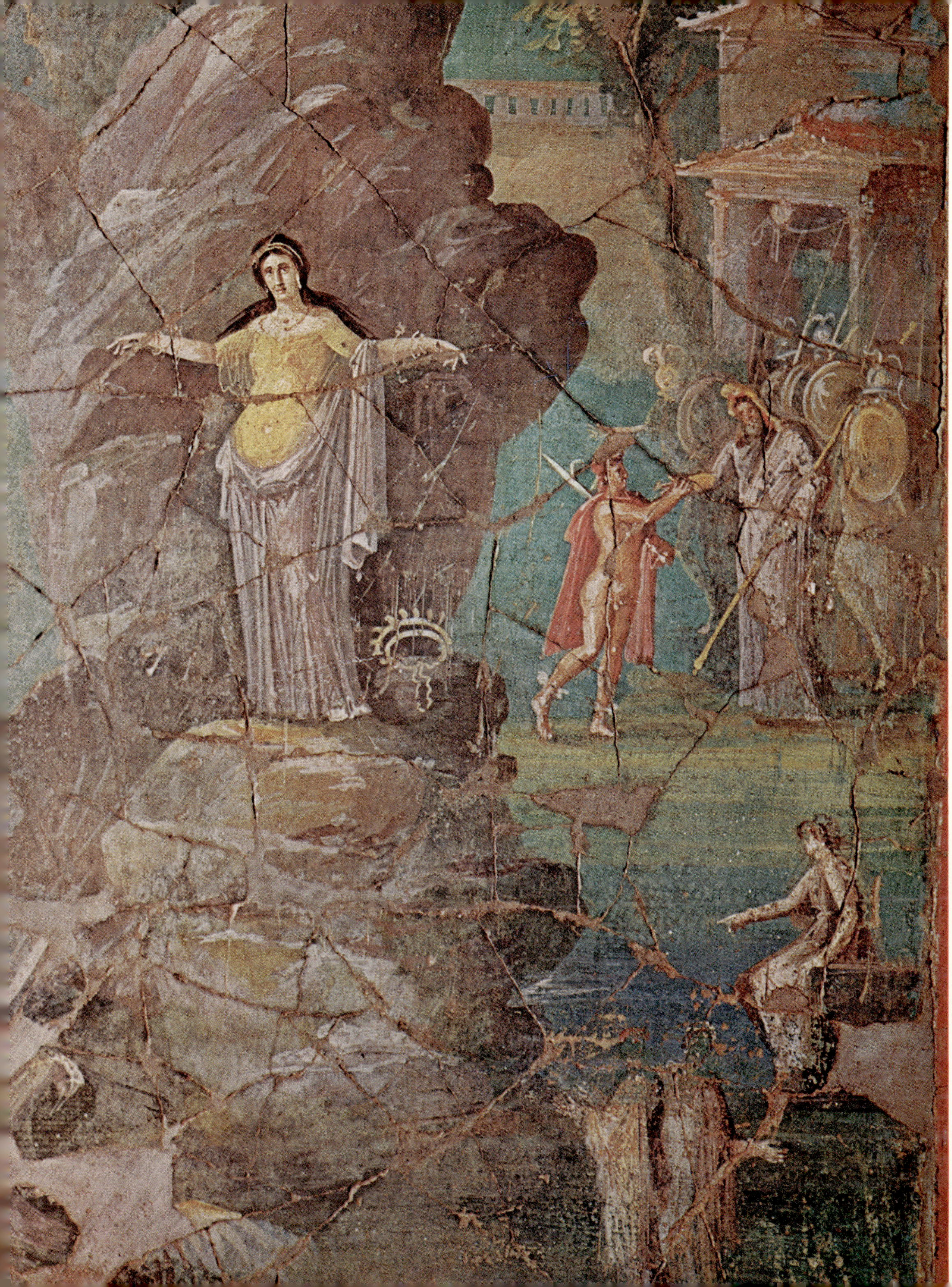

SONG OF THE FIELDS

Vergil fervently sang the praises of farm life. One of his poems, the *Georgics*, was a practical handbook for the farmer, telling him in detail how to rotate crops, fertilize the soil ("scruple not to enrich the dried-up soil with dung") and what to do "lest weeds should check the corn's exuberance."

LIVIA'S GARDEN, *a fresco from the country villa of Augustus' wife, is the kind of wall painting that created the illusion of spacious vistas inside the small rooms of Roman houses. The artist's birds and trees were as bright as those in an orchard (below) near Sorrento.*

"...*There is fresh wine, too, just drawn from the pitched jar,
 and a water-brook running noisily with hoarse murmur;
there are also chaplets of violet blossoms mixed with saffron,
 and yellow garlands blended with crimson roses...
There are little cheeses, too, dried in a basket of rushes.*"

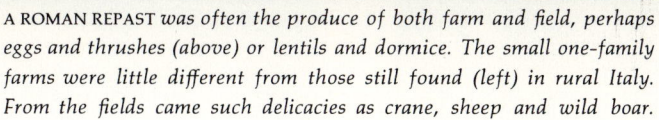

A ROMAN REPAST *was often the produce of both farm and field, perhaps eggs and thrushes (above) or lentils and dormice. The small one-family farms were little different from those still found (left) in rural Italy. From the fields came such delicacies as crane, sheep and wild boar.*

"There are waxen plums of autumn's season,
and chestnuts and sweetly blushing apples;
there is Ceres' pure gift, with Love and Bacchus;
there are blood-red mulberries with grapes in heavy clusters,
and from its stalk hangs the blue-grey melon..."
—ATTRIBUTED TO VERGIL

A RUSTIC RHYTHM

Horace was a great man who lived a simple life. Like the shepherd at right, he was at home among the rural shrines that dotted country roads outside Rome. His ideal of simplicity was summed up in his shrewd advice to young writers. "Be brief," he said. "More ought to be scratched out than left."

"Sharp winter melts with Spring's delicious birth;
The ships glide down on rollers to the sea;
The herds forsake their stalls, the hind his hearth;
No more with hoar-frost gleams the whitened lea....
With myrtle now 'tis time to wreathe our brows,
Or flowers up-springing from the earth let loose,
And in the shady grove to pay our vows
With lamb or kid, whichever Faunus choose...."

—HORACE

THE HERDSMAN'S SPRING, *celebrated by Horace in his ode, is caught in the painting at right with its shepherd, goat and cows. Patricians also enjoyed the pleasant country life, but preferred elegant settings like Hadrian's imperial villa, with its marble arcade and pool (above).*

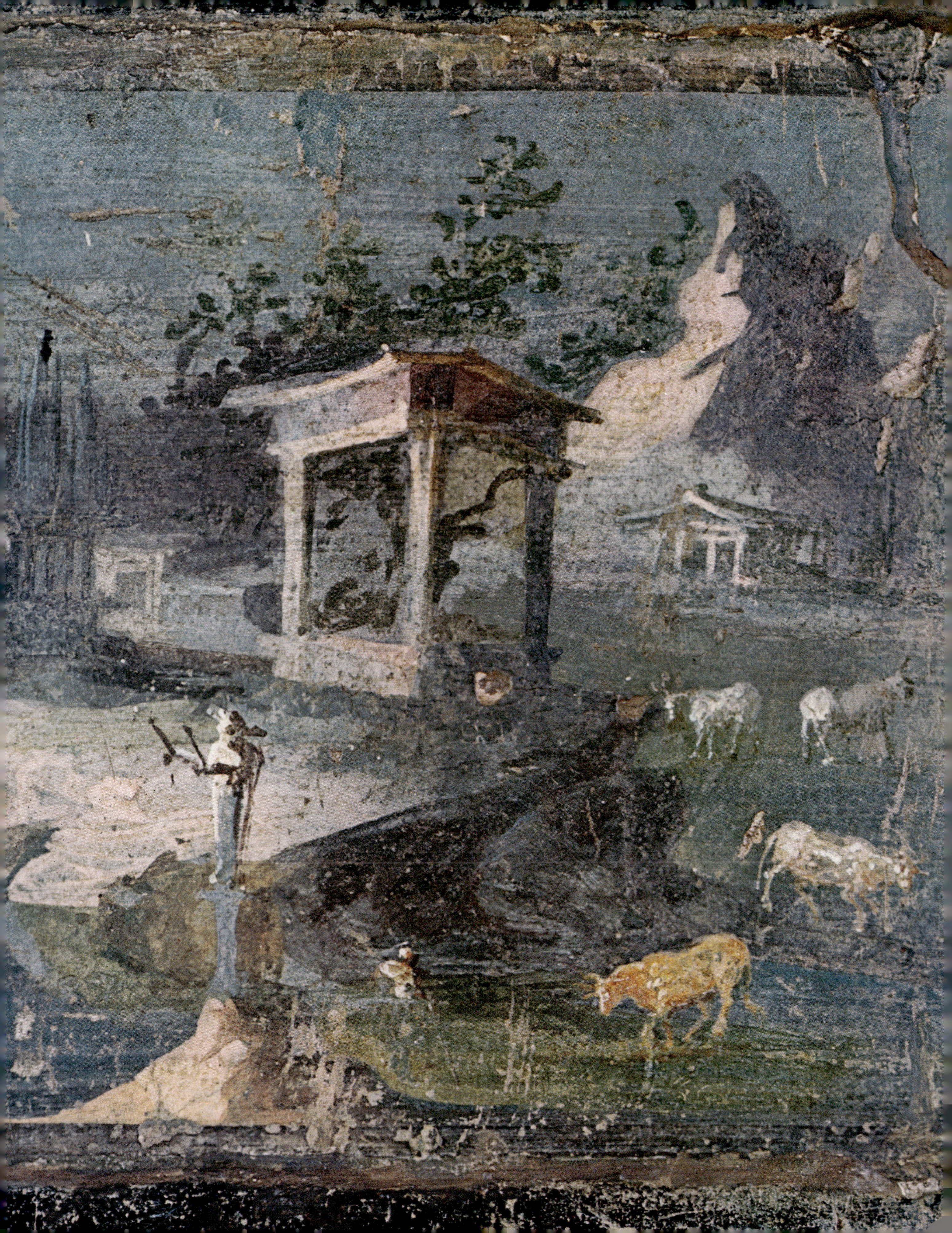

GODDESS FROM THE SEA

Venus, the legendary goddess of love, sometimes called Dione in Latin, was honored with a springtime Roman festival and often figured in the wall paintings and sculpture of rich villas and even in shop advertisements. Elaborate murals such as this, often covering all four walls of a room, served as more than simple decoration. Such mythological figures provided hosts with conversation pieces—tests of their guests' classical knowledge. An anonymous poem *(opposite)* describes the goddess rising from the sea.

A MAID OF MYTH, *Venus is seen below emerging from the surf, perhaps like that off the Italian coast (right). The artist showed the goddess in the classic pose, reclining on a shell and attended by cupids and a dolphin.*

"...'Twas on that day which saw the teeming flood
Swell round, impregnate with celestial blood;
Wand'ring in circles stood the finny crew,
The rest was left a void expanse of blue;
The parent ocean work'd with heaving throes,
And dripping wet the fair Dione rose.

Let those love now, who never loved before;
And those who always loved, now love the more...."
—ANONYMOUS

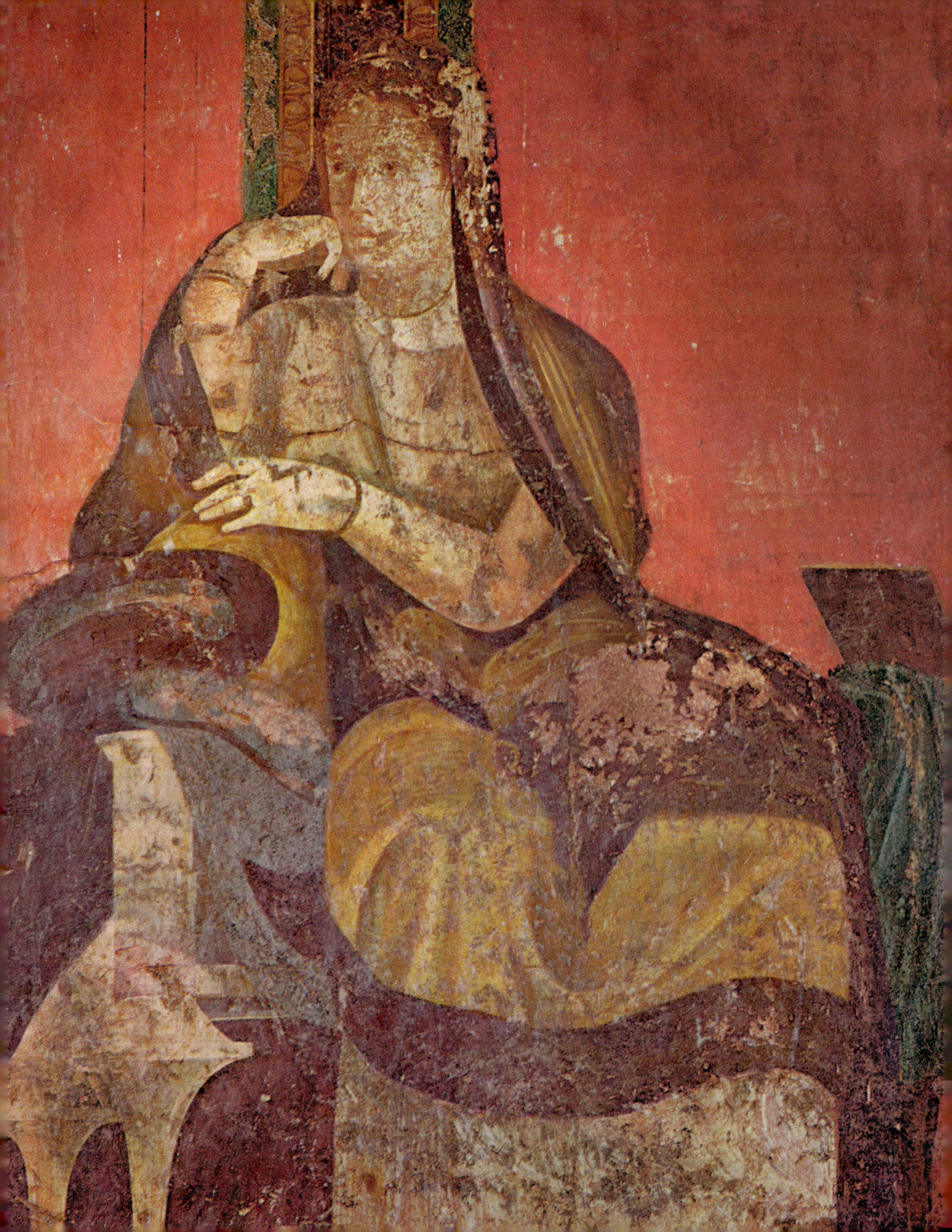

6
THE GODS OF ROME

A RELIGIOUS CULTIST, *this woman was mistress of a villa in which occurred initiation rites into one of Rome's many sects. The picture is from a huge Pompeian mural showing the only surviving details of these secret practices.*

Religion in Rome wore many faces and had many names: each new people the Romans encountered through conquest or trade seems to have added to the Roman pantheon. And yet for many centuries, almost until the birth of Christ, Roman religion, whatever its guise, had certain unchanging qualities. It was, to begin with, a religion of form, of ritual, with little emphasis on the spiritual. The Roman made a compact with his gods—you do something for me and I will do something for you —and his religion was largely a meticulous observance of that bargain. Second, it was an external, communal affair, rather than an internal experience. At first the religious community was the family; then, as Rome grew, it became the village, the city, the state and finally, the Empire. Only when these public formal observances became mechanical and meaningless did Rome turn, in reaction, to other kinds of religion whose appeal was intimate and emotional.

In its earliest form, when the ancestors of the Romans were still simple shepherds and farmers, this religion was almost pure animism. The gods were not persons, but impersonal spirits, and they resided in everything—in trees, in rocks, in birds and beasts, in the grass of the fields and the lightning in the sky. These spirits, or *numina*, were totally amoral, neither good nor bad, and with no special affinity for man. They could help or harm, depending on how they were treated, and it was the job of religion to deal with them in such a way that their powers would benefit man.

At first these dealings, or observances, were probably handled by the head of each household, the *pater familias*. Later they were taken over by the head of the community, the *rex*, and by groups of men, rather like priesthoods, who understood the often complex ritual of pleasing a particular *numen*. The king himself was advised on the proper conduct of religious matters by colleges of wise men called *pontifices* and *augures*; the first were specialists in religious law, the second in the interpretation of omens.

The earliest of the *numina* were the spirits that inhabited each Roman family and farm: Vesta, whose concern was the hearth fire, the Lares, who guarded the home and the boundary of each fam-

121

ily's fields, the Penates, spirits of the larder. Also dating from very early times were the *numina* of Jupiter and Mars: Jupiter in the days of the Italic tribes was an Indo-European sky god, but the Romans assigned him a home in a particular oak tree on Capitoline Hill; Mars was the spirit of the season of growth and harvest, which was also the season of warfare.

Finally, there was the spirit of a man himself, his *Genius*, which inhabited only the men of his family or clan. A man's *Genius* was a kind of spiritual double; it was his *Genius* that was being honored when he was tendered a banquet or a birthday gift. Many centuries later, when Augustus took for himself the role of central authority, making Rome Augustus and Augustus Rome, it was his *Genius* that received the homage, not Augustus himself.

Gradually, as the rites of propitiating the *numina* were taken over by the king and the priests, the *numina* proliferated until their number, origin and duties became a confusing welter. Many centuries later St. Augustine, making a case for Christianity, ridiculed the multiplicity of the Roman deities still honored by country people:

> *Do you think they dared trust one god with their lands? No, Rusina must look to the country, Jugatinus to the hilltops, Collatina to the rest of the hills, and Vallonia to the valleys. Nor could Segetia alone protect the grain: when it was in the ground Seia must look to it; when it was up and ready to mow, Segetia ... Proserpina they made goddess of the grain's first leaves and buds, Nodotus of the knots, Volutina of the blades, Patelena of the forming ears, Hostilina of the beards, Flora of the blooms, Lacturtia of the blooms whitening, Matuca of their being cut, and Runcina of the cut flower. . . . Their entry-ways had three gods: Forculus for the door, Cardea for the hinges, and Limentius for the threshold.*

HOUSEHOLD GODS *called Lares and Penates (opposite) were common objects in homes throughout the Roman world. The tiny bronze statuettes represented spirits of the home and the larder. At mealtime, bits of food were burned in their receptacles as offerings to the departed. Some households had miniature shrines like the one shown here, fashioned after Roman temples. This shrine, a particularly elaborate one, shows the family's special deity (center) flanked by the two household gods. Below the figures is the sacred serpent, a significant figure in temple rites.*

Left to themselves, the prosaic Romans might never have developed a system of religious thought any more profound than their *numina;* everything else in Roman religion was borrowed from outside. The first major external influence was the religion of their Etruscan neighbors. It was the Etruscans, with their strong sense of social order, who superimposed the idea of a larger religious community, the city, upon the old family-oriented tribal religion. It was also the Etruscans who added elaborate religious observances to the comparatively simple rites of the early Romans. They introduced temples and religious processions, the idea of gods with human forms, and the use of statues and images. Rome soon acquired a taste for them. When the Romans conquered the Etruscan stronghold of Veii in 396 B.C., they ceremoniously carried the Etruscans' wooden statue of the goddess Juno back to Rome and installed it on the Aventine Hill. They also absorbed the Etruscan goddess Minerva and added Etruscan attributes to Jupiter.

Through the Etruscans the Romans also learned about divination and prophecy. Etruscan priests deciphered the will of the gods by studying and interpreting such phenomena as the behavior of lightning or the birth of a two-headed calf. But their most trusted source of information was the entrails of sacrificial animals. The liver, in particular, was thought to be useful for this purpose because of the subtle variations evident in its size and shape, its color and the pattern of its veins.

In Roman religion divination also became associated with birds: "taking the auspices" literally meant bird-watching. According to legend, Romulus and Remus decided which of them should lay out the city of Rome by watching the flight of vultures: Remus, facing in one direction, spotted six of them, while Romulus, facing in another, saw 12, and claimed the honor on the basis of numerical superiority. Later, the taking of auspices involved the use

123

SYMBOLS OF GOOD AND EVIL

ROMAN SUPERSTITIONS *centered to a great extent on the world of nature. Romans read portents of disaster in the clatter of crows and found protection from the evil eye in the foliage of the holly bush. Along with this search for omens went a faith in the magical—usually medicinal—properties of many plants and animals. Some of these superstitions, and drawings of the animate and inanimate things which represent them, are shown on these pages.*

THE OWL

This bird was thought to herald disasters. Horace claimed witches used owl feathers in their brews.

THE CYCLAMEN

Romans believed that balding men could prevent further loss of hair by sniffing portions of this plant.

---

of chickens. During the first Punic War the commander of the Roman fleet, Claudius Pulcher, took a flock of sacred chickens to sea with him, expecting to read good omens or bad from the manner in which they pecked their food. But the chickens refused to eat and Pulcher, in a fit of pique, threw them overboard, exclaiming, "Then drink if you won't eat!" The Romans attributed Pulcher's disastrous defeat by the Carthaginians to this impious behavior toward the gods, and, when he returned to Rome, they tried and fined him.

It was the Etruscans also who gave Rome its earliest significant contact with the Greek gods and goddesses, many of whom the Romans eventually absorbed virtually unchanged. Jupiter now advanced still further to become synonymous with the Greek father god, Zeus. Venus, the *numen* of charm, became without effort the radiant and lovely Aphrodite. Similarly Juno took over the attributes of Hera, Greek goddess of women and marriage; Mars of Ares, god of war; Mercury of Hermes, the god's messenger; Diana of Artemis, goddess of the hunt; Minerva of Athena, goddess of wisdom. Some of the Greek gods, notably Apollo, came into the Roman pantheon unchanged even in name. For the pragmatic Romans this almost complete shift in the character of their deities apparently posed no great problem. Starting as impersonal *numina*, the Roman gods moved easily into the highly personal roles of a pantheon whose members were human in form and emotion and had human adventures.

Despite this wholesale borrowing from abroad, many elements of the old Roman religion survived intact. Publicly and privately individual Romans continued to honor the *numina*. One of the finest temples in the Forum Romanum was dedicated to Concord, the *numen* of political harmony, and each home had its own shrine, however humble, to domestic *numina*. The people of Rome scrupulously observed the old religious calendar, with its careful ordering of days of *fasti* and *nefasti* (days in which public business was permitted or forbidden) and its great annual festivals. The merriest of these was the Saturnalia held in December, a carnival that probably originated in the rustic celebrations that ended the autumn planting. At Saturnalia slaves were given temporary liberty to do as they pleased, and were waited on by their masters; people exchanged gifts such as small dolls and wax candles; and a mock-king was crowned.

With so many gods to choose from, the Romans naturally developed personal favorites; and just as naturally, the favorite gods of important men became the centers of elaborate cults, with special observances and holidays. Some of the cults had their own priests, but the role of the priest was seldom spiritual or moral. He was simply expected to know the ritual: the proper forms of addressing the god, the taboos associated with his worship, and the complicated liturgy. Over the centuries the sacred colleges of priests acquired impressive political and social powers; almost nothing in Roman

BELLS	BEES	THE PEONY	THE EAGLE
The ringing of bells near a woman in labor was supposed to ward off evil and ease the pain of childbirth.	These sacred insects were thought to be messengers of the gods whose presence signified good fortune.	This flower, named after Paeon, the god of healing, was considered to have magical curative properties.	The sacred bird of the Roman legions, the eagle was said to bring on lightning and thunderstorms.

life, from a business trip to a declaration of war, could be undertaken without the gods' sanction.

Besides the priests who served the needs of individuals, there were three religious institutions subscribed to by the entire population. One was the college of the Vestal Virgins, another was the Sibylline oracles, and the third was the person of the emperor in his role as Rome's spiritual head, or *pontifex maximus.*

The Vestals guarded the sacred fire of Vesta, once the spirit of the Roman hearth, but now the goddess of the flame that symbolized the Roman state. The fire of Vesta, enclosed in a round temple in the Forum Romanum, was never permitted to go out and was tended according to an ancient and intricate ritual. Its caretakers, the Vestals, were probably originally the daughters of the king, but after Rome became a Republic their members were usually drawn from leading families. To be a Vestal was a great honor, but it also entailed sacrifices. A girl was chosen for the office between the ages of six and 10, remained a Vestal for 30 years, and was sworn to chastity for the entire period of her service. If she broke her vow she was buried alive in an underground chamber. It was said that a Vestal spent the first decade of her service learning her duties, the second decade practicing them and the third teaching them to the novices.

The Sibylline oracles promoted the welfare of the state in a more tangible way. The oracles were a collection of ancient cryptic writings entered, according to legend, in nine Sibylline Books—although by the time Rome got them, their number had been reduced to three. The "books" actually consisted of a collection of odd scraps. The myth of their origin had it that they were brought to Rome by a sibyl, or prophetess, who tried to sell all nine of them to one of the early Etruscan kings. He turned her down, and the offended sibyl burned three. Then she offered him the remaining six, was rebuffed again and burned three more. Finally, with only three books left, she approached the king a third time and this time aroused his curiosity; he agreed to buy the three for the same price the sibyl had asked for the original nine.

The prestige of the oracles was enormous. They were consulted only on matters of great moment, in times of national emergency—a plague, a famine, a critical point in a war—and then not so much for direct advice on the problem itself as for advice on how to get the attention of the gods. The consultation was undertaken only on the Senate's orders and only through the offices of a sacred college of priests. In fact the actual content of the oracles is a complete mystery. None of them survives.

The third state religious institution involved worship of the emperor himself. This began with the deification of dead emperors, as a form of memorial, but later was applied to the living emperor. In his role as a quasi-deity the emperor became the symbol of the Empire, and his worship an expression of loyalty and unity.

JEWS UNDER ROME

Besides Christianity, the only major religion to survive the impact of Roman domination was Judaism—symbolized by this seven-branched candlestick, or Menorah, from a relief in the ancient Palestinian catacombs of Beth She'arim. Scattered in small settlements throughout the Empire, and surrounded by pagans, the Jews clung to their belief in one God, and to the literature, laws and language which had united them as a people for some 1,300 years.

Although they lived under chronic suspicion for their strict adherence to a monotheistic God, the Jews of Rome enjoyed periods of genuine toleration. Augustus even decreed that synagogues were inviolable and that Jews were exempt from appearing in court on their Sabbath. Indeed, the growing dissatisfaction which many Romans felt toward the proliferation of pagan cults led some to convert to Judaism.

Palestine, however, was a Jewish state which had been ruled by the Romans since 63 B.C. Seething under the supervision of unpopular procurators, the Jews rose up in fierce rebellion in 66 A.D. But this uprising and other sporadic revolts which followed were soon crushed by the legions. In 135 A.D. the Jews were driven out of Jerusalem and forbidden to re-enter—a dispersal that was to last until the 20th Century.

The association of the emperor with divinity also had another motive: it was an attempt to give Roman religion an inner meaning as well as an external form. As far back as the early Republic, Roman religion had passed from simple ceremony to elaborate public ritual in which the individual Roman played very little part. He was an obedient audience for whom an esoteric priesthood performed increasingly meaningless rites. Long before they began to deify their emperor, Romans had begun to look for a kind of spiritual sustenance that the old gods could no longer supply. Some of them gravitated to Greek philosophies whose values were essentially religious, while others found satisfaction in the more emotional rites of several religions of the East.

Epicureanism and Stoicism, two of the Greek philosophies, sought to give man *autarky*, a sense of self-sufficiency, but approached the goal from different directions. For the Epicurean, the natural world was formed by chance and without order, and man was therefore free to direct his own destiny. For the Stoic, the natural world was meticulously ordered by a universal reason which existed in all things, and man, by living in harmony with reason, could rise above the difficulties of his surroundings. Probably the most attractive feature of Epicurean philosophy for the disillusioned Roman was its doctrine that the goal of life was pleasure. To Epicurus, a Fourth Century B.C. Greek, pleasure had meant freedom from pain; no act could be pleasurable if its consequences also resulted in discomfort to the body or spirit, either of oneself or of others. But some cynical young Roman aristocrats debased this essentially noble idea into one of self-indulgence.

Stoicism, although it too was altered in Rome, fared far better. For one thing its stern ethics appealed to more serious-minded Romans. The good life, said the Stoics, was one that was lived according to pure reason. Possessed of this, a man realized that the things ordinary people value are not important: wealth, health and position are "things indifferent." Zeno, who had originated the philosophy in Athens (and preached it from a stoa, or porch, thus giving it its name), claimed that the appurtenances of religion—temples, statues, sacrifices, prayers—were also unimportant. But Roman Stoics could never bring themselves to discard their gods entirely; they continued to worship them on the theory that the gods were embodiments of various elements in Zeno's universal reason.

Although Stoicism attracted men like Cicero, Seneca and the Emperor Marcus Aurelius, it was generally far too ascetic for the Roman common man. He much preferred another sort of religious experience which now began to appear in Rome. From merchants, prisoners of war brought back as slaves, and the soldiers who served abroad, the Romans learned of such Eastern deities as Cybele, Isis and Mithras. The cult of Cybele, an Asian fertility goddess—known also as the *Magna Mater*—was in fact first brought to Rome by official invitation in 205 B.C. at the time of Hannibal's invasion of Italy, during the Second Punic War. The invitation was suggested by the Sibylline oracles, which indicated that the goddess' presence in Italy might help the Roman cause.

Cybele's powers seemed effective (Hannibal left Italy shortly after she arrived) and she was permitted to stay, but Rome had misgivings about her. Like many Asian fertility goddesses, Cybele was worshiped with orgiastic dancing, during which her devotees pricked and slashed themselves with swords and knives, literally turning the rite into a bath of blood. These aspects of Cybele's worship led to severe regulation of her cult by the state, and participation in the orgies was forbidden to Roman citizens.

Later, under the Empire, the government relaxed its restrictions and Cybele gained a new following. But she was never as popular as another fertility goddess, Isis, a far more gracious and gentle deity. Originally Egyptian, but later Hellenized, Isis was especially favored by Roman women, who were drawn to her elaborate and mystical initiation rites. These were reported to last 10 days and culminated in a nightlong religious dramatization of the story of the death and resurrection of Isis' husband, Osiris. This miraculous rebirth, supposedly achieved by Isis herself, through the depth and poignancy of her grief, was the central emotional appeal of Isis' cult. In reconstructing the event, her followers believed that they too were being reborn, and in fact, gained immortality.

The third of the three Eastern religions, which had an important influence in Rome, that of Mithras, surpassed both the others in number of adherents and had by far the highest moral tone. The origins of the God Mithras are shrouded in antiquity; by the time the Romans met him he had become associated with Persian Zoroastrianism, and was a deity of truth and light. Mithraism introduced Romans to the idea of a world divided between good and evil, the powers of light and the powers of darkness. Its followers joined Mithras in his militant fight against evil.

Mithraism was a man's religion, rigorous and virile, with orders of membership somewhat similar to the degrees of modern Freemasonry. With its sense of fraternity and its emphasis on combat in the cause of good, the cult of Mithras spread like wildfire through the Roman army; by the Third Century A.D. it was practically the army's unofficial religion. Even the Emperor Commodus was reputed to have been an adherent. In certain superficial elements its rites were not unlike Christianity's; there was, for example, a ceremony similar to baptism. In fact the two were for a time competitors for the religious affections of Rome.

Christianity alone among the many religions that came to Rome was banned everywhere and subjected to systematic repression. It was not that Rome disliked Christian theology—by this time the Romans had been exposed to so many religious beliefs that they were tolerant of all of them. Rather, they persecuted the Christians for the political disobedience that resulted from their religious scruples. The Christians insisted that they alone possessed the truth, and that all other religions, including the state ones, were false. They refused, for instance, to observe the ritual acts connected with the emperor—such as burning incense before his statue—on the grounds that such gestures were tantamount to worshiping the emperor as a god.

Yet much as they disliked the Christians, the very Romans who persecuted them often had to admire them for their bravery in the face of torture and hideous martyrdom. Around 112 A.D. a fascinating exchange occurred between Pliny the Younger, then governor of Bithynia-Pontus, and the Emperor Trajan. Full of misgivings about the government's standing order to execute Christians, Pliny wrote the Emperor:

> *Those who denied that they were or had been Christians I thought should be released, when they had repeated after me an invocation to the gods, offered incense and wine to your image (which I had ordered brought in for this purpose, along with the statues of the deities), and in addition cursed Christ. It is said that genuine Christians cannot be forced to perform any of these acts . . . Consequently I have postponed the inquiry and have resorted to consulting you . . . The infection of this religiosity has spread not only through the cities, but through the villages and countryside as well.*

To which Trajan replied: "These people are not to be sought out. If they should be denounced and convicted, they must be punished, but with this proviso: anyone who denies he is a Christian . . . shall . . . obtain pardon through his recantation. Information published anonymously should never be admitted in evidence. That constitutes a very bad precedent and is not in keeping with the spirit of our times."

By the Third Century A.D. Christianity was still accumulating converts, and had become less doctrinaire: Christian writers were conceding that it was possible to be both a good Christian and a good Roman. Nevertheless the struggle between Christians and non-Christians went on, even after 313 when Constantine issued an official edict of toleration. Thus, for instance, while Constantine's successor, Constantius, ordered the ancient pagan altar and statue of victory removed from the Senate in 357, Julian, who followed Constantius as Emperor, ordered them restored. Then Gratian, in 382, again ordered them removed. They were briefly restored to their time-honored place by a pagan insurrection in 392, but in 394 Theodosius once again ordered their removal, and this time the removal was permanent—neither altar nor statue ever came back.

By the Fourth Century Christian writers were claiming not only that it was possible to be both Christian and Roman, but that the long history of Rome was in fact the beginning of the Christian epic; Roman policies of peace and unity had prepared the way. The implication was that Rome had been divinely ordained, just as the Augustan writers said; only the name of the divinity had changed. As for Rome itself, it came to accept the Christian view, just as it had accepted Olympians, Sibylline oracles, philosophers and fertility goddesses. In a sense the true religion of Rome, the ultimate object of Roman worship, the embodiment of Roman ideals, was Rome itself.

A PRETTY POMPEIAN GIRL *muses over a book, reflecting the upper-class life of fine clothes and leisure to pursue cultured pastimes.*

POMPEII: A SELF-PORTRAIT

In 79 A.D. Pompeii is a thriving town, still rebuilding from a devastating earthquake 16 years earlier. Its new streets are lined with new shops. Expanding businesses are crowding out the resort villas of urban aristocrats and the old homes of the local gentry. Epitomizing the quest for quick gain, one merchant adorns his villa with the motto, "Hail, Profit." There is almost no warning when Vesuvius erupts—in the cataclysm, the whole town vanishes under volcanic ash.

In this essay, the remarkably preserved remains of Pompeii and nearby towns, unearthed in the last 200 years, provide a unique portrait of that community.

MEN OF AFFAIRS

The streets of Pompeii echoed with the sounds of commerce from the crack of dawn. Men seeking jobs might wait all night at a rich patron's door. Most of the wealthy men in Pompeii were merchants or manufacturers; often their shops or workrooms adjoined their villas. Sometimes tradesmen took over the ground floors of old aristocratic houses and even pushed the former owners out. After a busy morning spent making business deals or arguing over local politics, Pompeian men might also do the shopping for the household *(opposite)*.

STEPPINGSTONES *at crosswalks kept pedestrians dry-shod in wet weather. The stones were set apart, leaving clear space for chariot wheels.*

STREET MUSICIANS *such as these contributed to the clatter of Pompeian streets, attracting urchins as well as amusing shoppers. Passersby usually rewarded them with some small coins.*

A BAKER'S STALL *on the street (above) offered fresh bread and cakes. When Pompeii was excavated, charred loaves of bread were found, almost 1,800 years old, preserved in volcanic ash.*

131

LADIES OF LEISURE

For Pompeian women of the leisure class, with slaves to do the menial housework, there was ample time to keep up with the latest fashions in clothing, hair styles and cosmetics. They frequently spent an afternoon with a group of other women at a private bath or gambling with knucklebones *(right)*. The women's cultivated tastes were reflected in the exquisite furnishings and frescoes of their homes. Their persons, too, were the objects of careful decoration. They bleached their hair or wore wigs, used lipstick, eyeshadow and rouge. The exotic perfumes used prompted a dour comment from Plautus: "The right scent for a woman is none at all."

THE ELEGANT TRESSES *and complicated coiffures of Pompeian women required careful arranging, done here by a slave hairdresser.*

THE AIRY DECOR *of the bedroom of a villa, with wall paintings and mosaic on the floor, includes a garden scene painted on the far wall.*

LADYLIKE GAMBLERS *might spend an idle hour at knucklebones, a game handed down from the Greeks. This marble plaque pictures a mythical scene: Niobe and her daughters absorbed in the game.*

A PRIVATE BANQUET *is portrayed in this Pompeian scene. At left, a late arrival has his sandals taken off by a slave. At right, another slave is struggling to support an overstuffed diner.*

A SUNKEN FOUNTAIN *is the central feature of a wine merchant's dining room. The room is decorated with scenes portraying mythical animals and gods. Diners sat around the fountain as musicians played at the far end of the room.*

AN INTIMATE CONCERT *often followed a gargantuan banquet. Above, a woman musician entertains the guests, her left hand plucking a cithara and her right hand a small curved harp.*

PATRICIAN PLEASURES

At Pompeii's height the rich indulged themselves in both public and private. The public baths, almost as lavish as those at Rome, were radiant-heated. One bath stayed open at night, illuminated by over a thousand lamps. The baths served as fashionable clubs, for women as well as men. At home, the banquet table offered sumptuous entertainment. Men and women dined together, reclining on couches in a room like the one above. They dined throughout the late afternoon and evening. Flirtation added spice to these occasions. Drunkenness, Ovid noted, made audacity seem innocent.

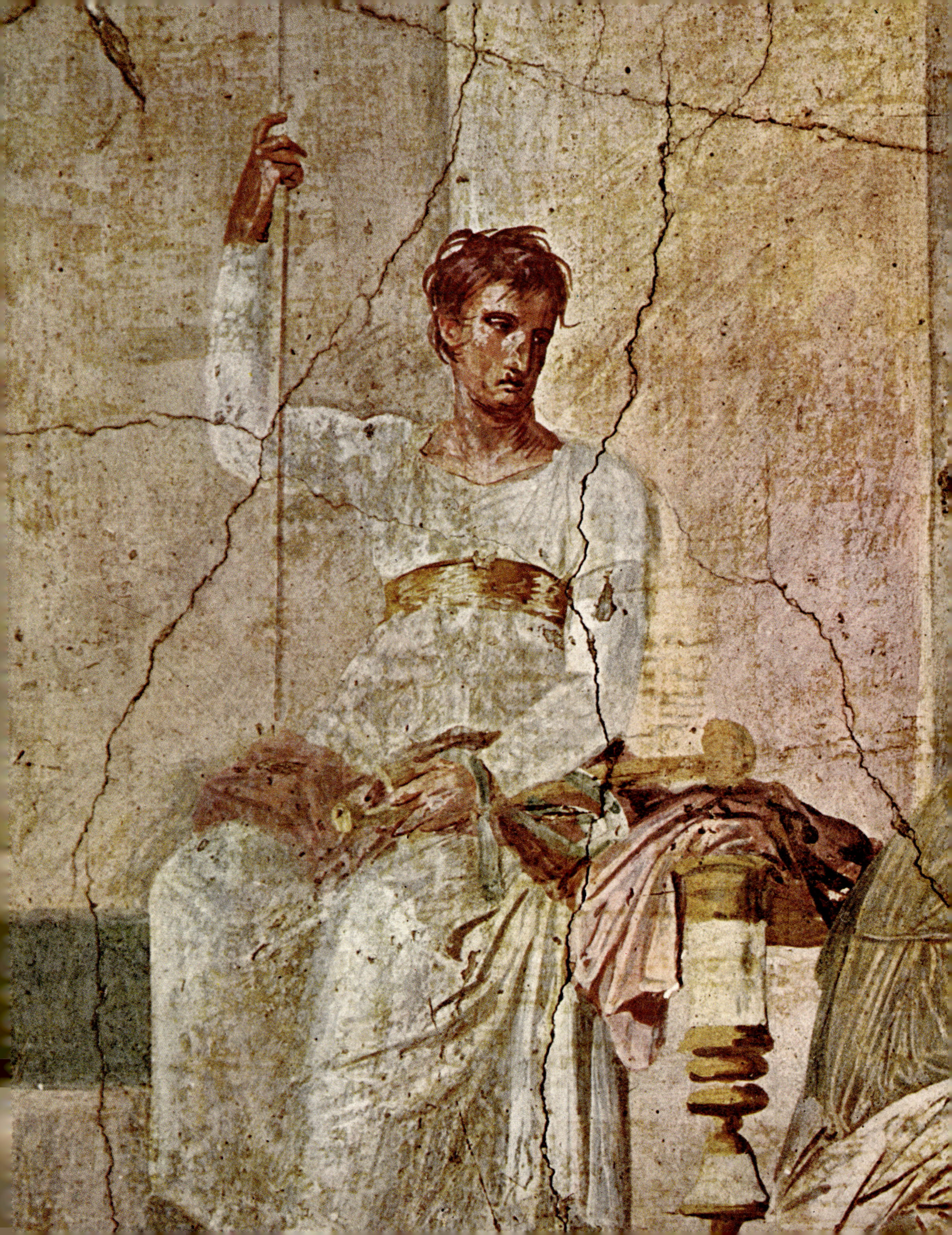

THE ODEON THEATER'S STAGE *is seen above through a vaulted entranceway. Steps lead up to the seats. This playhouse held an audience of about 1,200; the Great Theater next door about 5,000.*

VARIETY ON THE BOARDS

There were two theaters in Pompeii. The Great Theater offered open-air spectacles, Greek plays and—a local specialty—farces and burlesque mimes much like the Punch and Judy plays of later times. Pompeians laughed at stock figures of the stage— Pappus the Idiot as a candidate for office, or Bucco the Hunchback turned gladiator. On occasion a condemned criminal, cast in the part of a dying man, was put to death on stage. On sunny days, awnings shaded the audience. There was also the smaller, roofed-in Odeon *(above)*, where the more cultured Pompeians attended serious concerts, poetry readings, and intimate theatrical productions.

BEHIND THE SCENES *an actor (left) holds the scepter of a tragic king. With two other members of the troupe, he celebrates a success by dedicating a painting of a theatrical mask to the gods.*

A PERPETUAL THREAT *to the pleasant life of Pompeii, Vesuvius was depicted on one wall painting as covered with trees and terraced vineyards. Beside the ominous mountain is Bacchus, garlanded and dressed in grapes.*

A SOMBER WATCHER, *this tombstone statue of a shawled woman stands in a necropolis, or cemetery, outside Pompeii. The road (in background) running beside the city's walls was flanked by similar funeral monuments.*

A CITY'S SUDDEN DEATH

The first cloud over Vesuvius, wrote Pliny the Younger, looked like "a pine-tree, for it shot up a great height . . . into several branches." When the volcano erupted, on August 24, 79 A.D., the 18-year-old Pliny was near Pompeii. Vesuvius spewed clouds of ash and stone for three days. People, Pliny said, "tied pillows upon their heads with napkins" to protect themselves. Some Pompeians fell in the streets; children, overcome by noxious gas, were buried in a playroom; a laundryman died beside a hoard of coins. Almost everything in Pompeii, like the statue brooding over the dead *(opposite)*, was preserved as the town disappeared under a 30-foot layer of ash. Overhead, Pliny recalled, "a black and dreadful cloud . . . now and again yawned open to reveal long fantastic flames." Pliny escaped, but as he fled he thought "that all mankind was involved . . . and that I was perishing with the world itself."

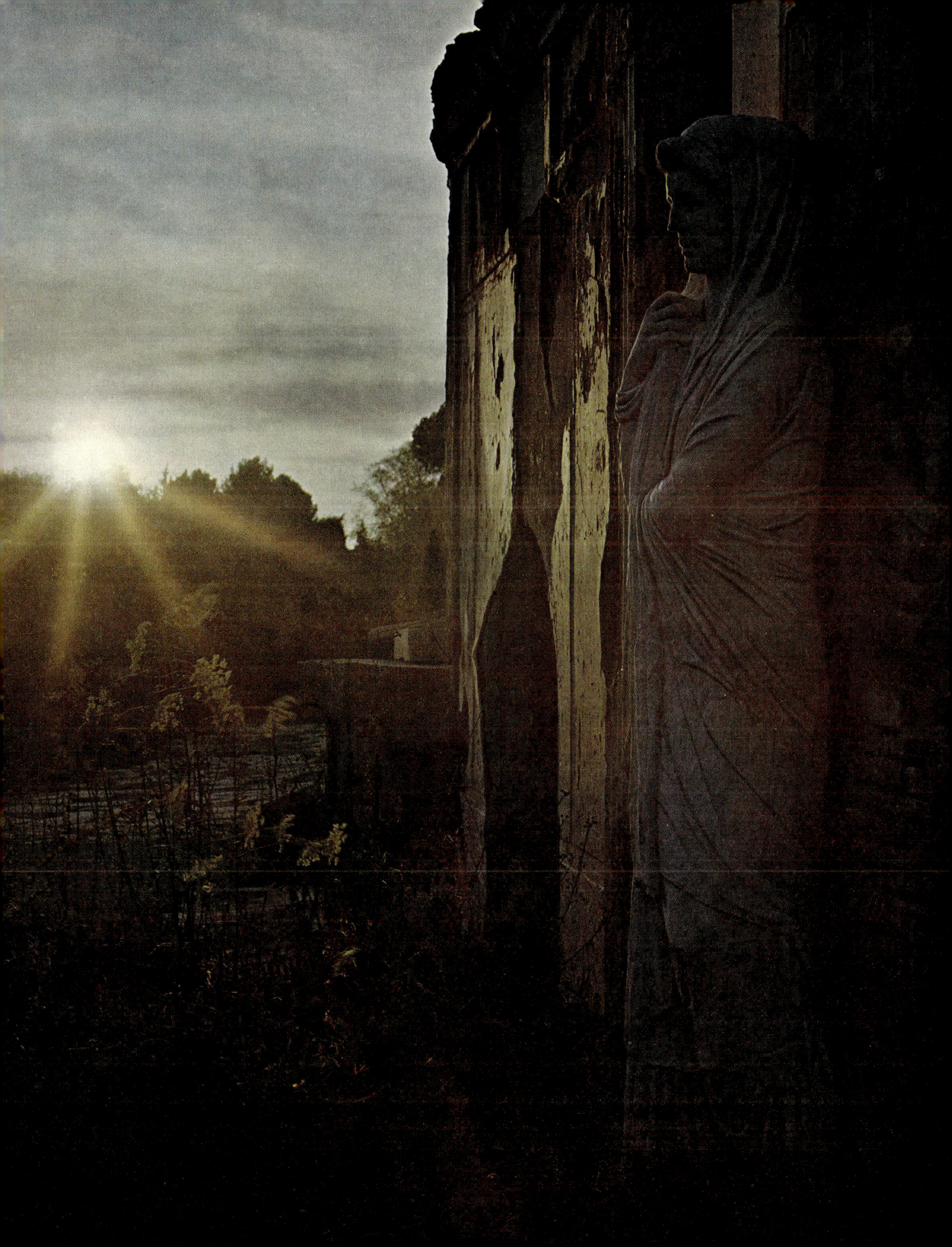

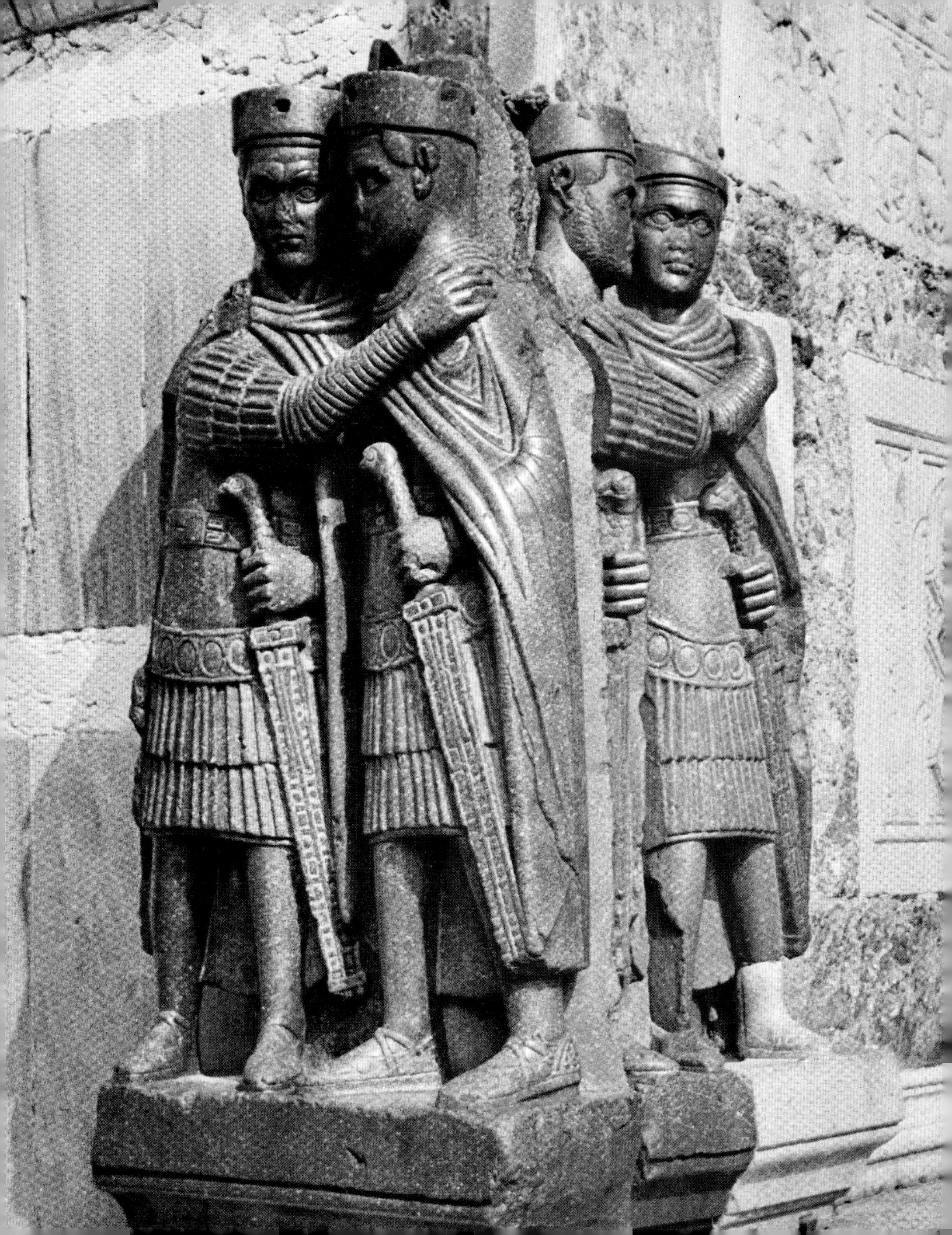

7
END OF GREATNESS

The three centuries between the great age of Marcus Aurelius and the overwhelming of Rome by barbarians in the Fifth Century A.D. is often called the epoch of Rome's "decline and fall." But Romans who lived in those centuries did not know it was falling. To them, the business of empire appeared to go on as usual: petty tyrants paraded as emperors; rich men dressed up in senatorial togas; Roman soldiers went forth to battle barbarians, even if they did it more for money than for the glory of Rome. It is only in the perspective of time that Rome's fall is evident.

When Marcus Aurelius died in 180, probably of the plague that was ravaging the Empire, he was succeeded by the first of many tyrants, his own son Commodus. According to one contemporary, the historian Cassius Dio, Commodus "was a greater curse to the Romans than any pestilence or crime." Vain and frivolous, he ordained that Rome be called Commodiana and gave himself up to the pleasures of executions, chariot races and lion baiting. His despotism so damaged and discredited the office of princeps that its prestige was all but destroyed. Finally, after 12 years of misrule, Commodus was assassinated. Three months later the Praetorian Guard, in a rampant display of power, proceeded to auction off the imperial office to the highest bidder. Cassius Dio describes this "most disgraceful business:

"The would-be buyers were Sulpicianus and Julianus, who vied to outbid each other, one from inside [the military camp], the other from the outside. . . . Some of the soldiers would carry the word to Julianus, 'Sulpicianus offers so much; how much more do you bid?' And to Sulpicianus in turn, 'Julianus promises so much; how much do you raise him?' Sulpicianus would have won the day, being inside and being a prefect of the city and also the first to name the figure of 20,000 sesterces per soldier, had not Julianus raised his bid no longer by a small amount but by 5,000 at one time, shouting it in a loud voice and also indicating the amount with his fingers." But Didius Julianus, which was the winner's full name, had bought himself a dubious claim. Armies based in several of the provinces had already proclaimed their own commanders as Emperor, and one of them, Septimius Severus, Afri-

SHARING THE RULE, *the tetrarchs whom Diocletian (second from right) established to help administer the Empire in 293 A.D. are shown embracing in this stone sculpture now standing in the Piazza di San Marco in Venice.*

can by birth and commander on the Danube, now marched on Rome and deposed the new Emperor-by-auction.

Severus' cardinal principle of government was simple: take care of the Army and the rest will take care of itself. "Enrich the soldiers," he advised the sons who were to succeed him, "and scorn all other men." Nevertheless, Severus was a competent administrator and an excellent soldier, and considering the problems he faced in both categories, he did reasonably well. To the north, German tribes continued to threaten the Empire's borders, while the Parthian Kingdom challenged Rome's frontiers in the East. The imperial coffers had been drained by the earlier military campaigns of Marcus Aurelius; finances were henceforth to be a problem that plagued all Roman leaders. Marcus Aurelius had made matters worse by devaluing the Roman currency 25 per cent and by selling imperial treasures to raise additional revenue. Now Severus devalued the money by another 25 per cent, and in addition raised existing taxes and devised new ones. One source of income came to be the wholesale confiscation of the property of Severus' political enemies, or of those citizens who contributed too slowly to his campaigns.

But none of these measures was sufficient. Just as the age of peace had brought Rome prosperity for which all emperors could take credit, so the age of wars brought economic and social difficulties which no emperor could resolve. The increasing taxation which war required depleted the treasuries of provincial cities and also of individual citizens: some members of the upper classes were driven to forfeit their rank and retire to lower social orders where the financial burdens were less. Thus, paradoxically, higher taxes led to a decline in revenues. At the same time, the numbers of the poor increased. To ease their burden—and allay their unrest—Severus systematically distributed food, money and medicine, putting an additional strain on the imperial budget. The state, it seemed, could not meet all the demands that were placed upon it, yet could not endure without meeting them.

First and foremost of the demands, of course, was the defense of the frontiers. Severus added three new legions to the regular Army, taking many barbarians into the ranks. He also improved his soldiers' pay and relaxed some of the restrictions of military life. The historian Herodian saw this as a cause of later troubles. Severus, he wrote, "granted [the soldiers] many privileges which they did not previously have: he was the first to increase their grain ration, and permitted them to wear gold rings [the insignia of equestrians] and to live with their wives . . . all of which used to be considered incompatible with military discipline and with preparedness and readiness for war. He was the first to undermine their famous vigor, . . . teaching them to covet money and turning them aside to luxurious living."

Gold rings on the hands of common soldiers signified Severus' aim to draw new blood into the equestrian rank, and then into the Government. The legions became a training ground for administrators as well as generals. Professional soldiers rose through the ranks to take high posts in the civil service alongside civilians. Former military men soon advanced in the imperial administration, giving the bureaucracy a military cast. "The emperor and his council," one historian has noted, "now resembled a general and his staff, with the equestrian civil servants as their executive officers."

The infiltration of the Army into the civil Government was a radical departure. But Severus was not unduly troubled by a feeling of reverence for the Empire's hallowed customs. He was a provincial from the old Phoenician town of Leptis Magna (he spoke Latin with a Punic accent), and his personal sympathies were with the provinces. During his reign, Punic and Celtic terms were allowed in legal documents, and in Gaul and the Rhine provinces, a Celtic measure of mileage replaced Latin on markers along newly repaired roads. Most of Severus' top officials were provincials from the East and Africa. And, continuing the practice of former rulers, he granted the right of citizenship to more and more towns and cities in the provinces.

Severus died in 211 at York, while directing the defense of the British frontier. For the next 24 years his sons and relatives, as the Severan Dynasty, directed the affairs of state. Following the course his father had set, Caracalla, the first of his successors, increased the Army's pay by 50 per cent and raised the bounties paid to barbarian chieftains to keep them from attacking weak points along the frontier. These bounties now began to equal the Army's whole payroll. Soon Caracalla had to raise the taxes and again debase the currency. His decision, in 212, to grant citizenship to all free men throughout the Empire was, says Dio, not dictated by an instinct for democracy: he wanted to include aliens on Rome's tax rolls "to increase his revenues."

The Severan Dynasty ended in 235 with the death of Severus Alexander, last of the line, who was murdered by his own troops on the Rhine frontier; they were outraged at his attempt to bribe invading barbarians whom they preferred to fight. In his place they proclaimed as Emperor a crude, towering Thracian soldier, Maximinus. A shepherd who had risen through the ranks, Maximinus had never even been to Rome. With his rise to power, the Roman soldiers took over the Empire. With his rise, also, the Empire's internal peace came to an end. The reign of Maximinus ushered in a half century of civil wars, compounded by barbarian incursions, financial collapse, spreading famine and recurring plague. The Severan policy of placating the Army had brought Rome to a state of military anarchy.

Under Maximinus, the demands of Rome upon its people and provinces grew more rapacious than ever. Herodian says that "after reducing most of the notable houses to poverty, and finding the income obtained thereby small and insufficient for his purpose, Maximinus began to lay hands on the public treasuries."

Maximinus lasted as Emperor only four years, but his successors did little better. In the chaotic 50 years from the death of Severus Alexander to the advent of Diocletian, there were some 20 emperors and a host of usurpers who held parts of the Empire for short times. The reign of these emperors averaged about two and a half years and, with the exception of one who died of the plague and another who was captured by Persians, emperors and usurpers alike all met violent deaths. Most of them were made and unmade at the whim of the Roman soldiers, who proclaimed and assassinated emperors mainly for their own profit.

During these dark years, enemies breached the Empire's frontier on almost all sides. In the East, the reviving Persian Empire menaced Syria, Egypt and the whole of Asia Minor; on the Rhine, Franks and Alemanni broke into Gaul and even Spain. In Africa, Berber tribes raided Roman cities and towns. Often the Roman armies sent against these invaders did as much damage to Roman communities as the aggressors.

As the wars raged—including civil wars: for 14 years Rome actually was governed as two separate nations—the finances of the Empire utterly collapsed. The denarius and the antoninianus, chief silver coins of the realm, lost more than 90 per cent of their silver content: in effect, they were copper coins washed with silver. Soldiers and civil servants were increasingly paid in goods and commodities. Inflation gripped the money market, and the price of goods soared. A peck of wheat which sold for half a denarius in the Second Century was fixed at 100 denarii by the end of the Third. In the Egyptian town of Oxyrhynchus, bankers refused to handle Roman money and tried to return to the Ptolemaic coins used some 300 years earlier.

As the prestige of Rome declined, the value of Roman citizenship declined with it. The position of magistrate in a city or town, once an honor, now became a burden. Aurelian made matters worse by insisting that local officials must raise their town's customary tribute even when some of the town's lands were no longer revenue-producing. Consequently, once-sought-after posts now had to be made obligatory. In Rome, even the Senate had only a remnant of its ancient prestige. Senators, by now excluded from holding military commands, issued fewer and fewer decrees. The assemblage, though it continued to meet in the historic Senate building and still called itself a Senate, was reduced in effect to serving as the city council of Rome.

The civil wars which made emperors of common soldiers ended when Diocletian took the scepter in 284. Although he too was an army man, a Dalmatian soldier who had risen to the rank of general, he restored to the Empire a sense of political order. Diocletian secured the frontiers and reorganized the state government, introducing a degree of discipline—and of regimentation—that would characterize Roman life to the end of the Empire. Abandoning even the pretense of Constitutional rule, Diocletian established the official doctrine of divine right to the Emperor's position; he went so far as to demand that all who approached him prostrate themselves in adoration.

Diocletian's measures to strengthen the frontiers consisted of establishing strong fortifications in the hinterlands. As the Greek historian Zosimus wrote, "the frontiers of the Roman empire were everywhere studded with cities and forts and towers . . . and the whole army was stationed along them, so that it was impossible for the barbarians to break through." Diocletian increased the size of the Army. But at the same time, he broke up the commands of the legions into smaller units, giving each general fewer men and thus less opportunity to attempt an insurrection. He reorganized the government of the provinces along similar lines, carving the existing 50 or so provinces into more than 100 smaller ones. Even Italy was divided into eight or more districts.

Naturally this fragmentation called for an increase in officials and paper work; the result was a great expansion of the imperial bureaucracy. A note written in 288 from one Roman official to another observes that, "It is apparent from the accounts alone that many persons wishing to batten on the estates of the treasury have devised titles for themselves, such as administrators, secretaries, or superintendents, whereby they procure no advantage for the treasury but eat up the revenues." To manage the growing civil service, Diocletian overhauled the whole structure of empire. The provinces were grouped into larger *dioceses*, each of which was directed by a *vicarius*, or vicar.

Finally, to oversee this enormous establishment, Diocletian created a ruling tetrarchy: two emperors with the title of Augustus to rule the Empire, and two heirs-apparent with the title of Caesar to succeed them. Diocletian (who took care that he never really lost his supremacy under this system) ran the East, controlling the provinces in Asia, Asia Minor, Egypt and Thrace; his co-Emperor, a fellow officer named Maximian, ruled the Western provinces. The two Caesars were given provincial assignments under their Emperors so that the Empire

A LONG-LIVED COIN, *the gold solidus, with a portrait of a reigning emperor on one side and a personification of Constantinople on the other, was first struck by Constantine around 312 A.D. Succeeding emperors reissued the solidus with their own portrait—the one at left shows the Emperor Honorius (395-423 A.D.). The solidus remained a medium of exchange until the 11th Century.*

was divided into four prefectures. This resulted in a further swelling of the establishment.

Diocletian's measures to make sense out of the Empire's monetary chaos were equally bureaucratic. As prices continued to soar unchecked, he issued an edict fixing maximum prices for goods and wages throughout the Empire, and prescribing the death penalty for violators. The edict was incredibly detailed. It set prices for wheat, barley and rye; for wild pheasant and fattened pheasant; for sparrows and dormice.

But Diocletian's edict boomeranged. When it was posted, Lactantius tells us, "nothing appeared on the market because of fear, and prices soared much higher." At last Diocletian let prices go unchecked. Four decades later, a peck of wheat price-fixed at 100 denarii was selling for 10,000 denarii.

For some time the government had been collecting revenues partly in the form of commodities rather than entirely in cash. Now Diocletian increased the amount of taxes collected in this form. In order to determine these new assessments, Diocletian sent out a vast army of census-takers to collect data in every corner of the Empire. When the census was complete, the state had remarkably extensive records on both its people and its land. It knew for example that one Dionysius the farmer lived at Mytelene, on the island of Lesbos in the Aegean Sea, and that he owned exactly 216 first-class olive trees.

The taking of the census became a regular affair, occurring at first every five years and later every 15 years. Eventually it imposed a new burden on the populace: people were required to remain on their land or stay at their jobs so that they would always be where the census-taker expected to find them (and also so they could continue to produce for the government). Eventually this regulation fixed every Roman citizen in a rigid economic caste system. Sons inherited their fathers' obligations; all men within the Empire labored and produced primarily for the benefit of the state.

Diocletian, a remarkable man in many ways, was perhaps most remarkable of all in being the first Roman Emperor to abdicate. Having voluntarily shared the office in 286, he stepped down of his own volition in 305, persuading his co-Emperor to retire at the same time.

Diocletian had meant the two Caesars to succeed as Augusti, and in time to turn the government over to their own appointed Caesars. But it took less than a year for this arrangement to break down. Soldiers once more tried to dictate the succession, and by 311 there were four rival Augusti.

One of them was Constantine, who was to emerge as one of the outstanding men of Rome's declining years. Marching on Rome to battle it out with a rival claimant, Maxentius, Constantine—according to his biographer Eusebius—had a vision. He saw a Cross in the sky and the inscription *hoc signo vince*, "By this sign win your victory." Immediately Constantine ordered the Christian monogram—the letters *chi* and *rho*, the first two in Christ's name—emblazoned on his soldiers' standards. When he emerged as sole Emperor in 324, he became known as the first Christian Emperor.

Ever since the reign of Nero, Christians had endured sporadic persecution. In spite of this, Christian congregations throughout the Empire had held their ground numerically, and had even made some converts among Rome's influential families. The conversion of Constantine, however, ultimately wedded Church and state, diverting Roman funds into Church coffers and bringing bishops into the service of the state—and imperial regulation into Church affairs.

Under Constantine the Roman Government became more autocratic than ever. All the energies of the state were spent on supplying and maintaining its huge bureaucracies and defensive armies, and all the energies of the people were harnessed to the same cause. Through the edicts of Constantine and his successors, the artisan was bound to his bench, the farmer to his land, the magistrate to his town council, the merchant to his guild. A son had no choice but to enroll in his father's guild and take up his father's obligations to the state. The sons of veterans had to serve in the Army.

Some of the social changes embodied in Constantine's edicts had actually begun long before his reign. Through custom and debt the tenant farmer, for example, had been more and more tied to his land. Often he had to purchase his seed and rent his plow and oxen from the landlord, and a crop failure could leave him deep in debt with little prospect of getting out. Constantine's edicts simply formalized this relationship, under the guise of guaranteeing the state its share of the farmer's crop and the landlord's profit. Thus he prohibited landlords from charging a tenant, or *colonus*, "more than it was customary to render . . . in former times," but at the same time he provided that "if someone wants to sell an estate . . . he has not the right to retain *coloni* . . . in order to transfer them to other places." In effect he bound both tenant and landlord in perpetuity to one piece of land.

Constantine's edicts did not halt the economic deterioration of the Empire any more than Diocletian's had. The western part of the Empire had very nearly been wrung dry; a Gallic writer protested to Constantine that tax assessments had "drained our very life." The once-great city of Rome was now no more than a symbol, and its decline was hastened in 324 when Constantine decided to build a new imperial capital in the East.

Constantine's new capital, Constantinople, constructed on the site of the old Greek city of Byzantium in what is now Turkey, was intended as a replica of Rome, even to the seven hills. There, Roman emperors continued to rule for another 1,100 years, long after the Western Roman Empire was lost to barbarians. It was in Constantinople that the two great Roman legal codes were issued, by the Emperor Theodosius in 438 and the Emperor Justinian between 529 and 534. Together these codes were the summation of centuries of Roman Government, a digest of edicts, laws and regulations dating back to the Republic. Combining both Roman and Christian ethical traditions, they were the last great achievement of the Empire.

As time passed, the barbarians could no longer be held back. In 376, several Germanic tribes broke through the Danube frontier, and others soon followed. The Visigoths, Suevi and Vandals set up their own kingdoms within the Empire. But the ravages of the last wars left the invaders little more of the once-great Empire than the land they occupied. Ammianus, the last great Roman historian, describes the Empire in the West as a land hounded by "the burden of tributes and the repeated increase in taxes . . . crushed by the severity of the dunning tax-collectors." As the barbarians swept over the countryside, Ammianus continues, one could see "women driven along by cracking whips, and stupefied with fear, still heavy with their unborn children, which before coming into the world endured many horrors."

The city of Rome itself was sacked by the Visigoths in 410 and by the Vandals in 455. But Rome could not be destroyed. It lived on as the seat of the Church and as a great monument: even in ruins it outshone the rising cities of Europe until the days of the Renaissance.

PAYING TAXES, *provincials hand coins to the collector. Romans were taxed on crops, slaves, estates and roads—and even had to pay local sales taxes.*

THE METROPOLIS

In the days of Augustus, about a million people lived in Rome, most of them jammed into stuffy, malodorous apartments. (They smelled so bad that Pliny suggested disguising the odor by burning bread.) People complained about the housing shortage, soaring rents, congested traffic, polluted air, crime in the streets and the high cost of living. Unemployment was a perennial problem, and it increased as farm families, dispossessed by changing agricultural methods, flooded into the city. To keep some semblance of order, the Government created a civil service with a multitude of agents—including tax collectors *(above)*, police, fire wardens, building inspectors and public health officials. For residents of the swarming imperial capital, daily life presented most of the complex problems—and provided all the excitement—found in a teeming modern metropolis.

A STOOPED FARMER, *shown in a relief of the First Century B.C., takes his cow to town past roadside shrines. By then there were few small, independent farmers; this man was probably a tenant.*

A PRIMITIVE PLOW, *used by Roman farmers in the early days of the Republic, was made of wood and rope, and was usually drawn by oxen. Plows like this one are still used in parts of southern Italy.*

THE FARMERS' FLIGHT TO THE CITY

To live in sprawling Rome, with all its drawbacks, was the cherished goal of the ambitious, the last hope of the impoverished. The city offered dazzling opportunities to a determined man; to the penniless, there was at least the promise of a meager dole.

Among the hordes of poverty-stricken freedmen, the most pathetic were the former farmers. Independent farmers had been the backbone of the early Republic. But by the Second Century B.C. they were in trouble; imported foodstuffs were being sold at prices lower than the small farmer could match. Large-scale farming—more efficient and economical—offered one solution, but only the rich could afford the great tracts of land that were needed. Furthermore, the big farms added to the problems of the small landholders; Pliny the Elder grumbled that "large holdings have ruined Italy." The displaced yeoman could become a tenant farmer on an estate, or he could leave the land. Many left and journeyed to Rome, there to be ridiculed as yokels for their *rusticitas*—their country simplicity—and to swell the numbers of the unemployed.

A GOATHERD *seated on a woven wicker stool milks an animal. This relief, carved about 270 A.D., shows his shelter as a lean-to constructed of wicker and bamboo. A clay pot at his feet holds the milk.*

AN OIL MERCHANT (right) ladles his merchandise out of a bowl and into a customer's jug. Olive oil was a mainstay of the Roman diet; it was used for sauces and salad dressings.

AN OIL PRESS, shown in a modern reconstruction, used a stone block that was screwed against a base, crushing olives in between. The oil flowed into vials set at the corners.

PROSPERITY IN THE SHOPS

The city hummed with trade; Pliny the Younger commented that "in Rome the merchandise of the whole world could be had all together." Indoors and in the streets a variety of tradesmen did business: barbers at one stand, grocers at the next, money changers, furniture merchants, book dealers. Boys sold sausages, and sooty, smoking shops offered cooked food ready to take out. Oil—used for lamps, for cooking and in soap—was Rome's single most important commodity, so much so that by 300 A.D. the city had 2,300 dealers in this product alone.

Though shopkeepers prospered, aristocrats looked down on them. Cicero wrote his son: "Contemptible is the business of the retail dealer, for he cannot succeed unless he is dishonest, and dishonesty is the most shameful thing in the world." Roman storekeepers were so eager for profit, it was said, that they would sell themselves for the right price.

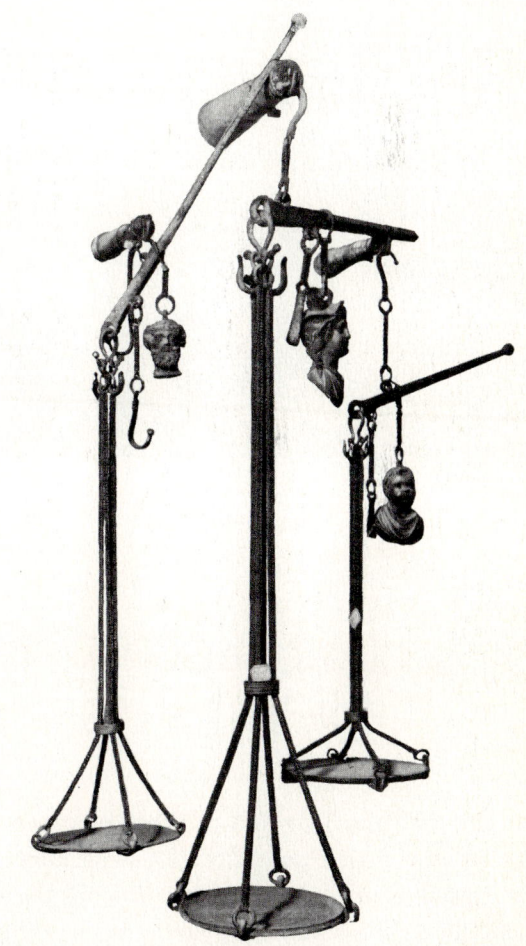

STOREKEEPERS' SCALES, *seen in replicas, were used in the First Century A.D. Goods placed in the pans were weighed by moving the sculptured weights along the horizontal bars.*

A ROMAN MATRON *selects a goose in a meat market (left), as a seated woman notes her purchases. Women worked in and sometimes owned small shops, and some widows grew rich in business.*

A ROMAN PHARMACY *might sell anything from herbs to groceries. At left, the goddess of healing, Meditrina, holds a libation dish; the girl behind her holds a phial of medicine.*

A PHARMACOPOEIA FOR THE SICK

In imperial Rome, it was said, the rich got sick from eating, the poor from not eating. The undernourished fell victim to epidemics of typhus, dysentery and tuberculosis. To fight the spread of disease, inspectors were appointed to check housing and sanitation, and by the Fourth Century there were also public doctors for the poor. Some physicians were highly sophisticated (they supplied amputees with artificial limbs, for example) but others were quacks who prescribed boiled lard for broken bones, goats' hair for drowsiness and owls' toes for fever.

A MEDICAL INSTRUMENT, *one of 200 medical tools found in Pompeii, was used for internal examinations of expectant mothers. Called a speculum, it closely resembles its modern counterpart.*

HEALING THE SICK *(opposite), a physician examines a child's swollen belly and wasted limbs. The best medical books were written in Greek, and Greek doctors were the most skillful in all Rome.*

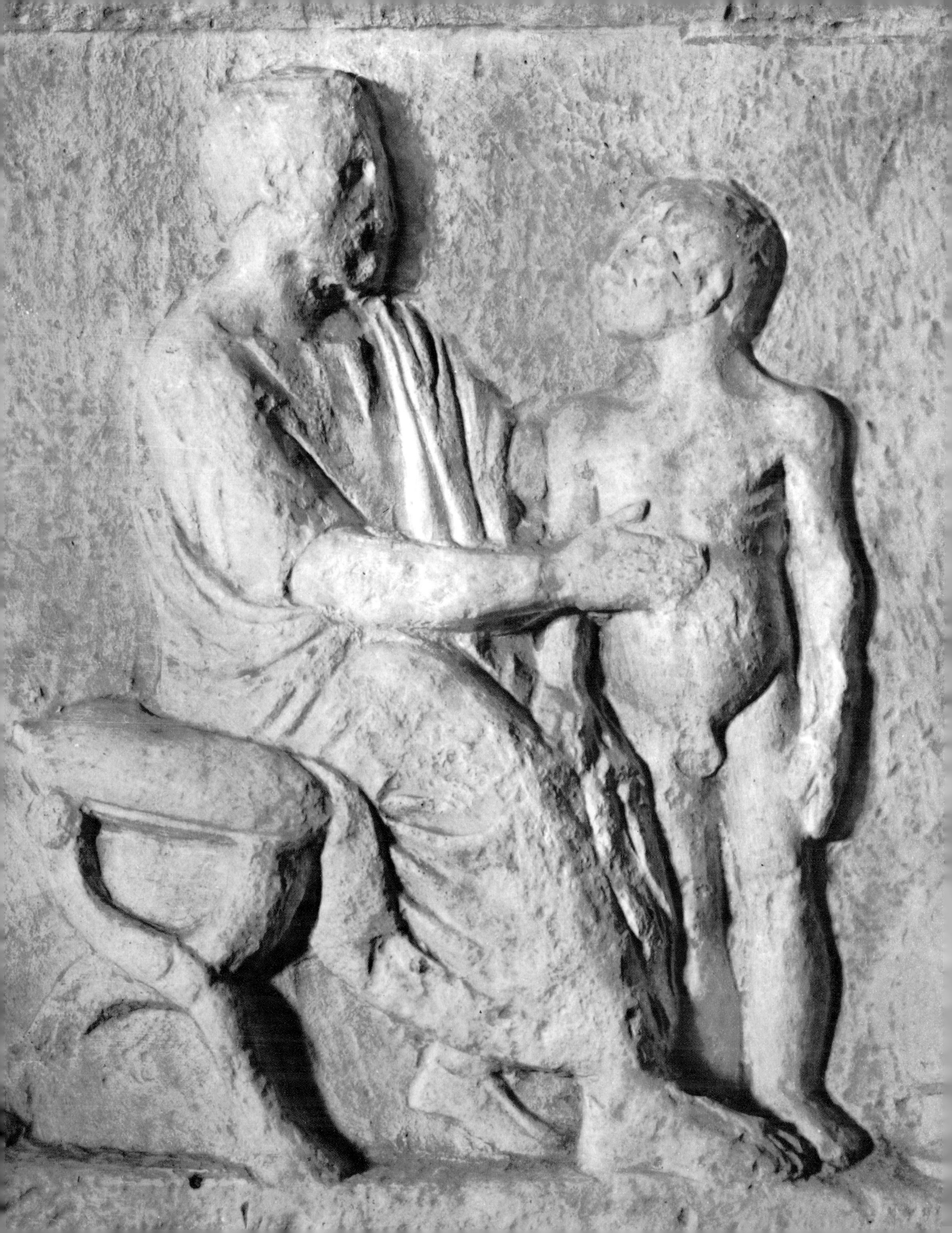

BOOMING TRADE, BUSY BUILDERS

"All that trade and ships may bring reaches Rome," said an orator in the Second Century. The city lived off its imports, and importers were among the wealthiest men of the Empire. Shipping became such big business that companies were formed to offer insurance against storms at sea.

Huge cargoes shipped from the provinces were unloaded at the seaport of Ostia and were carried daily up the Tiber on small boats to warehouses in the capital. Among the products carried upriver in this fashion were brick, marble, granite and wood, for Rome seemed always to be building and rebuilding itself. Juvenal spoke of "this aerial Rome which rests only on beams as long and thin as flutes." By imperial times, Roman builders had erected over 45,000 apartment houses. These tenements, scattered throughout the city, frequently rose to relatively great heights. Materials were often shoddy, construction was hurried, and the resultant cave-ins and fires eventually led the Emperor Augustus to prohibit the building of private dwellings more than 70 feet high on public streets.

Rents kept pace with the building boom. In one period rents in Rome were four times higher than in other Italian cities. Still landlords complained. "Two of my buildings have collapsed," protested Cicero; "in the others the walls are all cracked; not only the tenants, but even the mice, have left."

MERCHANT SHIPS, *fancifully portrayed below, reached Italian ports from all over the world, usually at speeds averaging more than 100 miles a day. The task*

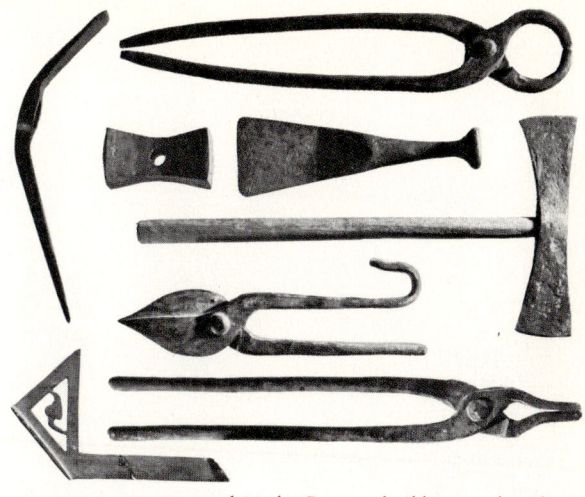

A DISPLAY OF TOOLS used in the Roman building trades shows tongs (top and bottom), a variety of cutting tools, a hammer head and trowel (top center), and a mason's square (lower left).

AN ELABORATE CRANE (left) was used to build multistoried structures. Materials were raised by ropes from the towering beam; power was supplied by workers treading on spokes of the wheel.

of moving their cargoes to the consumer provided many Romans with a wide range of jobs: as stevedores and clerks, money lenders and middlemen.

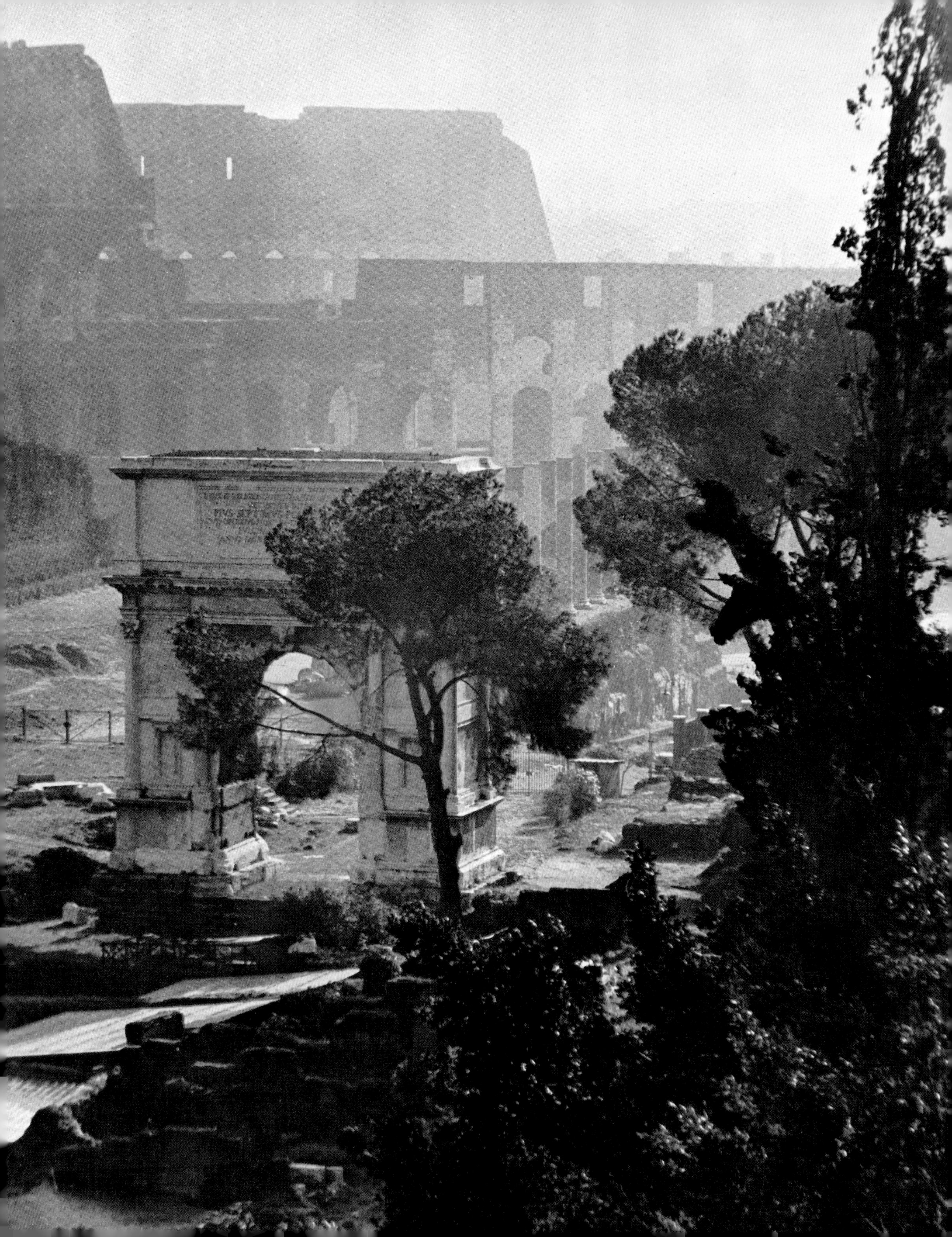

8
A PERSISTENT PRESENCE

Rome was not effaced by its fall. In earlier ages the decline of a state had often meant not only the collapse of its political structure, but the disappearance of its culture—the extinction of its way of life. Long before Rome fell from power, however, it had insured its cultural survival by Romanizing the far-flung parts of its Empire. Although the remote provinces resumed autonomy when the political threads which bound them to Rome were broken, each was now to some degree a replica of Rome. Rome fell, but Romanism went on.

Today, 1,500 years later, the heritage of Rome is an essential ingredient of Western culture: it has shaped and been embodied in the thought, the institutions and the languages of the Western world. Sometimes the influence of Rome is plain to see, as in the classic façade of a public building, or in scientific nomenclature constructed on Latin roots. Often, however, the Roman element is hard to distinguish, for it has been so woven into the web of daily experience that it takes on the appearance of a native growth.

But the route followed by Roman ideas and fashions is never difficult to discern. The heritage has been passed on to the modern world through three historic channels: through the Roman Empire of the East, which lasted until the Turks captured Constantinople in 1453; through the Roman Catholic Church; and through the conscious adoption of Roman styles by almost all who have encountered them.

The first channel, the Eastern Empire (sometimes called Byzantium), preserved the Roman way for a thousand years after Rome itself had fallen to the barbarians. Constantine's Eastern capital of Constantinople was a replica of old Rome on the Tiber. It had seven hills and 14 regions, as did Rome; many of its buildings were exact reproductions of Roman originals; it had a Senate patterned after the Roman version. It even had a genuine Roman mob, a proletarian group especially imported by Constantine from Italy to give the new capital an authentically Latin atmosphere.

The emperors who reigned from this Second Rome on the Bosporus did not regard the loss of the West as fatal. They continued, in the tradition

AN ARCHITECTURAL LEGACY, *the Colosseum and the Arch of Titus were constructed by the Flavian Emperors—Vespasian, who began work on the arena in 79 A.D., and his son Domitian, who built the arch soon afterward.*

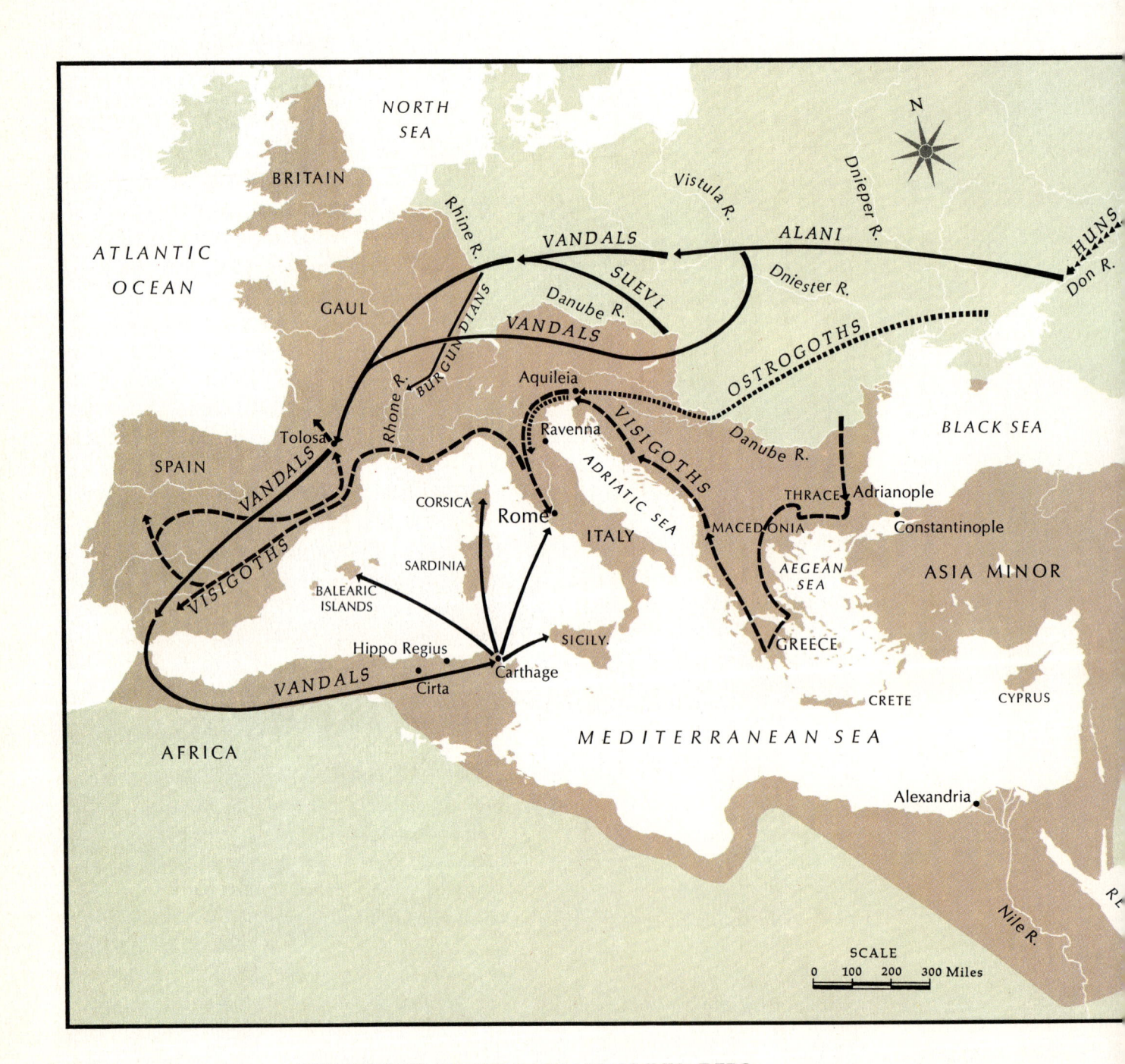

THE ROUTES OF THE BARBARIAN INVADERS

THE GERMANIC INCURSIONS of the Fourth and Fifth Centuries A.D. overwhelmed the Empire, while leaving intact the institutions that had made Rome great. The invasion process was triggered thousands of miles from Rome by the Huns. These Asiatic barbarians moved into Europe over many years, and displaced the Alani and ultimately the Ostrogoths and Visigoths. Those peoples retreated westward until most of the Empire (brown) was overrun. The city of Rome was sacked twice and finally occupied.

of Constantine, to rule as Christian emperors. The great civil service developed by the Caesars continued to function and expand. The army remained organized along Roman lines.

In the Eastern Empire, Roman elements were admixed with Hellenic and Oriental culture. Massive Roman-style buildings were decorated with lacy surfaces and ornate Byzantine mosaics, and Oriental domes were introduced. The Roman toga gave way to a brocaded robe that had come down in direct descent from the mandarins' robes of China. Latin remained the official state language (until the late Sixth Century), but the common spoken language was Greek—a somewhat vulgarized form of the classical language, and the direct ancestor of modern Greek.

In time communications between East and West broke down, and the Church of the East split with the Church of Rome. In 1053 the Patriarch of Constantinople closed all churches that adhered to the Roman liturgy, and the following year the Pope's legates reacted by excommunicating the Patriarch. Despite these conflicts the Eastern Empire remained a great preserve of Roman tradition and influence. As late as the 15th Century, inhabitants of Constantinople still referred to themselves as *Romaioi* —Romans.

From Byzantium, Romanism and Christianity spread even farther into the East. The Byzantine Church fathered the Church of Russia; for a time, the Patriarch of Constantinople appointed Church Fathers in that country. But when the Turks captured Constantinople the Grand Dukes of Moscow proclaimed themselves successors to the great Constantine, and 16th Century Moscow styled itself the Third Rome. The Grand Dukes even claimed to be descended from a brother of the first Roman Emperor, Augustus. Roman coins were used in Russia for many years, and parts of the Justinian code were worked into Russian law.

The second channel of Roman influence, the Catholic Church, remained throughout the Middle Ages as the only effective unifying force in the old territories of the Western Empire. Retaining Rome as its own capital, it kept Roman tradition alive through its organization, its laws, its language, and, above all, through its universal outlook: the unity of all Europe which the Church fostered was a conscious continuation of the unity which Rome had welded.

From the viewpoint of the Church, even Rome's pagan past was divinely ordained: the Empire had prepared the ground for the Church. The organization of the Church, in turn, was constructed largely on the Roman model. Regional dioceses corresponded to the Empire's territorial divisions; the word "diocese" had originally been used administratively by Diocletian. The hierarchy of the Church corresponded to the Roman administrative apparatus: for example, the early bishops were assigned to Roman districts called *curia*, each of which had its own civil official. Ecclesiastical law was strongly influenced by Roman jurisprudence, particularly as regarded the status of individual congregations within the Church (the guiding principle was Roman corporate law).

With the decline of the Roman state, the Church became the chief repository of Latin culture. Church schools continued to teach Latin; over the centuries, it endured as a functioning language only in Catholicism (the pronunciation is softer and a few prepositions have been added, but all else remains the same). In the years following Rome's decline a good Christian education continued to include the great works of Roman literature. "We should participate in the pagan literature," wrote Saint Basil, though he warned that "just as in plucking the blooms from a rose bed we avoid the thorns, so also in garnering from such writings whatever is useful, let us guard against what is harmful." The

Christians did not feel any incongruity in referring to Seneca as one of their own, or in writing hymns to Vergil.

The old Roman works were not only studied and taught; they were transcribed by monks and preserved in the libraries of monasteries and abbeys. In the Middle Ages, when education was at a low ebb, some classical writings were so rarely reproduced that by the time the Renaissance dawned copies were hard to find. But the Church had preserved them, and it was because of these Church copies that so much of the Roman heritage could be handed down. Even in that epoch, there was never a time when literate men did not know Vergil. Thus the great 14th Century poet Dante wrote the Roman poet Vergil into his masterpiece, *The Divine Comedy*—and in the lowest reach of the underworld, where archtraitors are punished, Dante placed Brutus and Cassius, the betrayers of Caesar, along with Judas Iscariot, the betrayer of Christ.

Third and most important of the ways in which Rome shaped later civilizations was the sheer impact of Roman ideas and objects on the cultures that followed. The actual relics of Rome—its language and literature, its architecture and its law—comprise perhaps its greatest legacy.

Not the least of these relics was the memory of Rome's grandeur, which inspired the leaders of Europe for centuries. When Clovis established a new Kingdom of the Franks in Gaul in the late Fifth Century, he paid token tribute to the sovereignty of the Roman emperors—in both Rome and Constantinople—although by that time their power had dwindled except in their own reduced realms. It was the *idea* of the Roman emperor to which Clovis bowed. Centuries later, when Charlemagne reunited most of western Europe under a single reign, he claimed to be reconstituting the old Roman Empire, and he dreamed of restoring the tradition of the Caesars. He journeyed to Rome for his coronation in 800, and was crowned in Saint Peter's Basilica while a chorus of notables chanted a salute: "To Charles Augustus, crowned by God, great and peaceful Roman emperor, long life and victory."

Successors to Charlemagne carried this process still further by naming the realm the Holy Roman Empire. Though this Empire ultimately shrank to a confederation of German principalities, emperors like Frederick Barbarossa and the aristocratic Hapsburgs continued to rule under the mantle of Rome from the time of Otto's coronation in 962 until 1806.

Not only imperial Rome, but the earlier Roman Republic served to inspire the politicians of later times. In 1347 the self-appointed savior of democracy, Cola di Rienzi, actually donned a wreath of flowers and had himself installed as Tribune of Rome. His restoration of the Republic was a short-lived fiasco—among other things, he apparently was under the impression that the old Romans had spent all their time at feasts and pageants—but it was also a symptom of reawakened interest in the ideals of ancient Rome.

The work of the political theorists who shaped modern thinking was largely a continuation of the dialogues of the ancients. The ideals of the Roman Republic infused the writings of men such as Machiavelli and Thomas More, Rabelais and Montaigne, and the *philosophes* who paved the way for the French Revolution.

The Founding Fathers of the American Republic also studied and consciously emulated the Romans. They quoted liberally from Roman authors and often signed themselves by Latin names. (Thomas Paine called himself Atlanticus and the American Tory Joseph Galloway referred to his correspondence with the British Whig leader Charles James Fox as "Letters from Cicero to Catiline the Second.") John Adams spent nights alone in his room declaiming the orations of Cicero aloud. In architecture, Thomas Jefferson led a Roman revival. He designed his own house, Monticello, in what was essentially the Roman style; he modeled the Virginia State Capitol after the Maison Carrée, an old Roman temple in Nîmes, France; and he designed the library of the University of Virginia as a small-scale Pantheon, of brick and wood instead of marble. The architecture of the old Roman Republic, he believed, was ideally suited to the structures of the new American Republic.

The Roman architectural forms have remained relevant in modern times partly because the Romans were so practical in their approach to the art of building. "The Romans had the best foresight in those matters which the Greeks took but little account of," wrote the First Century historian Strabo, "such as the construction of roads and aqueducts, and of sewers that could wash out the filth of the city."

The Roman concept of the architect reflected this concentration on the practical. Vitruvius, the great architect of Augustus' time, wrote that it was not enough for an architect to know architecture; he must be a man of many other talents. Only through a knowledge of medicine, for example, would he understand "questions of climate . . . air, the healthiness and unhealthiness of sites, and water supply." Knowledge of the law was needed to familiarize him with the building codes; and it was only through the study of optics that "light in buildings can be properly drawn from definite quarters of the sky."

Vitruvius' classic work, *On Architecture*, was an exhaustive, detailed treatise that was used as a basic textbook not only by the Romans but by the Renaissance architects. The magnificent Teatro Olimpico completed at Vicenza in 1584, for exam-

ADMINISTRATOR OF THE LAW, *the consul Magnus is shown in a leaf from an ivory panel carved in 518 A.D. The magistrate is seated between two figures personifying Rome (left) and his native Constantinople. In his left hand Magnus carries a scepter, the symbol of power and justice; in his right hand he holds a money bag, which represents his generosity.*

DOUBLE-TIER ARCH CONSTRUCTION

TUNNEL

INVERTED SIPHON

ple, was constructed according to Vitruvius' prescription, and it became a model for many later Renaissance theaters.

The city of Rome, showplace of the Empire, was the archetype of all the great metropolises of Europe in later centuries. Roman architects and builders seized on ancient concepts and coupled them with a new building material—concrete—that enabled them to overcome all ancient limits of height and space. Roman concrete was little different from the concrete still in use; the only improvement introduced in modern times has been the reinforcing of the concrete with steel rods. Using this relatively cheap, crude material, which could be easily handled by unskilled labor, Roman architects and engineers were able to devise grandiose structures without worrying much about the cost of executing their plans. Majestic arches and domes quickly became the distinctive feature of their work.

The original arch was a simple semicircle of bricks and stones, each slightly wedge-shaped to form the curve. The Romans, desiring to roof over great areas, adapted the arch to this purpose by lengthening it into a tunnel-like structure, called a barrel vault. To support such a vault, massive walls were required. But later Roman engineers devised the technique of building two barrel vaults that intersected at right angles; the result, called a groined vault, was supported at its corners by four great piers. With the weight thus distributed, the walls could be light because they were not bearing the full load of the structure. They were less expensive; furthermore, windows could be cut into them to brighten the interior. Roman methods of constructing such vaults served as a basis for architectural developments over the next thousand years, and are reflected in many of the resplendent cathedrals of medieval Europe.

The amphitheater was designed to accommodate great numbers of people. The Colosseum, which took 10 years to build, was more than 600 feet long and 500 feet wide, and it had four levels of seats with a capacity of about 50,000. Throughout the structure, there were stairways and ramps; elevators brought the animals, gladiators and scenery up from vaulted dens beneath the arena. Crowds were controlled by a system of numbering tickets to match gate numbers, and by stairs leading directly to the various levels—techniques still used in modern sports arenas.

As time passed, the great architecture of Rome fell into decay. The city's wealth and population dwindled after the Fourth Century, and building maintenance fell off. Nature and the heedlessness of man hastened the process of disintegration. A series of earthquakes in the Middle Ages toppled part of the Colosseum; the ruins were later used as a stone quarry. The Forum Romanum was similarly cannibalized. Many of its buildings were broken up, and supplied construction materials for churches and other buildings; the marble in them was burned to obtain lime. By the 15th Century the once-handsome Forum was in complete disrepair. In 1431 a Renaissance writer observed: "The Roman Forum, the most celebrated place in the city . . . and the nearby Comitium, where magistrates were chosen, are now deserted through the malignance of Fortune. The one is given over to

WATER CHANNEL

MONUMENTAL AQUEDUCTS *linked Rome with springs as far as 30 miles away. The diagram of a hypothetical aqueduct above illustrates several major engineering features. The water descended gently from a higher level to a lower one flowing through a concrete channel at the top of the aqueduct (one Roman writer, Vitruvius, recommended a fall of six inches to every 100 feet of aqueduct). Arches—sometimes single-tier, sometimes double or even triple—were used to cross steep valleys. Tunnels, burrowed through hills too difficult to skirt, were equipped with shafts for inspection and cleaning. The inverted siphon, sometimes employed when valleys were particularly steep, was based on the principle that water seeks its own level. The siphon effect forced water to flow uphill after it had descended from a higher place.*

swine and cattle; the other is enclosed as a vegetable garden."

Yet the old plan of the Forum Romanum has never lost its broad appeal; in the great cities of later centuries, the frequent arrangement of imposing structures around large areas of open space has continued the Roman ideal in practice—as in Washington, D.C., for example, where the Roman-style Capitol building stands at the end of the great Constitution Mall.

The Romans' accent on utility in building was nowhere more strikingly reflected than in their great roads and aqueducts, monuments of engineering skill. Rome laid down roads wherever its authority extended—to facilitate trade as well as troop movements. The Romans spent five centuries in completing a road system to every corner of the Empire. Roman roads eventually covered a distance equal to 10 times the circumference of the earth at the equator.

Each mile along the Roman roads was marked by a six-foot circular pillar, measured from the Golden Milestone in the Forum Romanum. The road markers usually were inscribed to the emperor who reigned at the time of their construction. Thus a marker erected in 100 A.D. in the Danubian province (part of modern Yugoslavia) reads: "The emperor [Trajan] . . . built this road by cutting through mountains and eliminating the curves." A marker from Egypt records that the Emperor Hadrian built that particular road "with copious cisterns, resting stations and garrisons at intervals along the route."

The Roman roads ran straight, level and flat. As the Danube road marker implies, the engineers did not hesitate to cut across country, tunnel through mountains, or bridge valleys. The main arteries were so well constructed that some are still in use today—including the first one, the Appian Way, built some 2,200 years ago.

The aqueducts, among the most splendid of all Roman structural creations, were a synthesis of practical engineering and architectural grace. The Romans were justly proud of them. "Water," said Strabo, "is brought into the city . . . in such quantities that veritable rivers flow through the city and the sewers." Eventually, there were 11 aqueducts, and they carried about 200 million gallons of water daily into Rome.

The first of these structures to use arches to elevate its conduits was the Aqua Marcia, built in 144 B.C. The stone arches, which extended along six miles of the aqueduct's 60-mile course, enabled the channel to maintain the same gradual slope all the way from the source of water in the distant hills into the city itself. The water was delivered to Rome at a level substantially above the Tiber, thus providing excellent water pressure. Like the roads, the aqueducts outlasted Rome. One of them, a towering structure at Segovia in Spain, is still in partial use *(see page 30).*

Rome left its mark in language as well as in stone, in culture as well as in concrete. The great Latin schools of Gaul, some of which were greater than those of Rome itself, made an impression on the native language of the province that endured long after Roman sovereignty was gone. The languages of such former provinces as France, Spain, Portugal and Romania are today almost as dependent on Latin as is the language of Italy itself.

English, too, relies heavily on words of Latin origin, although few of them stem directly from the Roman occupation of Britain. Many words were introduced into the language by those later settlers of Britain, the Anglo-Saxons, who had been ruled by Romans in their German homeland. The route from Latin to modern English via "Middle English" can be traced in such a word as "street"; the Middle English word was *strete*, a variant of the Latin *strata*, meaning paved. Still other Latin words arrived in the British Isles in the 11th Century with the French-speaking Normans; "empire," for example, stems from the Latin *imperium* via the Middle French *empirie*.

The Britons of later centuries admired Latin greatly, and often insisted that their own language suffered by comparison with the older tongue. Many modern rules of English grammar were superimposed by literary men who were following Latin usage.

The classic sense of style and the dignity of form which characterized the greatest Latin verse led early Renaissance poets like Boccaccio and Petrarch to emulate the authors of Roman antiquity. The only way to write an epic poem, taught Jerome Vida in the 16th Century, was to copy Vergil as closely as possible, as he himself did in his *Christiads*. Nor was the influence of Rome confined to the Renaissance. Like Boccaccio and Petrarch, the 19th Century poet Keats was a student of old Roman forms. His beautiful "Ode to a Nightingale," in fact, contains echoes of Horace. Throughout the ages, authors have drawn characters from the Romans: Shakespeare wrote of Caesar and Antony; Racine of Britannicus. Nero figures in a dozen plays; the demented Emperor Caligula becomes an existentialist hero in the writings of Albert Camus, the paralytic Claudius emerges as a shrewd intellectual in the hands of Robert Graves.

Of all Rome's intellectual bequests, the one that may have been most characteristic of the Roman mind was its thousand years of law. The word justice stems from the Latin word for law, *ius*, and the Roman concept of impartial justice, even more than the Roman laws themselves, has shaped Western legal tradition.

Cicero expressed the Roman spirit of justice in an oration: "What sort of thing is the civil law? It is of a sort that cannot be bent by influence or broken by power or spoiled by money." In the Acts of the Apostles in the New Testament, Saint Luke wrote: "It is not the Roman custom to condemn any man before the accused meets his accusers face to face and has an opportunity to defend himself against the charge."

Roman law had its foundation in the Twelve Tables promulgated by republican magistrates about 450 B.C. The Tables were the first compilation of legal rules to govern the Roman administration of justice. They were simply a series of terse commands dealing with court actions, family law, wills, property rights and public behavior of citizens. They were very much a product of their time: among other things, for example, they forbade a Roman to damage his neighbor's crops by the use of evil charms.

In the Tables, and for centuries afterward, Roman law was essentially civil law, primarily concerned with the rights of individuals. Not until late in the Empire did a specific body of criminal law appear, in which the state undertook the prosecution and punishment of criminals. In the early Republic, even murder came under civil law. It was the responsibility of the relatives of a murdered person to demand satisfaction. The accused and his accuser would go before a magistrate, who then weighed their testimony and passed judgment on whether the homicide was intentional or accidental. If it was intentional, the murderer forfeited the protection of his gods and revenge might be freely enacted by the dead man's family. Accidental death was not punishable.

RISE OF THE MAYAS

During the years when Rome was lapsing into its long decline, a civilization 6,000 miles to the west, on a continent unknown to the Romans, was approaching its peak.

By the Fourth Century A.D. the Mayas, who modeled the figure above from clay, had begun to build what was to be a great, glittering chain of temple cities throughout the rain forests of modern southern Mexico, Guatemala and British Honduras. Stucco pyramids looming hundreds of feet above the jungle floor honored a fantastic hierarchy of deities—sky serpents, dragons and earth monsters. Along the broad avenues and plazas which separated the pyramids and other temple buildings, pilgrims gathered to celebrate religious festivals. Maya engineers connected the cities with wide paved roads which, like the great Roman highways, are still in evidence today.

Skilled artists, these Indians glorified their rulers and represented daily life in brilliantly colored murals and masterful wood carvings. Maya astronomers recorded eclipses, solstices, equinoxes and the course of the sun and the moon, and also worked out an intricate calendar far more accurate than that used by the Europeans. It was not until the 16th Century, 600 years after the Mayas' sudden and mysterious collapse, that exploring Spaniards first came upon the ruins of their cities.

The Twelve Tables provided the basic legal code of Rome for almost a thousand years, while rulings of magistrates and the opinions of jurists developed a supplementary body of "case law," or legal precedent. Eventually, textbooks of law were published, lawyers emerged as a special professional group, and legal scholars became the close advisers of the emperors. Regardless of political changes—from Republic to Empire and under emperors liberal or authoritarian—Roman law based on human wisdom and consent continued its development. Then, around 527 a codification of the entire system was ordered by the Eastern Emperor Justinian—the Corpus Iuris Civilis, or Body of Civil Law. Earlier emperors, from Hadrian's time on, had encouraged the standardization and classification of laws, but it was this comprehensive work that summed up the entire legal experience of Rome. Ironically, the Justinian Code—the key part of the Corpus—was not completed until 529, a half-century after Rome itself had passed into the hands of the Goths.

The concept of justice, and of the rights of individuals, embodied in this Code remain in force in modern legal codes throughout the Western world. Just a few of the Code's provisions suffice to show its continuing relevance:

> *No one is compelled to defend a cause against his will.*
> *No one suffers a penalty for what he thinks.*
> *No one may be forcibly removed from his own house.*
> *Anything not permitted the defendant ought not be allowed the plaintiff.*
> *The burden of proof is upon the party affirming, not on the party denying.*
> *A father is not a competent witness for a son, nor a son for a father.*
> *The gravity of a past offense never increases ex post facto.*
> *In inflicting penalties, the age and inexperience of the guilty party must be taken into account.*

The law codes of most Western nations were influenced by the Justinian Code. The Napoleonic Code in France was directly and consciously modeled on it. In Germany Roman law was applied whenever it did not run counter to local legislation until 1900, when a national law system was devised. Although England and the countries it influenced developed a native "common law" of their own—which differed from Roman law in placing its emphasis on precedent rather than on written statutes—it too had roots in Roman judicial principles and practices. America took its law largely from the English system. The state law of Louisiana, however, still reflects some provisions of the ancient Justinian Code—a carry-over from the three-year period when the Louisiana Territory was governed by Napoleon.

The influence of Rome, whether seen in the practice of a courtroom or the facade of a church, in the style of a poem or the structure of a state, remains as a vital force, shaping the ideas and the material works of man. The world is a different place because Rome was once there. The Roman legacy has penetrated regions that Romans never ruled and continents they never dreamed of reaching.

Even as Rome was declining, a poet in Gaul envisioned the Empire's future greatness. Writing in 416, six years after the Goths had sacked the city, Rutilius Namatianus ended his eloquent farewell apostrophe to Rome with these words: "Spread forth the laws that are to last throughout the ages . . . thou alone needst not dread the distaffs of the Fates. . . . The span which doth remain is subject to no bounds, so long as earth shall stand and heaven uphold the stars!"

A ROMANIZED CHRIST *is shown as the Good Shepherd in this painting found in a Christian catacomb in Rome. The short-haired, beardless Jesus is represented as a simple herder wearing a Roman tunic.*

SEEDBED OF CHRISTIANITY

First Century Romans regarded Christ as a minor political rebel who, wrote Tacitus, "was crucified under Tiberius by the procurator Pontius Pilate." Although He preached for less than three years, in remote Palestine, His disciples were many, and they were soon traveling Roman roads to distant cities and provinces. In time, the whole Empire became a seedbed of the new religion.

Roman authorities used the Christians as political scapegoats for three centuries—until the reign of Constantine, who was converted in 337. From then on, Roman forms of government, legal tenets and architectural styles were increasingly reflected in the Church's administration, laws and buildings, and the city of Rome assumed a dual role—as seat of the Empire and center of the Church.

STURDY ROOTS IN ROME

In its early years, the Church, with congregations scattered through the Empire, had no central organization. Though there was a core of common beliefs, forms of worship differed from town to town, rivalries arose between disciples, and doctrinal disputes flourished. The disciples had to take local customs into account: "I am made all things to all men," said Saint Paul, "that I might by all means save some."

The organization of the Empire influenced the character of the Church. It was an empire of cities, so Christianity became an urban movement. The poor masses were ready converts, for they expected Christ's second coming to rid them of their rich masters. Indeed, the Church took such hold in urban centers that Christians used the Latin *paganus*, meaning "a rustic," to describe non-Christians—hence the word "pagan." Saint Peter himself, after his 30-year ministry in the East, came to make his headquarters in the Empire's foremost city, Rome.

CHRIST CRUCIFIED *and Judas hanging are shown in a panel done about 420 A.D. The Crucifixion, considered a disgrace, was rarely shown in earlier art.*

THE RESURRECTION *and Ascension of Christ, combined in this ivory panel, were depicted in many churches throughout the Empire.*

CATACOMB ART *often featured Old Testament scenes, like these three Hebrews in a fiery furnace. As they mourned their dead, Christians took comfort from reminders of other, earlier martyrs.*

THE DAYS OF WRATH

In the early years, Christians were blamed (and punished) by the Romans for all sorts of disasters—plagues, inflation, even barbarian incursions. The first Christians were put to death after they were held responsible by Nero for the fire that burned much of Rome in 64 A.D. "Their executions became sports events," wrote Tacitus. "They were covered with wild animal skins and torn apart by dogs." The Emperor Decius forced Christians to take loyalty oaths; Valerian organized mass murders of churchmen. Forbidden access to regular burial places, Christians buried their dead in the graves used by the poor—crowded underground vaults called catacombs *(opposite)*, built outside the city.

CHRIST AND THE APOSTLES *are seen in a fresco from a Roman catacomb. As in most Christian painting until the Middle Ages, Christ is portrayed clean-shaven, for the Romans regarded beards as the mark of barbarians.*

BURIAL PLACES *of the Christians, dug out under inhabited areas, had to meet strict building code specifications. Roman officials were not interested in Christians' burial practices, but they were afraid of possible cave-ins.*

AN AGE OF ACCORD

Constantine, who legalized Christianity, was baptized on his deathbed and is considered the first Christian emperor. By his time the clash between Church and Empire had abated, for Christians were seeking the millennium within the Church, not in political change. Constantine, trying to strengthen both Church and state, began to merge the two institutions. The Church was made tax exempt and the sign of the Cross appeared on Roman coins. In later years the Church braced the sagging state, while the powers of the state were used to unify the Church. The Roman title *Pontifex Maximus*, or "chief priest," was applied to the pope, or pontiff. And the shrines of old gods stood neglected.

CHAMPION OF THE CHURCH, *Constantine rebuilt and renamed the ancient Eastern city of Byzantium (now Istanbul). As Constantinople he dedicated it to the Holy Trinity and the Mother of God.*

BEARDED APOSTLE, *Peter is shown twice in this relief—with Christ at left, and at right making a convert among Roman legionaries. The rooster may symbolize the cock that crowed three times.*

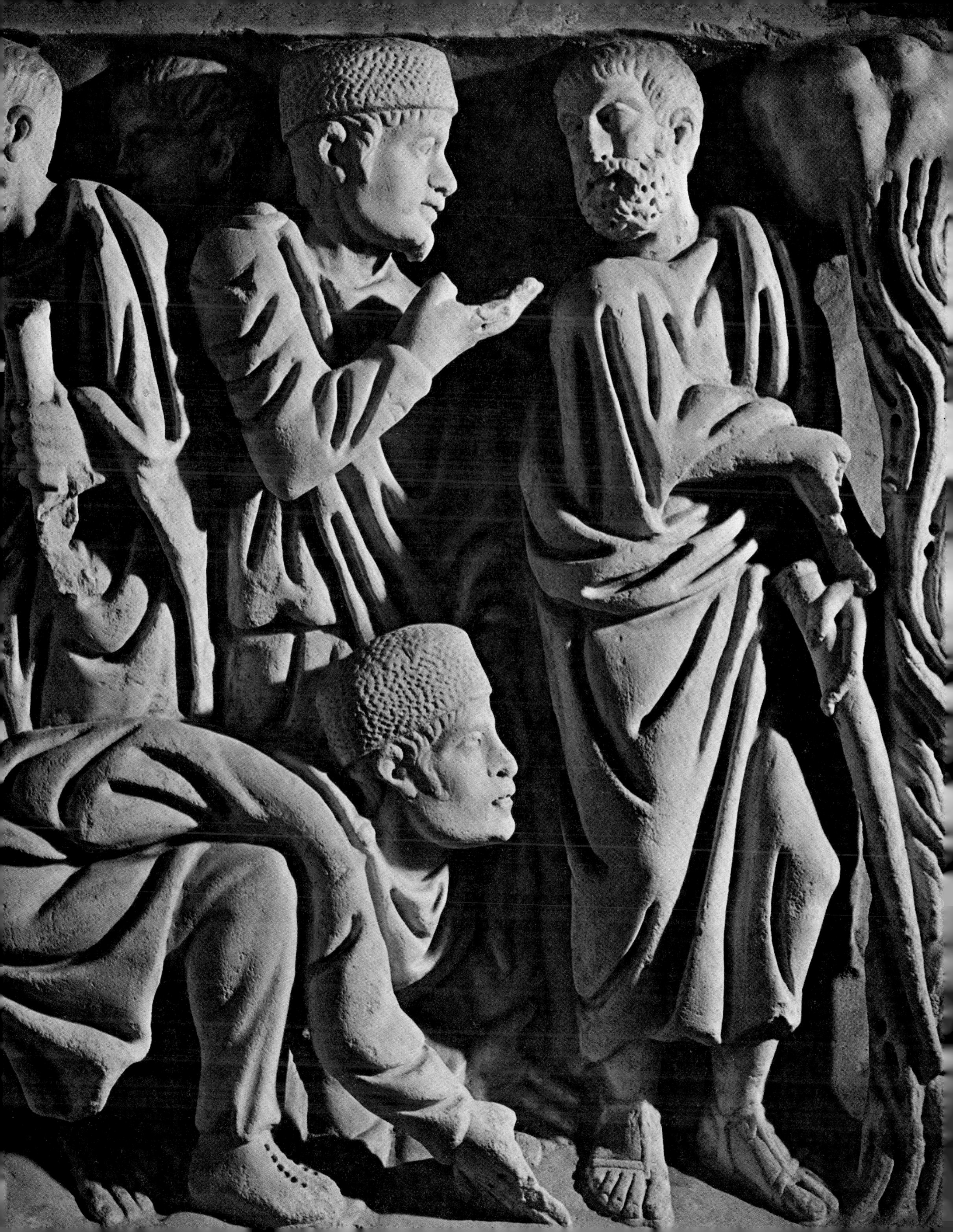

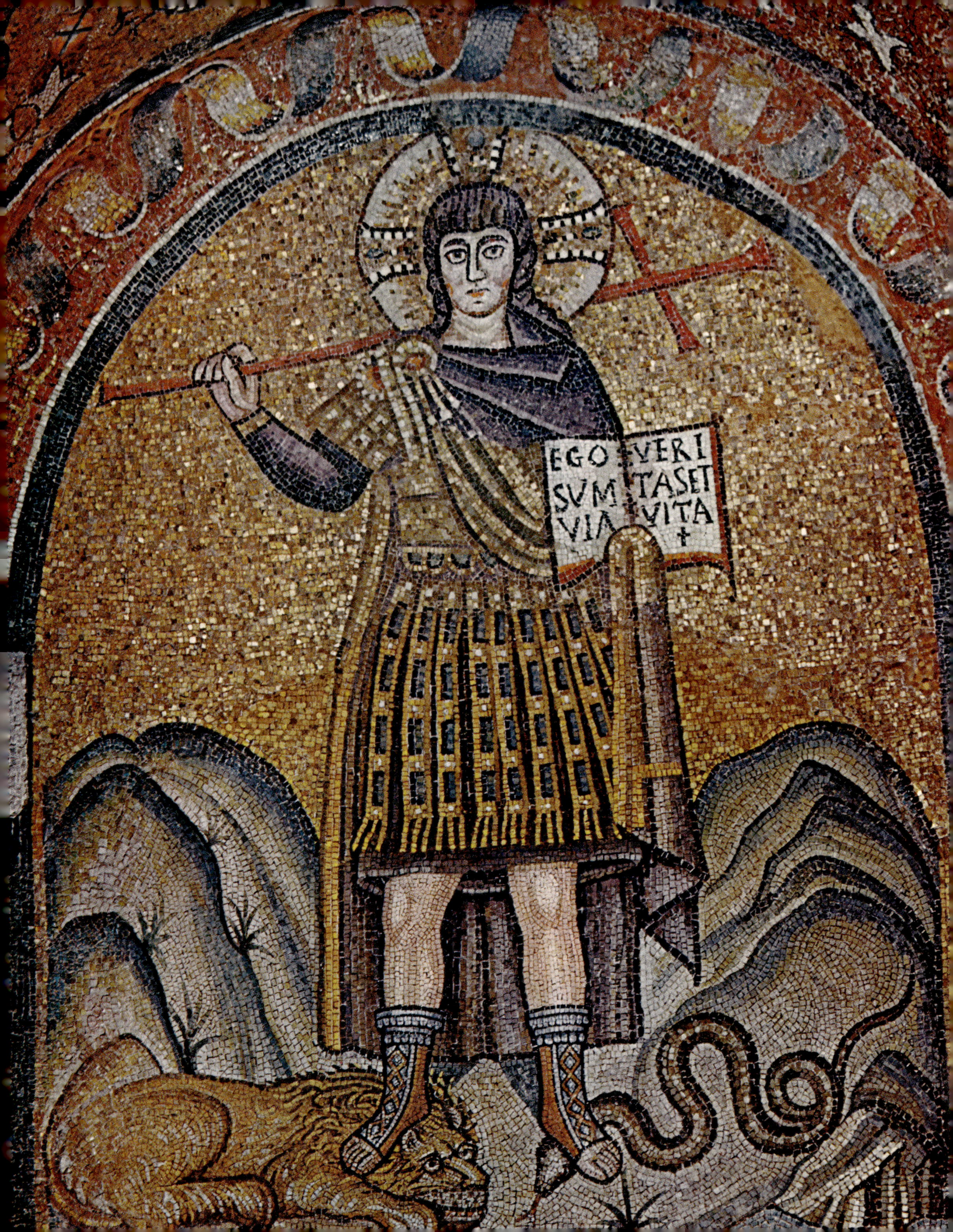
EGO
SUM
VIA
VERI
TASET
VITA

THE CHURCH TRIUMPHANT

From Constantine's time on, Christianity was the official religion of Rome. By 385 A.D., only 80 years after the last great wave of persecution of Christians, the Church was itself beginning to execute heretics, and its clerics were wielding power almost equivalent to that of the emperors. Indeed, in 390, when Emperor Theodosius ordered the massacre of every person in the town of Thessalonica as punishment for a riot, the angry Bishop of Milan, St. Ambrose, forced him to do public penance. As Church and state grew closer, basilicas, the old public buildings of Rome, were turned into churches; ecclesiastical and civil courts exchanged cases; bishops took a hand in municipal matters; and the state supervised internal affairs of the Church. When at last the political power of the emperors collapsed, the Church endured—and, in the dark ages that followed, helped preserve the Roman heritage.

A MILITANT CHRIST *is depicted in this late Fifth Century mosaic (opposite) as a triumphant warrior, dressed as a Roman legionary. He stands astride the heads of a serpent and a lion and holds a book inscribed in Latin: "I am the Way, the Truth and the Life."*

A CHRISTIAN MAUSOLEUM, *constructed in the Fourth Century for the Emperor Constantine's daughter Constantina and still in use as the Church of Santa Costanza in Rome, reflects the manner in which the Church absorbed the stateliness of Roman architecture.*

LATER CHRISTIAN ART, *though still influenced by the realistic style of the Romans, stood in marked contrast to the crude art of the catacombs. The*

176

panels of this Fifth Century book cover combine ornate Christian symbolism with gospel scenes. Details of the panels are identified on the next page.

DETAILS FROM A FIFTH CENTURY BOOK COVER

A key to the photographs on pages 176-177

1 *Lamb of God, a symbol of Christ.*
2 *A winged angel, the symbol of Matthew.*
3 *The Nativity.*
4 *A winged calf, the symbol of Luke.*
5 *Mary at the Temple, after the Virgin Birth.*
6 *Jesus among the doctors in the Temple of Jerusalem.*
7 *Jesus riding into Jerusalem on Palm Sunday.*
8 *Luke.*
9 *The Massacre of the Innocents.*
10 *Matthew.*
11 *The Baptism of Christ.*
12 *The Magi.*
13 *The Annunciation.*
14 *The Cross on the Mountain of Paradise, a symbol of Christ.*
15 *A winged lion, the symbol of Mark.*
16 *The Adoration of the Magi.*
17 *A winged eagle, the symbol of John.*
18 *Jesus between two of his apostles.*
19 *The Last Supper.*
20 *The Widow's Mite.*
21 *John.*
22 *The marriage feast at Cana, where Christ turned water to wine.*
23 *Mark.*
24 *The raising of Lazarus from the dead.*
25 *Jesus healing the lame.*
26 *Jesus healing the blind.*

APPENDIX

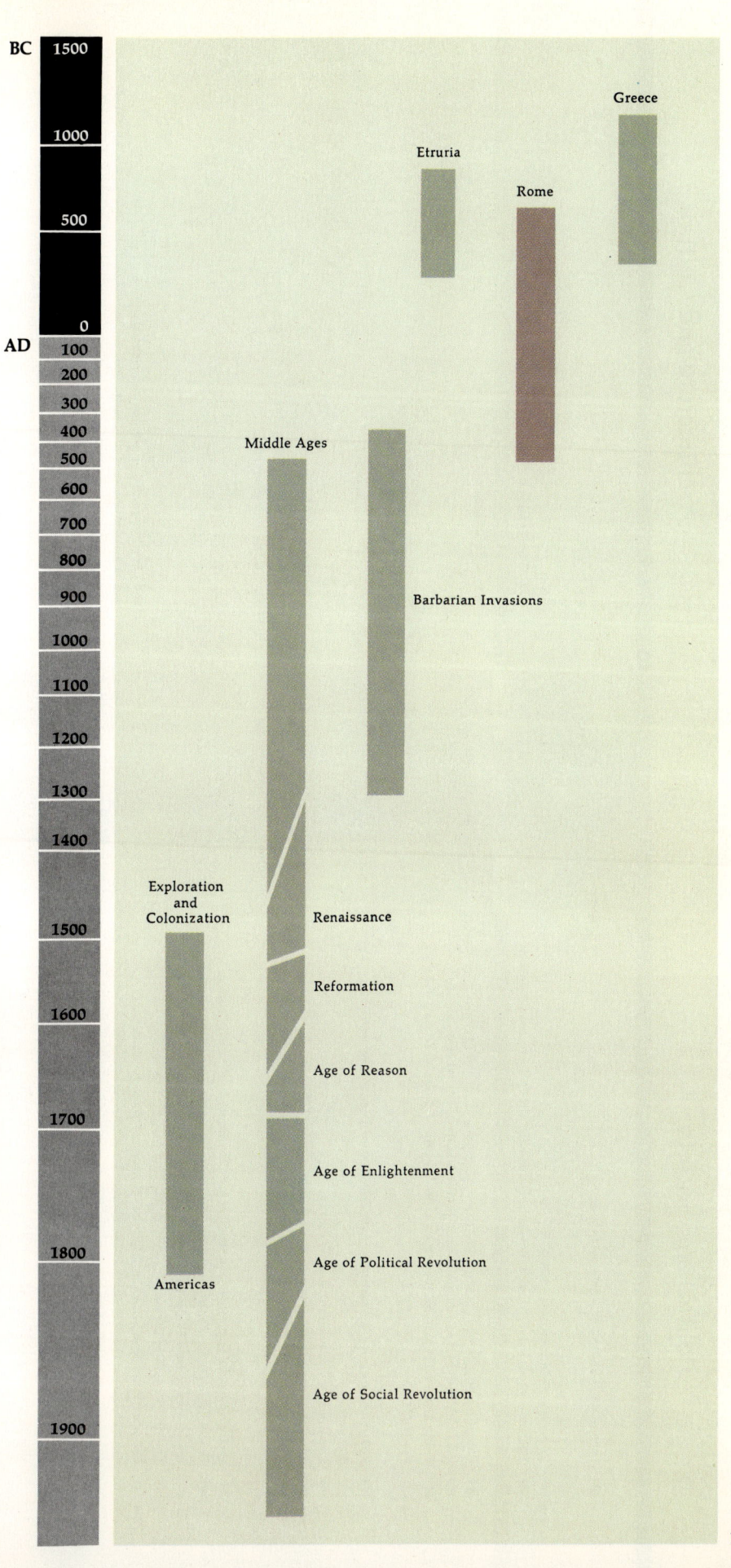

GREAT AGES OF WESTERN CIVILIZATION

The chart at right is designed to show the duration of the Roman culture that forms the subject matter of this volume, and to relate it to the other cultures of the Western world that are considered in one major group of volumes of this series. This chart is excerpted from a comprehensive world chronology which appears in the introductory booklet to the series. Comparison of the chart seen here with the world chronology will enable the reader to relate the great ages of Western civilization to important cultures in other parts of the world.

On the following two pages is printed a chronological table of the important events which took place throughout the Roman world during the era covered by this book.

CHRONOLOGY: A listing of events significant in the history of ancient Rome

Politics and Society

BC	
753	Legendary founding of Rome by Romulus
c. 616-509	Rome is ruled by Etruscan kings
509	The Republic is established, following expulsion of the last Etruscan monarch
494	The office of tribune is created to protect the rights of plebeians
493	Rome joins the Latin League formed by its neighbors for mutual defense
449	Publication is begun of the Law of the Twelve Tables, codifying existing Roman law
396	Rome violates its agreements with the Latin League by annexing new territory
390	The Gauls sack Rome but soon withdraw
340-338	Rome defeats and dissolves the Latin League
c. 290	Victory over the Samnites completes Rome's domination of central Italy
287	The Hortensian Law shifts legislative power from aristocrats to plebeians
275	Rome is undisputed ruler of southern Italy
268	The first Roman silver coins
264-241	The First Punic War with Carthage sees Romans ultimately victorious
218-201	The Second Punic War ends in Roman triumph despite Hannibal's remarkable invasion across the Alps
197	Rome defeats Philip V of Macedon at Cynoscephalae
190	Rome crushes Antiochus the Great of Syria at Magnesia
149-146	The Third Punic War; Rome besieges, then destroys Carthage
133-122	Land reforms of Gracchus brothers
121	Rome conquers southern Gaul
112-106	War with the North African King, Jugurtha
87	Violence erupts between partisans of the aristocrats and the populace
81	The aristocratic general Sulla becomes dictator; he restores the power of the Senate and improves the judicial system
73-71	Spartacus leads a slave revolt that ends with bloody reprisals against the rebels
63	Cicero becomes Consul
60	The First Triumvirate is formed: Pompey, Caesar and Crassus
58-51	Caesar conducts a series of great campaigns in Gaul

Architecture and Culture

BC	
509	The Temple of Jupiter, on the Capitol, is dedicated
498	The Temple of Saturn is built
312	Rome's first highway, the Via Appia, is built
312	Rome's first aqueduct
264	Earliest record of gladiatorial combats
240	Latin tragedy and comedy are inaugurated with the plays of Livius Andronicus
221	The Circus Flaminius is built
220	The Via Flaminia is constructed
c. 205	Plautus' comedy *Braggart Soldier* is performed
205	Cult worship from Asia Minor influences Rome
204	The poet Ennius comes to Rome
185	Town-planning activity flourishes
166	The playwright Terence's *Andria* is produced
c. 160	Cato composes his major treatise on agriculture
131	Satires by Lucilius are published
81	Cicero delivers his first oration
c. 62	The lyric poet Catullus arrives in Rome
c. 55	Pompey's Theater, the first stone theater in Rome, is constructed
c. 55	Death of Lucretius, author of the great philosophical poem *On the Nature of Things*

MONARCHY — REPUBLIC

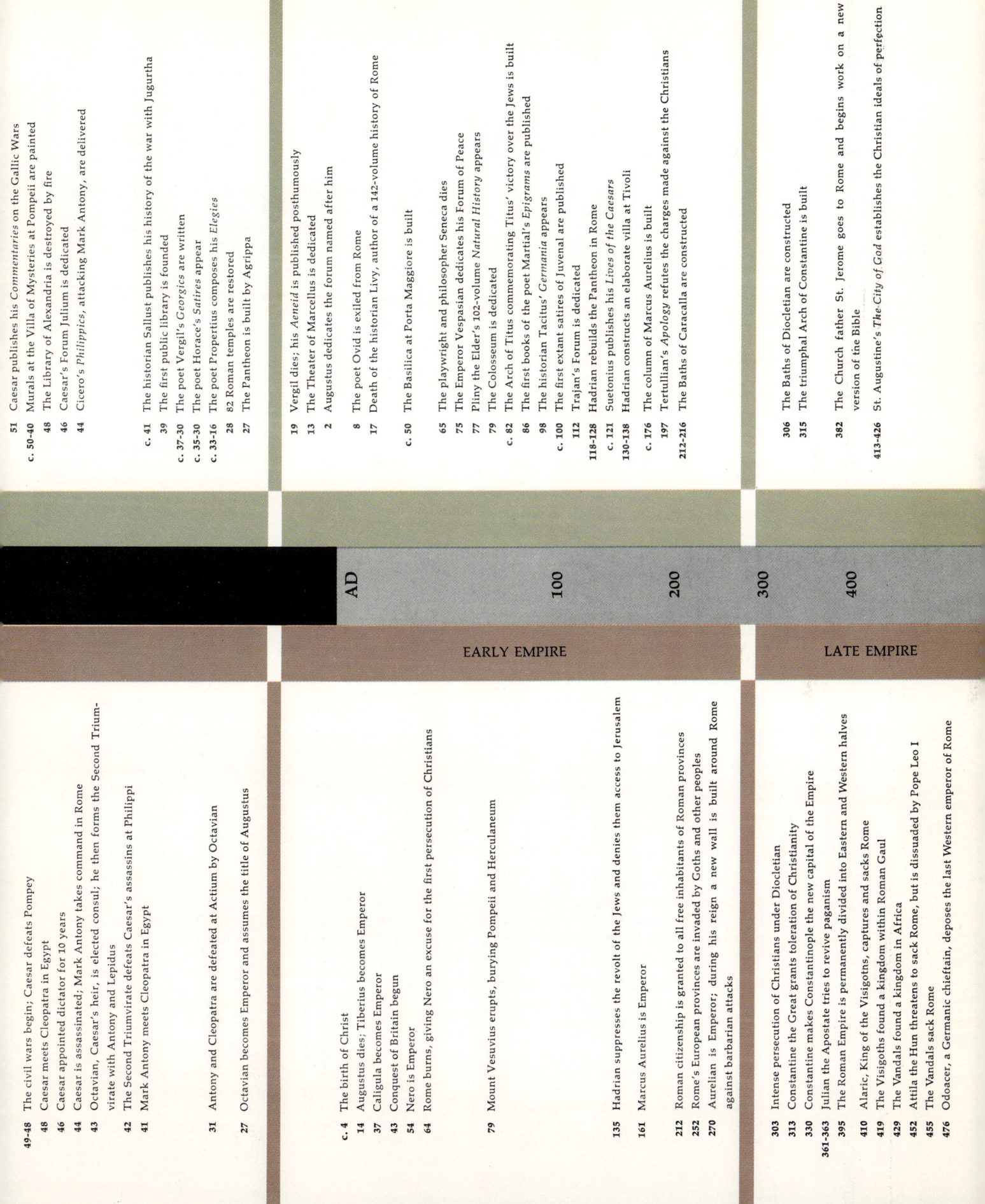

Date	Event
51	Caesar publishes his *Commentaries* on the Gallic Wars
c. 50-40	Murals at the Villa of Mysteries at Pompeii are painted
48	The Library of Alexandria is destroyed by fire
46	Caesar's Forum Julium is dedicated
44	Cicero's *Philippics*, attacking Mark Antony, are delivered
c. 41	The historian Sallust publishes his history of the war with Jugurtha
39	The first public library is founded
c. 37-30	The poet Vergil's *Georgics* are written
c. 35-30	The poet Horace's *Satires* appear
c. 33-16	The poet Propertius composes his *Elegies*
28	82 Roman temples are restored
27	The Pantheon is built by Agrippa
19	Vergil dies; his *Aeneid* is published posthumously
13	The Theater of Marcellus is dedicated
2	Augustus dedicates the forum named after him
8	The poet Ovid is exiled from Rome
17	Death of the historian Livy, author of a 142-volume history of Rome
c. 50	The Basilica at Porta Maggiore is built
65	The playwright and philosopher Seneca dies
75	The Emperor Vespasian dedicates his Forum of Peace
77	Pliny the Elder's 102-volume *Natural History* appears
79	The Colosseum is dedicated
c. 82	The Arch of Titus commemorating Titus' victory over the Jews is built
86	The first books of the poet Martial's *Epigrams* are published
98	The historian Tacitus' *Germania* appears
c. 100	The first extant satires of Juvenal are published
112	Trajan's Forum is dedicated
118-128	Hadrian rebuilds the Pantheon in Rome
c. 121	Suetonius publishes his *Lives of the Caesars*
130-138	Hadrian constructs an elaborate villa at Tivoli
c. 176	The column of Marcus Aurelius is built
197	Tertullian's *Apology* refutes the charges made against the Christians
212-216	The Baths of Caracalla are constructed
306	The Baths of Diocletian are constructed
315	The triumphal Arch of Constantine is built
382	The Church father St. Jerome goes to Rome and begins work on a new version of the Bible
413-426	St. Augustine's *The City of God* establishes the Christian ideals of perfection

AD 100 200 300 400

EARLY EMPIRE — **LATE EMPIRE**

Date	Event
49-48	The civil wars begin; Caesar defeats Pompey
48	Caesar meets Cleopatra in Egypt
46	Caesar appointed dictator for 10 years
44	Caesar is assassinated; Mark Antony takes command in Rome
43	Octavian, Caesar's heir, is elected consul; he then forms the Second Triumvirate with Antony and Lepidus
42	The Second Triumvirate defeats Caesar's assassins at Philippi
41	Mark Antony meets Cleopatra in Egypt
31	Antony and Cleopatra are defeated at Actium by Octavian
27	Octavian becomes Emperor and assumes the title of Augustus
c. 4	The birth of Christ
14	Augustus dies; Tiberius becomes Emperor
37	Caligula becomes Emperor
43	Conquest of Britain begun
54	Nero is Emperor
64	Rome burns, giving Nero an excuse for the first persecution of Christians
79	Mount Vesuvius erupts, burying Pompeii and Herculaneum
135	Hadrian suppresses the revolt of the Jews and denies them access to Jerusalem
161	Marcus Aurelius is Emperor
212	Roman citizenship is granted to all free inhabitants of Roman provinces
252	Rome's European provinces are invaded by Goths and other peoples
270	Aurelian is Emperor; during his reign a new wall is built around Rome against barbarian attacks
303	Intense persecution of Christians under Diocletian
313	Constantine the Great grants toleration of Christianity
330	Constantine makes Constantinople the new capital of the Empire
361-363	Julian the Apostate tries to revive paganism
395	The Roman Empire is permanently divided into Eastern and Western halves
410	Alaric, King of the Visigoths, captures and sacks Rome
419	The Visigoths found a kingdom within Roman Gaul
429	The Vandals found a kingdom in Africa
452	Attila the Hun threatens to sack Rome, but is dissuaded by Pope Leo I
455	The Vandals sack Rome
476	Odoacer, a Germanic chieftain, deposes the last Western emperor of Rome

THE IMMORTAL ROMANS

Imperial Rome, and the earlier Republic, may be measured by the greatness of their men as well as by the breadth of their conquests. The great Romans, 41 of whom are named below, usually excelled in more than one field—and saw no conflict between lives of action and thought. The annals of Rome are full of soldier-poets and philosopher-politicians, but here they are classified as public men and men of letters.

PUBLIC MEN

MARK ANTONY (82-30 B.C.) — A soldier and statesman in the last years of the Republic. After Caesar's assassination he contended for power with Octavian, who was later to be called Augustus (below). Antony's affair with Cleopatra in Egypt became a legend. He took his own life after Octavian defeated his forces at Actium.

AUGUSTUS (63 B.C.-14 A.D.) — Rome's first Emperor. After the murder of Julius Caesar, whose heir he was, he emerged from a triumvirate of rulers to reorganize the state, dominate the Senate. Adding the title Augustus to his given name, Octavian, he governed brilliantly for over 40 years.

BRUTUS (c.85-42 B.C.) — A leader in the cabal that murdered Caesar. Honored as a general, Brutus took his own life after his troops were defeated in Macedonia.

JULIUS CAESAR (c.100-44 B.C.) — An extraordinary soldier and dictator of Rome. He recorded his triumphs in distinctive essays on the Gallic Wars. Appointed dictator for life in 44 B.C., he was assassinated the same year.

CATILINE (c.108-63 B.C.) — Leader of a political conspiracy. Twice defeated by Cicero in elections for the consulship, Catiline tried to stage an uprising in Rome in order to secure the office by force. When his plot was exposed, he fled and died near Gaul, fighting against Roman troops.

CATO (234-149 B.C.) — An influential Senator during the Republic. Known as Cato the Censor for his vigorous execution of that office, he became famous for ending his speeches with the warning, "Carthage must be destroyed"—and led Rome into the Third Punic War, which did see Carthage utterly destroyed.

CICERO (106-43 B.C.) — A distinguished politician, lawyer and writer. He was considered the greatest of all Roman orators. One fiery speech stirred the Senate to execute a group of conspirators without a trial, but afterward, Caesar had Cicero banished.

CONSTANTINE (274-337 A.D.) — The first Christian Emperor. It was Constantine's Edict of Milan, issued in 313, which granted freedom of religion throughout the Empire. In the East, Constantine established Byzantium (present-day Istanbul) as a Christian capital, naming it Constantinople.

CRASSUS (c.112-53 B.C.) — A soldier, briefly co-ruler of the Republic with Pompey and Caesar. Crassus led the forces which crushed Spartacus' slave rebellion. Although a poor politician, he amassed a fortune in business—and often lent Caesar large sums.

DIOCLETIAN (245-313 A.D.) — Emperor who reformed the Government. He was the first to split the administration of the Empire into Eastern and Western domains. He ruled the West; a colleague reigned in the East.

GRACCHUS, TIBERIUS (162-133 B.C.)
GRACCHUS, GAIUS (154-121 B.C.) — Brothers who were political reformers during the Republic. Both Gracchi brothers served as tribunes, carried out extensive agrarian reforms, and were murdered while in office. Besides distributing land to the landless, they tried to augment the political rights of the people, at the expense of the Senate.

HADRIAN (76-138 A.D.) — Emperor who built a great defensive wall against barbarian incursions in England. He was the adopted son and successor of the Emperor Trajan. Occupied with defending the Empire abroad, Hadrian also cultivated the arts and brought touches of Greek culture into Roman life. His own villa was an artistic triumph.

JUSTINIAN (483-565 A.D.) — A great Emperor who reigned from Constantinople. His comprehensive legal code was the capstone of centuries of Roman law, and it provided a foundation, centuries later, for many modern European legal codes.

MARCUS AURELIUS (121-180 A.D.) — Emperor who was both a great soldier and a Stoic philosopher. Although he sought peace, he had to wage incessant wars. He wrote his famous *Meditations* while encamped with his armies.

MARIUS (157-86 B.C.) — An outstanding soldier who won great victories in Spain and Africa. Despite his humble birth, he became a general and served as consul seven times. His career was marked by bitter conflict with a rival general, Sulla.

NERO (37-68 A.D.) — A most depraved Emperor. He began the mass persecution of Christians, blaming them for the burning of Rome. Treating senators like slaves, he put them in arenas with wild beasts.

POMPEY (106-48 B.C.) — Renowned soldier who for a time ruled Rome with Caesar and Crassus. His campaigns added Asia Minor to the Empire and cleared the Mediterranean of pirate armadas. His wife was Caesar's daughter, Julia.

ROMULUS AND REMUS (date unknown) — Twins who, according to legend, established Rome. Cast into the Tiber as babes, they floated ashore and were nursed by a she-wolf. Young Romulus founded Rome on the Palatine Hill, killing Remus in a dispute over the site.

SCIPIO (c.236-184 B.C.) — General who defeated Hannibal in the Second Punic War. For his part in the destruction of Carthage, he was given the name Scipio Africanus.

SULLA
(138-78 B.C.)
An outstanding soldier of conservative views. He achieved fame as a general, provincial governor and consul. After defeating a rival general, Marius, he was proclaimed dictator. He was deposed three years later.

TRAJAN
(53-117 A.D.)
The Emperor whose campaigns brought the Empire to its greatest territorial extent. Born in Spain, Trajan became a great general and excellent ruler, administering many public works and welfare programs. To mark his triumph in the Dacian War, he built his famous column in Rome.

MEN OF LETTERS

CATULLUS
(c.84-54 B.C.)
A master of lyric, erotic and epigrammatic poetry. As a young man he attacked Julius Caesar in verse; later his poetry dealt with the pangs of a lover scorned. His adaptation of Greek meters influenced both Horace and Vergil.

ENNIUS
(239-169 B.C.)
A poet whose masterpiece was the *Annals*. This was an epic history of Rome, in Greek hexameter form. He was often quoted by such orators as Cicero and Quintilian.

HORACE
(65-8 B.C.)
Poet who became Augustus' unofficial laureate after the death of Vergil. Most famous for his magnificent Odes, Horace was an accomplished satirist, critic and love-poet. He lived most of his life on a farm some distance from Rome.

LIVY
(59 B.C.-17 A.D.)
The foremost Roman historian in Augustus' time. Livy's magnum opus was a 142-book history of Rome from the time of its foundation. His portrait of the remote past was drawn from legend and folklore and makes no pretense to realism. In dealing with later ages, he was regarded as an accurate, analytical writer.

LUCRETIUS
(c.96-c.52 B.C.)
A philosopher and poet. He elaborated on the teachings of the famous Greek philosopher, Epicurus. His great work, *De Rerum Natura*, or *The Laws of Nature*, treated in verse such subjects as the atomic nature of matter.

MARTIAL
(c.40-c.104 A.D.)
A poet famous for his barbed and witty epigrams. Although he often attacked noted men or women in his verse, he took care to flatter the emperors. His output ran to 1,561 poems.

OVID
(43 B.C.-c.18 A.D.)
One of Rome's most popular poets. Ovid was a master of love lyrics and mythological verse. In a fit of pique he burned his greatest collection of poems, *The Metamorphoses*—but he had previously given copies to friends, who published them.

PLINY THE ELDER
(23-79 A.D.)
A prodigious writer, cavalry officer and government official. In addition to an active public life, Pliny wrote volumes on natural history, war, weapons, contemporary history and rhetoric. He died of suffocation while making first-hand observations of the catastrophic eruption of Mount Vesuvius.

PLINY THE YOUNGER
(c.61-c.113 A.D.)
A lawyer, writer and orator, the nephew of the elder Pliny. He served the Emperor Trajan as consul and provincial governor. His letters to prominent Romans, including Trajan, fill ten volumes. Pliny published most of them himself.

PROPERTIUS
(c.47-c.15 B.C.)
An elegiac poet. His great reputation rested on the impassioned verses he wrote to his unfaithful mistress. Along with Vergil and Horace, he shared the patronage of Augustus' court.

QUINTILIAN
(c.35-c.95 A.D.)
A famous orator, legal counselor and teacher of rhetoric. Pliny the Younger was one of his students. His major work, *Institutio Oratorio*, became a standard textbook of Latin oratory.

SALLUST
(86-35 B.C.)
An historian who fought beside Caesar in Africa. He also served the Republic as governor of Numidia and in the office of magistrate. One of his books records the conspiracy of Catiline against the Roman Senate.

SENECA
(c.5 B.C.-65 A.D.)
A Stoic, writer and lawyer. Famous for his philosophical treatise, the *Dialogues*, Seneca also had a mercurial public career: banished from the Senate by the Emperor Claudius, he returned to Rome as Nero's tutor—and later committed suicide at Nero's order.

SUETONIUS
(c.69-c.140 A.D.)
A political biographer, author of *The Lives of the Twelve Caesars*. Drawing on his friendship with Rome's most important public men, Suetonius left a record of the inner workings, scandals and treacheries of the Government.

TACITUS
(c.55-c.116 A.D.)
The greatest of the Roman historians. Silenced during the despotic reign of Domitian, Tacitus later wrote his exhaustive *Histories* and *Annals*. One of his aims as an historian, he said, was "to hold out the reprobation of posterity as a terror to evil words and deeds."

TERENCE
(c.195-159 B.C.)
A popular playwright who came to Rome from Africa as a slave. Accused of plagiarizing the Greek dramatist Menander, he wrote: "Nothing is ever said which has not been said before." All six of his comedies survive.

TIBULLUS
(c.55-19 B.C.)
A pastoral poet prominent in Republican literary circles. He was famous for his terse and elegant elegies on fickle and wicked women.

VERGIL
(70-19 B.C.)
Pre-eminent among the great poets of the Augustan Age. In early works like the *Georgics*, Vergil made classic verse of mundane subjects, such as the agricultural policies of Augustus. He spent the last ten years of his life working on the *Aeneid*, his immortal epic on the Trojan heroes who founded Rome, but died before he could complete his final revision.

BIBLIOGRAPHY

These books were selected during the preparation of the volume for their interest and authority, and for their usefulness to readers seeking additional information on specific points. An asterisk (*) marks works available in both hard-cover and paperback editions; a dagger (†) indicates availability only in paperback.

GENERAL HISTORY

Adcock, Frank E., *The Roman Art of War Under the Republic*. Barnes & Noble, 1960.
*Adcock, Frank E., *Roman Political Ideas and Practices*. University of Michigan Press, 1959.
Boak, Arthur E. R., *A History of Rome to 565 A.D.* (5th ed.). Macmillan, 1965.
†Caesar, Julius, *War Commentaries of Caesar*. Transl. by Rex Warner. Mentor, 1962.
The Cambridge Ancient History, Vols. VII-XII. Cambridge University Press, 1926; *Cambridge Medieval History*, Vols. I and II. Cambridge University Press, 1930.
Frank, Tenney, *A History of Rome*. Holt, Rinehart and Winston, 1923.
*Hadas, Moses, *A History of Rome*. G. Bell & Sons, Ltd., 1958.
†Haywood, Richard, *The Myth of Rome's Fall*. Apollo, 1962.
Lewis, Naphtali and Meyer Reinhold, *Roman Civilization*. 2 vols. Columbia University Press, Vol. I, 1951; Vol. II, 1959.
*Mattingly, Harold, *Roman Imperial Civilization*. St. Martin's Press, 1957.
Methuen's *A History of the Greek and Roman World. A History of the Roman World from 753 to 146 B.C.* Vol. IV. By H. H. Scullard (3rd ed.). Barnes & Noble, 1961; *A History of the Roman World from 146-30 B.C.* Vol. V. By Frank B. Marsh (3rd ed.). Barnes & Noble, 1963; *A History of the Roman World from 30 B.C. to 138 A.D.* Vol. VI. By H.M.D. Parker (3rd ed.). Barnes & Noble, 1959; *A History of the Roman World from 138-337 A.D.* Vol. VII. By H.M.D. Parker (2nd ed.). Barnes & Noble, 1958.
Mommsen, Theodor, *A History of Rome*. 5 vols. Free Press, 1947.
Moore, Ralph W., *The Roman Commonwealth*. Botsford (London), 1942.
†Nilsson, Martin P., *Imperial Rome*. Schocken, 1962.
Oxford Classical Dictionary. Ed. by M. Cary and others. Oxford University Press, 1953.
*Rostovtzeff, M., *History of the Ancient World*. Vol. II. Oxford University Press, 1930.
Rostovtzeff, M., *Social and Economic History of the Roman Empire*. 2 vols. (2nd ed.). Oxford University Press, 1957.
Sandys, John Edwin, *A Companion to Latin Studies* (3rd ed.). Hafner, 1935.
Webster, Graham, *The Roman Army*. Grovenor Museum Publications, 1956.
Wolff, Hans J., *Roman Law*. University of Oklahoma, 1951.
*Wormser, René, *The Story of the Law* (Rev. ed.). Simon & Schuster, 1962.

ART, ARCHITECTURE AND ARCHEOLOGY

Brion, Marcel, *Pompeii and Herculaneum: The Glory and the Grief*. Crown, 1960.
Brown, Frank E., *Roman Architecture*. Braziller, 1961.
Grant, Michael, *The Birth of Western Civilization; Greece and Rome*. McGraw-Hill, 1964.
Grimal, Pierre, *In Search of Ancient Italy*. Transl. by Phyllis Cummins. Hill & Wang, 1964.
Hanfmann, George M. A., *Roman Art*. New York Graphic Society, 1964.
Kahler, Heinz, *The Art of Rome and her Empire*. Crown, 1963.
MacKendrick, Paul, *The Mute Stones Speak*. St. Martin's Press, 1960.
Maiuri, Amedeo and Albert Skira, *Roman Painting*. World Publishing Co., 1953.
Masson, Georgina, *Italian Gardens*. Abrams, 1961.
Robertson, Donald Struance, *Greek and Roman Architecture* (2nd ed.). Cambridge University Press, 1943.
Scherer, Margaret R., *Marvels of Ancient Rome*. Phaidon Press Ltd., New York Graphic Society, 1955.
Stobart, J. C., *The Grandeur That Was Rome* (4th ed.). Revised by W. S. Maguinness and H. H. Scullard. Hawthorne, 1962.
Toynbee, Jocelyn, *Art in Roman Britain*. Phaidon Press Ltd., New York Graphic Society, 1962.
Volbach, W. F., *Early Christian Art*. Abrams, 1962.

LITERATURE

†Apuleius, *The Golden Ass*. Transl. by Jack Lindsay. Indiana University Press, 1962.
The Basic Works of Cicero. Transl. by Moses Hadas. Modern Library, 1951.
Davenport, Basil, *The Portable Roman Reader*. Viking, 1951.
Duckworth, George E., *The Complete Roman Drama* (2 vols.). Random House, 1942.
Godolphin, Francis R. B., *The Latin Poets*. Modern Library, 1949.
*Hadas, Moses, *A History of Latin Literature*. Columbia University Press, 1952.
Horace, *The Complete Works of Horace*. Ed. by Casper J. Kraemer Jr. Modern Library, 1936.
†Juvenal, *The Satires of Juvenal*. Transl. by Rolfe Humphries. Indiana University Press, 1958.
Livy, *A History of Rome*. Transl. by Moses Hadas. Modern Library, 1962.
†Lucan, *Pharsalia*. Transl. by Robert Graves. Penguin Books, 1957.
†Lucretius, *Nature of the Universe*. Transl. by R. E. Latham. Penguin Books, 1962.
†Martial, *Selected Epigrams*. Transl. by Rolfe Humphries. Indiana University Press, 1963.
†Ovid, *The Art of Love*. Transl. by Rolfe Humphries. Indiana University Press, 1958.
Ovid, *The Metamorphoses*. Transl. by Horace Gregory. New American Library, 1964.
The Oxford Book of Latin Verse. Oxford University Press, 1912.
*Pliny, *Natural History* (9 vols.). The Loeb Classical Library. Harvard University Press, 1951.
†Pliny, *The Letters of Pliny*. Transl. by Betty Radice. Penguin Books, 1963.
†Plutarch, *Plutarch's Essays*. Transl. by Moses Hadas. Mentor, 1957.
Plutarch, *Plutarch's Lives*. Ed. by Paul Turner. Southern Illinois Press, 1963.
Polybius, *Histories* (6 vols.). Transl. by Evelyn S. Schuckburgh. Indiana University Press, 1962.
Suetonius, *The Lives of the Twelve Caesars*. Transl. by Robert Graves. Penguin Books, 1957.
Tacitus, *The Complete Works of Tacitus*. Transl. by Moses Hadas. Modern Library, 1942.
Vergil, *Aeneid*. Bantam Books, 1963.
Vergil, *Georgics*. Transl. by Paul Bovie. University of Chicago Press, 1956.

RELIGION AND PHILOSOPHY

Durant, Will, *The Story of Civilization. Caesar and Christ*. Vol. 3. Simon & Schuster, 1944.
Latourette, Kenneth S., *A History of Christianity*. Harper, 1953.
*Seneca, *The Stoic Philosophy of Seneca*. Transl. by Moses Hadas. Doubleday, 1958.
†MacKendrick, Paul, *The Roman Mind at Work*. Van Nostrand, 1958.

ROMAN DAILY LIFE

Balsdon, J.P.V.D., *Roman Women*. Dufour, 1963.
*Barrow, R. H., *The Romans*. Aldine, 1964.
†Carcopino, Jérôme, *Daily Life in Ancient Rome*. Yale University Press, 1940.
Dill, Samuel, *Roman Society from Nero to Marcus Aurelius*. Meridian, 1958.
Friedlander, Ludwig, *Roman Life and Manners under the Early Empire*. 4 vols. Transl. by L. A. Magnus. Dutton, 1909.
Hamilton, Edith, *The Roman Way*. Norton, 1932.
Mattingly, Harold, *Man in the Roman Street*. Numismatic Review, 1947.
Paoli, Ugo E., *Rome, Its People, Life and Customs*. Transl. by R. D. Macnaghten. McKay, 1964.

ACKNOWLEDGMENT OF QUOTATIONS

P. 12—Prudentius: from *A History of Rome*, by M. Hadas, Doubleday Anchor Books, 1956. Cicero: from "On Moral Duties," in *The Basic Works of Cicero*, ed. by M. Hadas, Book I, transl. by G. B. Gardiner, Modern Library, Random House, 1951. P. 13—*Ibid.* P. 15—Vergil: from *Vergil, The Aeneid*, ed. by M. Hadas, transl. by T. H. Delabere May, Bantam Books, 1963. P. 16—Propertius: from *The Poems of Propertius*, transl. by C. Carrier, Indiana University Press, 1963. P. 33—Tacitus: from *The Complete Works of Tacitus*, transl. by A. J. Church and W. J. Brodribb, Modern Library, 1942. P. 45—Suetonius: from *The Lives of the Twelve Caesars*, ed. by J. Gavorse, Modern Library, 1957. P. 52—Tacitus, op. cit. P. 57—Tacitus, op. cit. P. 59—Suetonius, op. cit. P. 60—*Ibid.* P. 86—Seneca from *Rome: Its People, Life and Customs*, by U. E. Paoli, transl. by R. D. Macnaghten, McKay, 1963. P. 104—Cicero: from "Concerning Old Age," in *The Portable Roman Reader*, transl. by W. A. Falconer, Viking Press, 1951. P. 105—Catullus: from *The Poems of Catullus*, transl. by H. Gregory, Grove Press, 1956. P. 106—Vergil: from *Georgics and Eclogues*, transl. by T. C. Williams, Harvard University Press, 1915. Vergil: from the *Aeneid*, transl. by L. R. Lind, Indiana University Press, 1963. P. 107—Horace: from *The Odes and Epodes of Horace*, transl. by J. P. Clancy, Phoenix Books, 1960. P. 108—Seneca: from *Agamemnon*, in *The Complete Roman Drama*, ed. by G. E. Duckworth, transl. by F. J. Miller, Random House, 1942. Martial: from *Martial, the Twelve Books of Epigrams*, transl. by J. A. Pott and F. A. Wright, Dutton, 1924. P. 109—Juvenal: from *The Satires of Juvenal*, transl. by R. Humphries, Indiana University Press, 1958. P. 110—St. Augustine: from his "Confessions," in *Masterworks of Autobiography*, ed. by R. D. Mallery, Doubleday, 1946. P. 112—Ovid: from *Metamorphoses*, transl. by Eusden and S. Garth, Heritage Press, 1961. Pp. 114-115—"Copa," attrib. to Vergil, in *Virgil*, Vol. II, transl. by H. R. Fairclough, The Loeb Classical Library, Harvard University Press, 1947. P. 116—Horace: from *The Complete Works of Horace*, transl. by J. C. Baring, Modern Library, 1936. P. 119—Anon., transl. by T. Parnell in *The Latin Poets*, ed. by F. R. B. Godolphin, Modern Library, 1949. P. 138—Pliny the Younger: from his *Letters*, in *Roman Literature in Translation*, ed. by G. Howe, G. A. Harrer and A. Suskin, rev. by A. Suskin, Harper & Row, 1959. P. 166—Justinian: from his *Digest*, in *Roman Civilization*, Vol. II, ed. by N. Lewis and M. Reinhold, Columbia University Press, 1959.

ACKNOWLEDGMENTS

The editors of this book are indebted to T. Robert S. Broughton, Professor of Latin, Bryn Mawr College; Cornelius Vermeule, Curator, Department of Classical Art, Museum of Fine Arts, Boston; Charles W. Dunmore, Assistant Professor of Classics, New York University; Colonel John R. Elting, Acting Deputy Head, Department of Military Art and Engineering, U.S. Military Academy, West Point; Frederick P. Todd, Director, New Windsor Cantonment; Raymond V. Schoder, S.J., Loyola University, Chicago; Paul P. Vouras, Associate Professor of Geography, and Livio C. Stecchini, Assistant Professor of History, Paterson State College; Bruno Molajoli, Director General of Antiquities and

Fine Arts, Ministero della Pubblica Istruzione, Rome; Antonio Pietrogrande, Eleanora Bracco, Caterina Caprino, Museo Nazionale, Rome; Mario Moretti and Giovanni Scichilone, Museo Nazionale de Villa Giulia, Rome; Maria Floriani Squarciapino, Ostia Antica; Gianfilippo Carettoni, and Itala Dondero, Foro Romano, Rome; Carlo Pietrangeli, Capitoline Museums and Museo della Civiltà Romana, Rome; Antonio Ferrua, S.J., Pontificio Istituto di Archeologia Cristiana, Rome; Irene Kircher, Deutsches Archaeologisches Institut, Rome; Ernest Nash, American Academy, Rome; Giacomo Caputo, Florence; Vatican Library, Rome; Erminia Speyer, Vatican Galleries and Museums, Rome; Alfonso de Franciscis and Giuseppe Maggi, Museo Nazionale, Naples; Bernabò Brea, Syracuse; Gianguido Belloni, Civico Gabinetto Numismatico, Castello Sforzesco, Milan; Munich Antiquarium; Georg Daltrop, Museum für Kunst and Gewerbe, Hamburg; Rheinisches Landesmuseum, Trier; H. Klumbach, Christa Belting-Ihm, Römisch-Germanisches Zentralmuseum, Mainz; Erwin M. Auer, Rudolf Noll, Kunsthistorisches Museum, Vienna; The staff of the London Museum; Denys Haynes, British Museum, London.

PICTURE CREDITS

The sources for the illustrations in this book are set forth below. Descriptive notes on the works of art are included. Credits for pictures positioned from left to right are separated by semicolons, from top to bottom by dashes. Photographers' names which follow a descriptive note appear in parentheses. Abbreviations include "c." for century and "ca." for circa.

Cover—Detail from Trajan's Column, marble, dedicated 113 A.D. (Aldo Durazzi).

CHAPTER 1: 10: Bronze wolf, Capitoline Hill, copy of original in Capitoline Museum, Rome, ca. 500 B.C., twins attributed to Antonio Pollaiuolo, 15th c. A.D. (David Lees). 14-15—Miniature from *Aeneid* manuscript, 4th c. A.D., Codex Vaticanus Latinus 3225, Vatican Library. 17—Via Appia (James Burke). 18-19—Model of Rome ca. 350 A.D., Museo della Civiltà Romana, Rome (Emmett Bright; flexichrome by Peter Bitlisian). 20-21—Forum Romanum (Roloff Beny). 22-23—Marcus Aurelius, bronze, ca. 173 A.D., Piazza del Campidoglio, Rome (Dmitri Kessel)—round temple in sacred area of Forum Boarium, late 1st c. B.C. (Roloff Beny); Pantheon dome, completed ca. 125 A.D. (John G. Ross from Photo Researchers, Inc.). 24-25—Hadrian's Villa, Tivoli, pool and marine pavilion, early 2nd c. A.D. (Roloff Beny); detail of mosaic from Piazza Armerina, Sicily, 4th century A.D. (Emmett Bright). 26-27—Treasury, Petra, Jordan, rose limestone, 1st c. A.D. (Roloff Beny); Aphrodite of Aphrodisias, white marble and black basalt, ca. 100 A.D., Antiquarium in the Residenz, Munich (Walter Sanders)—market foundations, Smyrna (Izmir), 2nd c. A.D. (Roloff Beny). 28-29—Timgad, Algeria, 2nd c. A.D. (Ray Delvert); wall painting from Pompeii, 1st c. A.D., Museo Nazionale, Naples (Emmett Bright). 30-31—Two prisoners, detail from Arch of Carpentras, 1st c. A.D. (Erich Lessing from Magnum); Aqueduct, Segovia, 1st c. A.D. (Walter Sanders). 32-33—Cernunnus, Celtic god, 4th c. A.D. Musée Saint Remy, Rheims, France (Erich Lessing from Magnum)—Hadrian's wall, England, early 2nd c. A.D. (Dmitri Kessel).

CHAPTER 2: 34—Bust of Gaius Julius Caesar, marble, ca. 50 B.C., toga ca. 16th c., Antiquarium in the Residenz, Munich (Walter Sanders). 39—Drawing by Nicholas N. Solovioff. 43—Great Wall of China (Seiya Toyama from Black Star). 45—Circus scene, terra cotta relief from Campagna, probably 1st c. A.D., Museo Nazionale, Rome (Erich Lessing from Magnum). 46-47—Hunt mosaic, end 3rd c. A.D., Musée Archéologique d'Hippone, Algeria (Pierre Belzeaux from Rapho-Guillumette). 48-49—Amphitheater at Arles, France, 1st c. B.C. (Marc Riboud from Magnum); stone sculpture, probably 4th c. A.D., Musée Denon, Chalon-sur-Saône (Marc Riboud). 50-51—Mosaic of the Dar Buc Ammera from Zliten, 2nd c. A.D., Musée des Antiquités de Tripoli, Libya (Pierre Belzeaux from Rapho-Guillumette). 52-53—Mosaic from Piazza Armerina, Sicily, 4th c. A.D. (D. Edwards, from Free Lance Photographers Guild). 54-55—Circus mosaic, 3rd c. A.D., Musée de la Civilisation Gallo-Romaine, Lyons, France (Erich Lessing from Magnum).

CHAPTER 3: 56—Detail from Trajan's Column, marble, dedicated 113 A.D. (Aldo Durazzi). 58-61—Drawing by Nicholas N. Solovioff. 64—Augustus, head, ca. 20 B.C., Capitoline Museum, Rome; Julian, 4th c. A.D., Louvre, Paris (Alinari)—Tiberius, 1st c. A.D., Archeological Museum, Madrid (Alinari); Diocletian, late 3rd c. A.D., Villa Doria-Pamphilj, Rome (Istituto Archeologico Germanico)—Caligula, 1st c. A.D., Museo Nazionale, Naples (Alinari); Caracalla, early 3rd c. A.D., Museo Nazionale, Naples (Alinari)—Claudius, 1st c. A.D., Vatican Museum, Rome (Anderson); Septimius Severus, ca. 200 A.D., restored, Capitoline Museum, Rome—Nero, 1st c. A.D., restored, Capitoline Museum, Rome (Alinari); Domitian, ca. 90 A.D., Museo Comunale Antiquarium, Rome (Alinari); Trajan, 1st-2nd c. A.D. British Museum, London; Hadrian, 2nd c. A.D., Capitoline Museum, Rome (Anderson). 69—Sard intaglio, plaster impression, from Hadrumetum, ca. 30 B.C., Museum of Fine Arts, Boston (John McQuade). 70-71—Mosaic, ca. 2nd c. A.D., Museo Archeològico Prenestino (Emmett Bright). 72-73—Reconstruction of Roman Forum by Samuel Bronston for *The Fall of the Roman Empire* (John Cabrera); jasper seal, gold mounting, 1st c. B.C., Archeological Museum, Florence (Erich Lessing from Magnum). 74-75—Relief from altar from Temple of Vespasian, 1st c. B.C.-1st c. A.D., Pompeii Excavations (Erich Lessing from Magnum). 76-77—Chalcedony gem, early 1st c. A.D., Kunsthistorisches Museum, Vienna. Grand Camée de la Sainte Chapelle, 1st c. A.D., Bibliothèque Nationale, Paris.

CHAPTER 4: 78—Wall painting from Pompeii, 1st c. A.D. (Scala). 80,81—Head, ca. 90 A.D., Capitoline Museum, Rome (Alinari); Antonia, 1st-2nd c. A.D., wife of Drusus, Museo Nazionale, Naples (Alinari); Annia Faustina, 3rd c. A.D., Capitoline Museum, Rome (Alinari); head, late 1st c. A.D., Vatican Museum, Rome (Alinari); Faustina the Elder, 2nd c. A.D., Vatican Museum, Rome (Alinari); Minazia Pollas, 1st c. A.D., Museo Nazionale, Rome (Alinari). 85—Mosaic from the Dar Buc Ammera at Zliten, 2nd c. A.D., Musée des Antiquités de Tripoli, Libya (Pierre Belzeaux from Rapho-Guillumette). 86, 87—Drawing by Nicholas N. Solovioff. 89-101: Roman and Macedonian soldiers from West Point Museum Collections, United States Military Academy, by John A. Greenwood and John Fleming Scheid. Gauls and Roman war machines by John Fleming Scheid. 89-97: Model of Avaricum by Edward M. Godschalk (Ben Rose). 89-101: Model of Cynoscephalae by Matt Greene (Ralph Morse).

CHAPTER 5: 102—Manuscript miniature, Vergil's *Georgics III*, Codex Vaticanus Latinus 3867, 6th c. A.D., Vatican Library (William J. Sumits). 105—Inkpot, Museo Nazionale, Naples (Aldo Durazzi)—wax tablet, modern reproduction, Museo della Civiltà Romana, Rome (Aldo Durazzi)—iron styli, courtesy Trustees of the London Museum (Heinz Zinram)—bucket with papyrus rolls, modern reconstruction, Museo della Civiltà Romana, Rome (Aldo Durazzi). 109—Mosaic from Pompeii, 1st c. A.D., Museo Nazionale, Naples (Alinari). 111—Detail from wall painting, House of the Marine Venus, Pompeii, 1st c. A.D. (Erich Lessing from Magnum). 112, 113—Siren's rock, Aeolian Islands off Sicily (Giac Casale); Perseus and Andromeda, wall painting, House of the Priest Amandus, Pompeii, 1st c. A.D. (Erich Lessing from Magnum). 114, 115—Wall painting from House of Livia, Prima Porte, late 1st c. B.C.-early 1st c. A.D., Museo Nazionale, Rome (Erich Lessing from Magnum)—Erich Lessing from Magnum; wall painting from House of Julia Felix, Pompeii, 1st c. B.C., Museo Nazionale, Naples (Emmett Bright)—haystacks in Tibertine Valley (James Burke). 116, 117—Swans in Canopus pool, Hadrian's Villa, Tivoli (Roloff Beny); wall painting from Pompeii, late 1st c. B.C.-early 1st c. A.D., Museo Nazionale, Naples (Emmett Bright). 118, 119—Coastline with sea spray off Camogli (Walter Sanders)—wall painting from Pompeii, 1st c. A.D. (Raymond V. Schoder, S.J.).

CHAPTER 6: 120—Domina, detail from wall painting, Villa of the Mysteries, Pompeii, 1st c. B.C. (Erich Lessing from Magnum). 122, 123—Bronze Lares, Louvre Museum, Paris (Giraudon); Lararium, House of the Vettii, Pompeii, after 62 A.D. (Emmett Bright). 124, 125—Drawings by Nicholas N. Solovioff. 126—Menorah from lead sarcophagus, necropolis, Beth She'arim, Israel, ca. 300 A.D. (S. J. Schweig for Department of Archaeology, Hebrew University, Jerusalem). 129—Wall painting from Pompeii (sometimes identified as Sappho), 1st c. A.D., Museo Nazionale, Naples (Erich Lessing from Magnum). 130, 131—Street scene, Pompeii (Erich Lessing from Magnum)— street musicians, mosaic from Cicero's Villa, Pompeii, by Dioscuris of Samos, 1st c. A.D., Museo Nazionale, Naples (Erich Lessing from Magnum); wall painting from the House of the Baker, Pompeii, 1st c. A.D., Museo Nazionale, Naples (Erich Lessing from Magnum). 132, 133—Wall painting from Herculaneum, 1st c. A.D., Museo Nazionale, Naples (Erich Lessing from Magnum); cubiculum found at Boscoreale, 1st c. B.C., The Metropolitan Museum of Art, Rogers Fund, 1903; encaustic on marble by Alexander Ateniese, from Herculaneum, probably 1st c. A.D., Museo Nazionale, Naples (Erich Lessing from Magnum). 134, 135—Wall painting from Pompeii, 1st c. A.D., Museo Nazionale, Naples (Emmett Bright); wall painting from Stabia, probably 1st c. A.D., Museo Nazionale, Naples (Raymond V. Schoder, S.J.); nymphaeum and triclinium of the House of Neptune and Amphitrite, Herculaneum, 1st c. A.D. (Erich Lessing from Magnum). 136, 137—Wall painting from Herculaneum, 1st c. A.D., copy of 4th c. B.C. Greek original, Museo Nazionale, Naples (Erich Lessing from Magnum). Odeon, or "Theatrum Tectum," Pompeii, 80-75 B.C. (Erich Lessing from Magnum). 138, 139—Wall painting from Pompeii, 1st c. A.D., Museo Nazionale, Naples (Emmett Bright); necropolis on Via Nucerina, Pompeii, 1st c. A.D. (Erich Lessing from Magnum).

CHAPTER 7: 140—Tetrarchs, porphyry, ca. 300 A.D., Piazza San Marco, Venice (Roloff Beny). 145—Gold solidus, Honorius, 395-423 A.D., Civico Gabinetto Numismatico, Castello Sforzesco, Milan. 147—Sandstone relief, after 200 A.D., Landesmuseum, Trier. 148, 149—Marble relief, late 1st c. B.C., Staatliche Antikensammlungen, Munich—Roman plow, modern model, Museo della Civiltà Romana, Rome (Alinari); bas relief, ca. 270 A.D., Museo Nazionale, Rome (Alinari). 150, 151—Oil press, model, Museo della Civiltà Romana, Rome (David Lees)—Marble sepulchral relief, Museo Torlonia, Rome (Alinari); oil shop, stone funerary stele, 2nd or 3rd c. A.D., Cherchel Museum, Algiers—Roman scales, bronze, 1st c. A.D., Museo Nazionale, Naples (Alinari-Giraudon). 152, 153—Protective goddess of healing, Meditrina (sometimes identified as soap factory), stone funerary stele, 2nd or 3rd century A.D., Musée Departemental des Vosges, Epinal (Alinari); bronze vaginal speculum from Pompeii, 1st c. A.D., Museo Nazionale, Naples (Erich Lessing from Magnum); doctor examining a child, marble relief, 2nd c. A.D., British Museum (Alinari). 154, 155—Mausoleum of the Aterii family, ca. 90 A.D., Via Labicana, Rome (Alinari), Roman tools, reproductions, Museo della Civiltà Romana, Rome (David Lees)—Sarcophagus from Ostia, marble, 2nd or 3rd c. A.D., Ny Carlsberg Glyptotek, Copenhagen (Alinari).

CHAPTER 8: 156—Arch of Titus and Colosseum, end 1st c. A.D. (Roloff Beny). 161—Ivory diptych of the consul Magnus, Constantinople, 518 A.D., Cabinet des Medailles, Bibliothèque Nationale, Paris. 162, 163—Drawing by Nicholas N. Solovioff. 165—Maya figure, Tzakol phase, from Uaxactún, Peten, Guatemala, National Museum of Archeology and Ethnology, Guatemala City, Guatemala (Dmitri Kessel). 167—Fresco from catacomb of St. Priscilla, Rome, second half of 3rd c. A.D. (Erich Lessing from Magnum). 168, 169—Crucifixion, ivory, ca. 420 A.D., British Museum (Heinz Zinram); ivory panel, ca. 400 A.D., Bavarian National Museum, Munich (Friedrich Rauch). 170, 171—Fresco from the catacomb of St. Domitilla, Rome, first half of 4th c. A.D. (Erich Lessing from Magnum)—fresco from the catacomb of St. Priscilla, Rome, second half of 3rd c. A.D. (Erich Lessing from Magnum); catacomb of St. Callisto, 2nd-4th c. A.D., Pontificia Commissione de Archeologica Sacra. 172, 173—Head of Constantine, marble, 4th c. A.D., Capitoline Museum, Rome (Erich Lessing from Magnum); bas-relief from marble sarcophagus, late 4th c. A.D., Musée d'Art Chrétien, Arles, France (Erich Lessing from Magnum). 174-175—Mosaic from Chapel of the Bishop's Palace, Ravenna, Italy, ca. 494-519 A.D. (Erich Lessing from Magnum); Santa Costanza Mausoleum, Rome, 4th c. A.D. (David Lees). 176, 177—Ivory book-cover, late 5th c. A.D., cross and lamb probably 8th c. A.D., Treasury of the Cathedral, Milan, Italy (Erich Lessing from Magnum). 178: Matt Greene.

INDEX

*This symbol in front of a page number indicates a photograph or painting of the subject mentioned.

MAPS IN THIS VOLUME
All maps by David Greenspan

The Roman World	8-9
Italy in the Sixth Century B.C.	37
The Roman Empire, 117 A.D.	66-67
Routes of Barbarian Invaders	158-159

A

Achaea (Greece), *map* 9, *map* 67
Actium, *map* 9; battle of, 44, *69
Adams, John, 160-161
Adrianople, *map* 158
Adriatic Sea, *map* 8, *map* 37, *map* 66
Aedile, office of, 40
Aegean Sea, *map* 9, *map* 67
Aeneas, *14, 16, 106, 107
Aeneid, Vergil, 14, 15, 75, 106
Aequi, tribe, *map* 37; invasion of Rome by, 15-16
Aesculapius, Temple of, Rome, *18-19
Africa. *See* North Africa
Agamemnon, Seneca, 108
Agriculture, 147, 149; barbarian labor, 68; homeland, early, 16; North Africa and Egypt, 29, 71; reform proposals of Gracchi, 40; small-scale replaced by large-scale, 149; tools, *148-149. *See also* Farmers
Agrigentum, *map* 37
Agrippina, 61
Alani, migration of, *map* 158
Alba Longa, 16
Alemanni, Germanic tribe, 143
Alexander the Great, 37, 43, 73
Alexandria, *map* 9, *map* 67
Algeria, Roman ruins in, *28-29
Alimenta, 67
Alps, *map* 8, *map* 37, *map* 66; Hannibal's crossing of, 38
Ammianus, 146
Amores, Ovid, 107
Amphitheaters, 45, *48, *156, 162
Amulius, King, 16
Anastasius, Emperor, 64
Ancyra (Ankara), *map* 9, *map* 67
Andromeda and Perseus, in Roman poetry and painting, *112-113
Andronicus, Livius, 103
Anglo-American law systems, 166
Animals: hunt, *46-47; husbandry, *102, *116-117, *148-149; war elephants, 38, *100-101; wild, in games, *45, 46, *48-51
Animism, 121, *124-125
Annals, Ennius, 103
Annals, Tacitus, 109
Anthemius, Emperor, 64
Antioch, *map* 9, 27, *map* 67
Antiochus III, King of Syria, 38
Antiochus IV, King of Syria, 38
Antoninianus, coin, 143
Antoninus Pius, Emperor, 64, 65, 68
Antony, Mark, 44, 57, 69, 71, 104, 164
Apennines, *map* 8
Aphorisms and maxims, 104, 109
Aphrodisias, *map* 9, 27
Aphrodite, 124
Apicius, 85
Apollo, *32, 124
Apollonia, *map* 66
Appian, quoted, 44
Appian Way, *17, 164
Apuleius, 110; quoted, 82
Apulum, *map* 66
Aqua Marcia, 164
Aqueducts, 11, *18-19, 22, *30-31, 87, 161, *162-163, 164
Aquileia, *map* 8, *map* 158
Aquincum (Budapest), *map* 8
Aquitania, *map* 66
Arabia, *map* 9, *map* 67
Arcadius, Emperor, 64
Arch, architectural use of, 22, *27, *28, *30-31, *156, *162-163, 164
Architecture, 11, *18-31, *72-73, 88, *156, 161-164; Byzantine, 159; Etruscan influences, 22; forms, 22, 162 (*see also* Arch; Dome; Vaults); Greek influences, *22, *24-25; heritage of Roman, 161-162, 163, *175; materials, 13, 22, 162; North African influences, *29. *See also* Amphitheaters; Aqueducts; Temples; Villas
Architecture, On, Vitruvius, 161
Arelate (Arles), *map* 8; amphitheater at, *48
Ares, 124
Aristides, quoted, 68
Aristocracy: landowners, 40; military leadership, 89; political leadership, 36, 39. *See also Nobiles*; Patricians; Upper class
Arles, *map* 8; amphitheater at, *48
Armenia, *map* 9; Romans in, 62, 65, *map* 67, 68
Army, 36, 73, 89, 90, *91-93, *96-101; barbarians in, 30, 142; citizenship privileges, 63; discipline, 63; discipline relaxed, 142; Eastern Empire, 159; infantry, 89, *98-101; infiltrates civil service, 142, 144; late Emperors installed and deposed by, 143-144, 145; leadership, 89; myth of invincibility, 15; a noble profession, 83; policy of placation of, and resulting degeneration, 142, 143; power of generals, late Republic, 41, 42; professionalism introduced, 41; rebellion of 68 A.D., 62, 63; reorganization by Diocletian, 144; superiority of, 89; triumphal procession, *58-61. *See also* Warfare; Weapons
Arno River, *map* 37
Arretium, *map* 37
Art, 11; Byzantine, 159; Christian, *167-177; Greek influence, 11, 111; patrons, 83, 106, 107; realism, 12, 176. *See also* Architecture; Literature; Mosaics; Painting; Sculpture
Art of Love, The, Ovid, 107
Artaxata, *map* 9
Artemis, 124
Artillery, *91-95
Ascanius, 16
Asoka, King of India, 43
Assemblies, 36
Assyria, *map* 67

Asturica Augusta, *map* 8
Athena, 124
Athens, *map* 9, *map* 67, 127; learning, 82; Sulla's assault on, 41
Atrium, 84
Augures, 121
Augusta Treverorum (Trier), *map* 8, *map* 66
Augusta Vindelicorum (Augsburg), *map* 66
Augustan Age of literature, 105-108
Augustine. *See* St. Augustine
Augustus, Emperor (Octavian), 44, 63, *64, 68, 69, 71, *74-75, 83; administration of, 58-59, 69, 73, 76, 126, 154; and Antony, 44, 69; beautification of Rome, 18, 58, 73; deification of, *69, *76-77, 122; and Egypt, 71; as literary sponsor, 75, 106, 107-108; offices and powers of, 57, 73; policy of containment of Empire, 60; *princeps*, 57; his *res gestae*, 58; seal of, *73; quoted, 71, 73, 76; mentioned, 86, 109, 110, 114, 147, 159, 161
Augustus, as title, 57, 62, 63, 144, 145
Aurelian, Emperor, 64, 144
Aurelius. *See* Marcus Aurelius
Auspices, taking of, 123-124
Autocracy: of Constantine, 146; of Diocletian, 144
Avaricum, siege of, *89-97
Avitus, Emperor, 64

B

Babylon, *map* 9
Bacchus, *138
Baetica, *map* 66
Balearic Islands, *map* 8, *map* 66; Vandals in, *map* 158
Ballista, *94-95
Banquets, 85-86, *134-135
Barbarians, *30; in Army and militia, 30, 142; as farm help, 68; invasions by, 143, 146, *map* 158; payment of bounties to, 143; settlements of, in provinces, 68
Barrel vault, 162
Basilica Julia, Rome, *18-19
Basilicas, 175
Baths, public, 86, *87, 88, 135
Belgica, *map* 66
Berber tribes, raids by, 143
Berenice, *map* 9
Bible, Vulgate, 110
Biblical scenes on book cover, *176-177
Birds, religious significance of, 123-124
Bithynia, *map* 67
Black Sea, *map* 9, *map* 67
Boccaccio, Giovanni, 164
Bononia (Bologna), *map* 8, *map* 66
Books and book trade, 82-83
Bostra, *map* 67
Boys: education of, 82; sports and games, *52-53
Brick: manufacture of, 13; use of, 22
Britain, Romans in, *map* 8, 33, 60, 62, 67, 143; Hadrian's Wall, *32-33, 67; roads and settlements, 63, *map* 66
Britannicus, 61, 164
Britons, 33
Brundisium, *map* 8, 17, *map* 66
Brutus, 160
Bucolics, Vergil, 106
Buddhism, in India, 43
Burdigala (Bordeaux), *map* 8, *map* 66
Bureaucracy. *See* Civil service
Burgundians, tribe, *map* 158
Burial, 88; catacombs, 170, *171
Business, 130; equestrians in, 39, 79, 83; regarded as vulgar, 13, 83, 151; retail, *131, *150-151
Byzantine Church, 159

Byzantium, *map* 9, *map* 66, 146, 157, 172. *See also* Constantinople; Eastern Empire

C

Caere, *map* 37
Caesar, C. Julius, *34, 42-44, 58, 60, 68, 89; career of, 43; and Cleopatra, 43-44; in First Triumvirate, 42-43; in Gaul, 42, 43, 90; murder of, 21, 44, 160; opposes Pompey and Senate, 43, 44; writings of, 43, 104-105; quoted, 104; mentioned, 57, 69, 107, 110, 164
Caesar, as title, 62, 63, 144, 145
Caesaraugusta (Saragossa), *map* 8, *map* 66
Caesarea, Judaea, *map* 9, *map* 67
Caesarea, Mauretania, *map* 8, *map* 66
Caesariensis, *map* 66
Calendar, 44, 124; Mayan, 165
Caligula, Emperor, 60, *64, *76, 164
Campus Martius, Rome, 13
Camus, Albert, 164
Cannae, *map* 8
Capitoline Hill, Rome, 22, 122; statue on, *10
Cappadocia, *map* 67
Capua, *map* 37, *map* 66
Caracalla, Emperor, *64, 143; baths of, *87, 88
Carinus, Emperor, 64
Carpathian Mountains, *map* 8
Carrhae, *map* 9
Carthage, *map* 8, *map* 37, *map* 66; Aeneas in, *14; colonies on Sicily, *map* 37, 38; Punic Wars, 16, *37-39, 38; razed, 29, 39; rebuilt, 29; Vandals in, *map* 158
Carthago Nova (Cartagena), *map* 8
Carus, Emperor, 64
Caspian Sea, *map* 9, *map* 67
Cassius (Caesar's betrayer), 160
Cassius Dio, quoted, 68, 73, 141
Catacombs, 170, *171; art, *167, *170
Catholic Church. *See* Roman Catholic Church
Catiline, 42, 104
Catullus, 105; quoted, 105, 109
Caucasus Mountains, *map* 9
Cave canem, mosaic, *109
Celtic tribes, 41, 60; deity, *32
Cena, meal, 86
Census-taking, 145
Centuriata (comitia), 36
Ceremonies and rituals, 12-13; boys' coming of age, 82; betrothal, 80; birth, 81; funeral, 88; traditionalism in, 13, 88; war declarations, 12; wedding, 81. *See also* Religion; Religious festivals
Cernunnus, Celtic deity, *32
Chariot races, 45, *54-55; children's, *52-53
Charlemagne, Emperor, 160
Children: sports and games, *52-53; upbringing of, 81-82; welfare program (*alimenta*), 67
Chinese Great Wall, *43
Christiads, Vida, 164
Christianity, 122, 127-128, 159, 167; art of, *167-177; early history, 168, 170, 172, 175; East-West schism, 159; legalization of, 128, 145-146, 172, 175; and Roman literature, 110, 159-160; persecutions, 128, 145, 167, 170; symbolism, *176-177. *See also* Roman Catholic Church
Cicero, 44, 47, 104, 127; master of prose, 104; murder of, 44, 104; on old age, 104; on the law, 165; on vulgarity of business, 13, 151; quoted, 12, 104, 105, 109, 132, 154; mentioned, 21, 80, 84

186

Cilicia, 47, *map 67*
Cincinnatus, 15-16
Circus Maximus, Rome, *18-19, 45
Circuses, 45, *54-55, 86; free admission, 67, 86
Cirta, *map 8, map 66, map 158*
Cities, 17; government, 65, 67-68, 144, 147, 175; Italian, 40, 41; Latin right, 61, 63, 68; provincial, 17, 21, *26-31, 60, 61, 65, 67-68, 143; as religious communities, 121, 123; status of *colonia*, 68; status of *municipium*, 68
Citizenship, 36, 40, 60-61, 68; army, 63; coming of age, 82; extension to all Italian cities, 41; extension to provincials, 11, 60, 63, 67-68, 143; freedmen's limited, 79; Latin right, 61, 63, 68; *municipia*, 68; overall extension of, 143; Third Century loss of value of, 144; withdrawal from Christians, 145
City of God, St. Augustine, 110
Civil law, 165
Civil service: beginnings under Augustus, 58-59; Eastern Empire, 159; extensions of, early Empire, 59, 60, 63; growth of bureaucracy, 65, 144, 146, 147; military infiltration of, 142; military replaced by lawyers, 144
Civil wars: Caesar's *Commentaries* on, 104; late Empire, 143-144; late Republic, 43-44; Social War, 41; Year of Four Emperors, 62
Class war: early Republic, 36; late Republic, 39, 40-41, 43
Classes. *See* Social classes
Claudius, Emperor, 59, 60-61, *64, 109, 164; temple of, *18-19
Claudius Gothicus, Emperor, 64
Claudius Pulcher, 124
Cleopatra, 43-44
Clients (social institution), 83
Clothing, *78, 86; boys' *vs.* men's, 82; Byzantine, 159; class distinctions, 79, 86
Clovis, King of Franks, 160
Clusium, *map 37*
Clytemnaestra, in Seneca's *Agamemnon*, 108
Coemptio, marriage, 81
Coins, 143, *145; loss of value, 143-144
Colonia, city status, 68
Colonia Agrippina (Cologne), *map 8*
Colonus, tenant farmer, 146
Colosseum, Rome, 11, *18-19, 45, *156, 162
Column, Greek, Roman use of, *22
Comedy, 103-104
Comitia centuriata, curiata, tributa, 36
Comitium, 162
Commentaries, Caesar, 43, 104-105
Commerce. *See* Business; Trade
Commodia, 141
Commodus, Emperor, 64, 76, 127, 141
Como, 65
Concord, Temple of, Rome, 124
Concrete, use of, 22, 162
Confarreatio, marriage, 80, 81
Confessions, St. Augustine, 110
Conservatism: general attitude of, 13; political, of *optimates*, 39
Constantine, Emperor, 64, 145-146, 157, 159, *172, 175; accepts Christianity, 128, *145, 167; Arch of, *18-19; Baths of, *18-19
Constantine, Licinius, Emperor, 64
Constantinople, *map 9*, 64, *map 66*, 110, 146, *map 158*, 159, 172; replica of Rome, 157; Turkish capture of, 157. *See also* Eastern Empire
Construction. *See* Engineering
Constantius, Emperor, 128
Consul, office of, 36, 39-40, *161; advancement to, 40; Marius' tenure, 40-41; Pompey's tenure, powers of, 36; Sulla's tenure, 41-42; term of office, 36
Corduba, *map 8, map 66*
Corinth, *map 9*; destruction by Rome, 38
Corpus Iuris Civilis, 166
Corsica, *map 8, map 37, map 66*; Vandals in, *map 158*
Corvus, 38, *39

Courts: early Empire, 59; language, 104. *See also* Judges; Law
Crassus, 42-43
Cremona: battle of, 62; Tacitus on occupation of, 62
Crete, *map 9, map 67*
Crime, 88
Criminal law, 165
Criminals as gladiators, 48, 50
Crossbow, *95
Croton, *map 37*
Ctesiphon, *map 9*
Cumae, *map 37*
Curators, municipal government, 65
Curia, Church districts, 159
Curia, Senate, *18-19
Curiata (comitia), 36
Currency: devaluations, 142, 143; inflation, 143-144; replaced by commodity payments, 143, 145. *See also* Coins
Cybele, cult of, 127
Cynoscephalae, *map 9*; battle of, 38, *98-101
Cyprus, *map 9, map 67*
Cyrenaica, *map 9, map 66*
Cyrene, *map 9, map 67*

D

Dacia, Romans in, 65, *map 66*
Dacians, victory over, *56, *58-61
Damascus, *map 9*, 27
Dante, 160
Danube, *map 8-9*; army insurrection of 68 A.D., 62; Augustan border, 60; barbarian invasions across, 68, 146, *map 158*; Roman extension beyond, 65, *map 66*
Dead Sea, *map 9*
Death penalty, uses of, 79, 84, 145, 165
Decius, Emperor, 64, 170
Denarius, coin, 143
Dialogues, Seneca, 108
Diana, 124
Didius Julianus, Emperor, 64, 141-142
Dio Cassius. *See* Cassius Dio
Dioceses: provinces grouped in, 144; in Church, 159
Diocletian, Emperor, *64, *140, 143, 144-145, 159
Dione, 118. *See also* Venus
Disease, 152. *See also* Plague
Divine Comedy, The, Dante, 160
Dome, architectural use of, 22, *23, 162
Domitian, Emperor, 58, *64, 65, 157; mentioned, 109, 110
Drama, 103-104, 108, 137
Drusus, Marcus Livius (tribune), 41
Drusus, Nero Claudius (general), 106; mentioned, 80
Durocortorum (Reims), *map 8*
Dyrrhachium (Durazzo), *map 8, map 66*

E

Eastern Empire, 146, 157-159; culture, 159; Emperors of, *table 64*, 157-159; language, 159; law, 166
Eastern provinces: border fortifications, 63; border threats, late Empire, 142, 143; cities of, *26-27, map 66-67*; Mark Antony in control of, 44; Pompey in, 42; Roman expansion, 38, 41, 42, 65, *map 66-67*; Sulla in, 41
Eastern religious influences, 126, 127
Eburacum (York), *map 8, map 66*
Ecclesiastical law, 159
Eclogues, Vergil, 106
Economy: city of Rome, 39; disparities between rich and poor, as source of political strife, 39, 40; farmers' problems, 39, 40, 68, 146, 149; importance of North African grain, 29, 62, 71; late Republic, 39, 40; prices and price controls, 143-144, 145; prosperity of early Empire, 65, 142; provincial, 65, 142, 144; troubles of late Empire, 142, 143-144, 145, 146;

wage controls, 145. *See also* Currency; Public finance; Taxation; Trade
Education, 82-83
Egypt, *map 9*, 62, *map 67*, *70-71; Antony and Cleopatra, 44; Caesar in, 43-44; economic importance, 29, 71; Persian threat to, 143; Ptolemaic Empire, 37
Elagabalus, Emperor, 64
Elephants, in warfare, 38, *100-101
Emerita Augusta (Merida), *map 8, map 66*
Emperors, 12, *table 64*; deification of, *69, *76-77, 122, 125-126; doctrine of divine rights, 144; excesses of some, 14, 59-60, 62, 65, 109-110, 141; *principes*, 57-58; provincials as, 11, 65, 67, 142-143, 144; succession problem, 59, 60, 65, 67, 144, 145; succession dictated by Army, 62, 143-144, 145
Empire, 11-12, 35, 57-68, 71, 76, 141-146; administration, 58-59, 60, 63, 65, 67-68, 76, 142, 144-145, 146 (*see also* Government; Public finance); Augustan policy of containment of, 60; autocracy of late, 144, 146; citizenship, 60-61, 63, 68, 143, 144; a commonwealth, 67-68; constitutional basis of, 57, 62-63; constitutional pretenses abandoned, 144; decline and fall, 141-146, 157; establishment of, 57-58, 73; expansion under Trajan, 65; at its height, 65, *map 66-67*; late, border threats, 142, 143; late, civil wars, 143-144; late, law statutes, 146, 165, 166; permanent split, 64, 146 (*see also* Eastern Empire); restoration in Holy Roman Empire, 160; structural reorganization of Diocletian, 144; temporary division during Third Century, 143; tetrarchy of Diocletian, *140, 144-145; Western, collapse of, 146, 157
Empires outside Rome, *43, *165; Hellenistic, 37
Engineering, 22, 163-164; construction, 154, 162, 163-164; crane and tools, *155; public baths, *87, 88; weaponry, *89-97. *See also* Aqueducts; Roads
English language, Latin elements in, 164
Ennius, Quintus, 103; quoted, 109
Entertainment, 86; banquets, 85-86, *134-135; brutality of, 14; children's, *52-53; free admission, 67, 86; mass, *45, *48-51, *54-55, 67, 86; patrician, 25, *134-135; theater, 67, 86, *136-137
Ephesus, *map 9, map 67*
Epic, historical, *14, 15, 103, 106
Epicurean philosophy, 105, 126
Epicurus, 126
Epigrams, 108
Epistles from Pontus, Ovid, 108
Equestrians, 39, 79, 83, 142, 145; dress, 86; in imperial household, 63
Etruscans, 15, 35, *map 37*; cultural influences on Rome, 22, 123-124; Kings of Rome, 35-36, 125; Roman subjugation of, 36
Euphrates, *map 9*; Romans on, 60, *map 67*, 68
Eusebius, 145
Expansion, 35; Augustan limits, 60; to Britain, 60; in East, 38, 41, 42, 65; in Italian peninsula, 16, 35, 36-37; maximum, under Trajan, 65, *map 66-67*; to Sicily, 38

F

Family: as legal and social unit, 12, 79-80; as religious unit, 121
Family life, 81-82, 84-86
Farm loan system, 67
Farmers and farm life, 12, 14, *116-117, *148-149; economic plight, 39, 40, 149; a noble profession, 83; tenant-to-landlord relationship, 146; urban migration, 147, 149; Vergil's handbook on, *102, 106, 114-115
Fashions, 86, 132; hairdos, 29, *80-81, 86, *132; North African influences, 29

Fasti and *nefasti*, 124
Felsina (Bologna), *map 37*
Festivals, 45. *See also* Ceremonies; Religious festivals
Fetiales, 13
Finance. *See* Public finance
Flavian dynasty, 63, 65, 157
Florian, Emperor, 64
Food, 85-86, *115; distribution to poor, 67, 142; imports, 29, 149; prices and price controls, 143-144, 145; shops, *131, 150-151; shortages, 143; staples, 86
Foreign policy: of geographical and political containment (Augustus), 60; late Republic, 40; of military preparedness, 89; of neutralization, 36-37, 38; placation of barbarians by bounties, 143. *See also* Expansion
Fortifications, on exposed border, 63, *map 66-67*, 144; Hadrian's Wall, *32-33, 67
Forum Romanum, *18-21, *72-73, 88, 124, 125, 162-163
Four Emperors, Year of, 62
Fox, James, 160
Franks, 143; Kingdom in Gaul, 160
Frederick Barbarossa, Emperor, 160
Freedmen, 79, 84, 149; in administrative service, 58, 59, 63; relation to patrons, 65
Fuel, lamp, 151
Funerals, 88
Furniture, 85

G

Gades (Cadiz), *map 8*
Galatia, *map 67*
Galba, Emperor, 62, 64
Galilee, Sea of, *map 9*
Gallic Wars, 43, 84, *89-93, *96-97; Caesar's *Commentaries* on, 43, 104
Gallienus, Emperor, 64
Galloway, Joseph, 160
Gallus (poet), 107
Gambling, 50, 132, *133
Games, *45, *48-51, *54-55, 86; children's, *52-53
Gaul, *map 8*, 30; army rebellion of 68 A.D., 62; Caesar in, 42, 43 (*see also* Gallic Wars); cities, 17, *map 8*; invasion by Germanic tribes, 143, *map 158*; Kingdom of the Franks, 160; Latin schools, 11, 164; provinces and roads, *map 66*
Gauls: destruction of city of Rome by, 390 B.C., 36; in Senate, 60
Generals, 83, 89; power of, 41; power curbed, 42
Genius, religious concept of, 122
Gens, 80
Genua, *map 8*
Georgics, Vergil, *102, 106, 114
Germania, Romans in, *map 8*, 63, *map 66*
Germanic tribes, invasions by, 41, 142, 143, 146, *map 158*
Geta, Emperor, 64
Girls, 80; education of, 82
Gladiatorial contests, 14, *45, *48-51, 86
Glycerius, Emperor, 64
Gods: early, *numina*, 121-123; foreign, Roman adaptation of, *32, 124, 126, 127; household, 121, *122-123; Roman attitudes toward, 121. *See also* Religion
Golden Age of Roman literature, 105-108
Golden Ass, The, Apuleius, 82, 110
Golden Milestone, Rome, 21, 163
Gordian I, II, III, Emperors, 64
Government: autocracy of late Empire, 144, 146; beginnings of civil service (imperial household), 58-59, 63; bureaucracy, 65, 144, 146; early Empire, 57-59, 60, 63, 65, 67-68, 73, 76; early Republic, 36; Eastern Empire, 159; late Empire, 142, 144-145, 146; late Republic, 39-40; military infiltration of, 142; military replaced by lawyers, 144; monarchial, 35-36; municipal, 65, 67-68; provincial, 40, 59, 60, 63, 65, 67-68, 71, 144; reorganization by Diocletian, 144; tetrarchy, *140, 144-145. *See also* Officials

187

Governors, provincial, 40, 60, 65
Gracchus, Gaius, 40
Gracchus, Tiberius, 40
Grain, Egypt and North Africa, 29, 62, 71
Grammaticus, teacher, 82
Gratian, Emperor, 128
Graves, Robert, 164
Great Wall, China, *43
Greece, map 8-9; Caesar *vs.* Pompey in, 43; comparisons with Rome, 12, 13, 84; cultural influences on Rome, 11, *22, *24-25, 103, 111, 124, 126-127; influence on Byzantium, 159; philosophy, 126-127; Roman subjugation of, 38, 41, map 66, 98; Visigoths in, map 158
Greek colonies in Italy and Sicily, 35, map 37; Roman subjugation of, 37
Greek gods, Roman adaptation of, 124
Greek mythology: as theme of Latin literature, 107, 108, 112, 119; as theme of Roman painting, 85, *112-113, *118-119
Greeks: as educators, 82; in Senate, 17
Groined vault, 162
Guadalquivir River, map 8
Guadiana River, map 8
Gymnasia, *87

H

Hadrian, Emperor, *64, 65, 67-68, 110, 166; villas of, *24-25, *116; Wall in Britain, *32-33, 67; mentioned, 76, 108, 109, 163
Hairdo fashions, 29, *80-81, 86, *132
Hannibal, 38, 107, 127
Hapsburg emperors, 160
Hellenistic kingdoms, 37
Hera, 124
Heraclea, map 8; battle of, 37
Hermes, 124
Herodian, quoted, 142, 143
Heroides, Ovid, 107
Himera, map 37
Hippo Regius, map 8, map 66, map 158
Hispalis (Seville), map 8
Hispania, map 8, map 66. See also Spain
Histories, Tacitus, 109
History: and legend, 16; Roman writing of, 15, 103, 104, 106-107, 109-110
Holy Roman Empire, 160
Homer, 103
Honorius, Emperor, 64; on coin, *145
Horace, 15, 16, 75, 84, 105, 106, 107, 111, 116, 164; *Odes*, 107; quoted, 11, 52, 76, 107, 116
Horatius Cocles, 15
Hospitium, 88
Housing, 84-85; apartment tenements, 147, 154; early Roman, 22, 84; official inspections, 152; patrician villas, *24-25, *116, *132, *134-135; rents, 147, 154; shortage in city of Rome, 147
Huns, migration of, map 158
Hunting, *46-47, 52, *53

I

Iapyges, map 37
Iconium, map 9
Ilium, map 9. See also Troy
Illyricum, map 66
Imperial Forums, Rome, *18-19
Imperial household, 58, 63
Imperium, 36
India, in Third Century B.C., 43
Indo-European gods, 122
Indo-European migrations, 16
Inflation, 143-144, 145; control measures, 145
Ink, *105
Ionian Sea, map 37
Irrigation, 29
Isis, cult of, 127
Italian alliance: extension of citizenship to, 41; secession move (Social War), 41
Italic tribes, 36, map 37; gods of, 122
Italy: barbarian invasions of, 146, map 158; cities, map 8, map 37, 40, 41, map 66; division into districts, by Diocletian, 144; early history of, 16, 35; Etruscan domination of, 35-36; Greek colonies in, 35, map 37; Hannibal in, 38; roads, map 66; Roman conquest of, 16, 35, 36-37; in Sixth Century B.C., map 37

J

Jefferson, Thomas, 161
Jerusalem, map 9, 126
Jews. See Judaism
Jordan River, map 9
Josephus, 89
Judaea, map 9, map 67; insurrection of 66-70 A.D., 62, 84, 126
Judaism, *126
Judges, 40, 42, *161, 165
Jugurtha, 40, 41
Julia, daughter of Caesar, 42-43
Julia, granddaughter of Augustus, 107
Julian calendar, 44
Julian the Apostate, Emperor, *64, 128
Juno, 123, 124
Jupiter, 11, *58, 122, 123, 124
Jupiter Capitolinus, Temple of, Rome, *18-19
Jupiter Victor, Temple of, Rome, *18-19
Jurors, 40
Justin I, Emperor, 64
Justinian, Emperor, 64, 146, 166
Justinian Code of Law, 146, 159, 166
Juvenal, 14-15, 108-109; quoted, 25, 82, 85, 109, 154

K

Keats, John, 164
Kings, of early Rome, 35-36, 121, 122, 125
Knights. See Equestrians

L

Labor, 13; agricultural, 68, 146, 149; construction, 162; slaves, 84
Lactantius, quoted, 145
Land reform proposals of Gracchi, 40
Landowners, 40, 146, 149
Landscape, Italian, 112, *114-115, *119
Lares, deities, 121, *122
Latin language, 103, 104; Bible translated into, 110; in Byzantium, 159; Greek works translated into, 103; heritage of, 110, 157, 164; in Roman Catholic Church, 159
Latin right, 61, 63, 68
Latins, tribe, 16, map 37
Latium, 16, 36, map 37, 106
Lavinium, 16
Law, Roman, 11, 164-166; "case law," 166; civil *vs.* criminal, 165; Theodosius' and Justinian's codifications, 146, 166; concept of justice, 165, 166; individual liberties, 166; lasting influence of, 159, 164-165, 166; marriage, 36, 73, 80-81; officials, 40, 42, *161, 165; patriarchal powers, 12, 79-80; standardization by Hadrian, 67, 166; study of, 68, 166; Twelve Tables, 165-166
Lawyers, 13, 166; in civil service posts, 144; a noble profession, 83
Legend, *14, 15-16, 35; of founding of Rome, *10, 16, 106, 123; and history, 16; of Sibylline Books, 125
Legislation: by Augustus, 58, 73; by Caesar, 44; powers of, in Republic, 36; price and wage controls, of Diocletian, 145; social regimentation, of Constantine, 146
Leisure, use of, 86, 132, *133-135; reading, 82-83, *129. See also Entertainment
Leo I, Emperor, 64
Lepidus, 44
Leptis Magna, map 9, map 66, 142
Liberalism, political, 39. See also Populares; Reform
Libraries, 65, 83, *87
Ligurians, map 37
Literature, 11, 103-110, 159; early (Republican era), 103-105; Greek influence, 11, 103; Golden (Augustan) Age, 105-108, 112, 114-116; history writing, 15, 103, 104, 106-107, 109-110; legend *vs.* history in, 15-16, 35; maxims and aphorisms, 104, 109; nationalistic and moralistic, 15, 75, 106-107, 109; patrons, 83, 106, 107; political, 104; Roman-Christian, 110; satire, 103, 107, 108-109; Silver Age, 108-110. See also Poetry; Prose
Litterator, teacher, 82
Lives of the Caesars, Suetonius, 110
Livy, 15, 105, 106-107; quoted, 15, 35
Londinium (London), map 8, map 66
Lucilius, 103
Lucius Verus, Emperor, 64
Lucretia, legend, 36
Lucretius (poet), 105
Lugdunensis, map 66
Lugdunum (Lyons), map 8, map 66
Lusitania, map 66
Lutetia (Paris), map 8, map 66
Lycia, map 67
Lyric poetry, 105, 107-108, 112, 114-116, 119

M

Macedonia, map 66, map 158; Empire, 37; war with, 38, *98-101
Machiavelli, 160
Macrinus, Emperor, 64
Maecenas, 106, 107
Magistrates. See Officials
Magnesia, map 9; battle of, 38
Magnus, consul, *161
Majorian, Emperor, 64
Marcellus, Theater of, Rome, *18-19
Marcian, Emperor, 64
Marcus Aurelius, Emperor, 64, 65, 68, 127, 141, 142; statue of, *22
Marius, Gaius, 40-41
Mark Antony. See Antony
Markets, *27
Marriage: ceremony, 81; forms of, 80-81; girls' age, 80; laws, 36, 73
Mars, 16, 122, 124
Mars the Avenger, Temple of, Rome, *18-19
Martial, 108-109; quoted, 108
Mauretania, map 8, map 66
Maxentius, 145; Basilica of, Rome, *18-19
Maximian, Emperor, 64, 144; villa in Sicily, *25
Maximinus, Emperor, 64, 143
Maximus, Emperor, 64
Maya civilization, *165
Meals, 85-86
Medicine, *152-153
Mediolanum (Milan), map 8, map 66
Meditations, Marcus Aurelius, 68
Mediterranean Sea, map 8-9, map 66-67
Meditrina, goddess of healing, *152
Memphis, map 9, map 67
Menander, 103
Merchant class, 39, 83, 146
Mercury, *32, 124
Mesopotamia, map 9; Romans in, 65, map 67, 68
Messana, map 37
Messapii, map 37
Metamorphoses, Ovid, 107, 112
Middle Ages, 159, 160, 170; architecture, 162
Middle class, 39, 79. See also Equestrians
Military tradition, 89. See also Army; Warfare
Minerva, 123, 124
Mithras and Mithraism, 127
Mithridates, King of Pontus, 41, 42
Modestinus, 80
Moesia, map 66
Monarchy, in early Rome, 35-36
Money. See Coins; Currency

Montaigne, Michel Eyquem de, 160
Moral Letters, Seneca, 108
More, Thomas, 160
Mos maiorum, 12
Mosaics, *25, *46-47, *50-55, *70-71, 85, *109, *130, *132; Byzantine, 159; Christian, *174
Municipium, city status, 68
Murals, *29, 85, *111-114, *118-119, *120, *132, *134-135, *138
Murder, law on, 165
Music, *134, 137; instruments, *50-51, *58, *59, *134
Musical comedy, 103
Musicus, freedman, 59
Mythology. See Greek mythology; Legend

N

Naevius, 103
Namatianus, Rutilius, 166
Names, 80
Napoleonic code of law, 166
Narbo, map 8, map 66
Narbonensis, map 66
Natural History, Pliny the Elder, 109
Nature, as theme in Roman art, *102, 106, *111, *114-117
Nature of Things, On the, Lucretius, 105
Naval warfare, 38, *39
Neapolis, map 8, map 37
Near East. See Eastern provinces; Orient
Nepos, Emperor, 64
Nepos, Cornelius, quoted, 109
Neptune, Augustus shown as, *69
Nero, Emperor, 58, 61-62, *64, 108; aqueduct of, *18-19; in literature, 110, 164; persecution of Christians, 145, 170; mentioned, 59, 63, 76, 109
Nerva, Emperor, 64, 65, 68
Neutralization policy of Rome, 36-37, 38
Nicaea, Asia Minor, map 9
Nicaea (Nice), map 8
Nicomedia, map 9
Nile River, map 9, map 67; mosaic, *70-71
Niobe, *133
Nisibis, map 9, map 67
Nobiles, 79
Noricum, map 66
North Africa, map 8-9; army rebellion of 68 A.D., 62; Berber raids, 143; cities, map 8-9, 17, *28-29; cultural influences on Rome, 29; economic importance, 29; Lepidus in control of, 44; Roman provinces, map 66-67; Vandals in, map 158. See also Carthage; Egypt
Numidia, 40
Numina, 121-123, 124

O

Occupations, *148-151; liberal *vs.* vulgar, 13, 83, 151; passed from father to son, 146
Octavian. See Augustus
Odes, Horace, 107
Odyssey, Latin translation of, 103
Oea (Tripoli), map 8
Officials, 36, 40, 59, 144; city of Rome, 147; class restrictions, 36, 39-40, 79; course of advancement, 40; Imperial household, 58, 63; provincial magistrates, 65, 68, 144; tax collector, *147; Third Century posts become burden, 144. See also Civil service; Judges; *and specific offices, e.g.,* Consul; Tribune
Olbia, map 9
Olisipo Chisbon, map 8, map 66
Olive oil, 150, 151; press, *150
Olybrius, Emperor, 64
Onager, *95
Optimates, 39, 41, 43
Oratory, 104
Orient, *26-27. See also Eastern provinces
Oscans, tribe, map 37
Ostia, map 8, 154
Ostrogoths, migration of, map 158

188

Otho, Emperor, 62, 64
Otto I, Holy Roman Emperor, 160
Ovid, 107-108, 111, 112, 135; quoted, 80, 107, 112

P

Paedagogus, 82
Paeon, deity, 125
Paestum, *map* 37
Pageantry, 12-13
Paine, Thomas, 160
Painting, 111; early Christian, *167, *170; Greek influence, 111; myths as subject of, *14, 85, *112-113, *118-119; nature and landscape, *102, *111, *114, *116-117, *132; portraiture, *78, *120, *129; still life, *115. *See also* Murals
Palestine, 126, 167. *See also* Judaea
Palestrina, mosaic from, *70-71
Pallas, freedman, 59
Palmyra, *map* 9, 27, *map* 67
Pamphylia, *map* 67
Pannonia, *map* 66
Pantheon, Rome, 11, 22, *23, 161
Panticapaeum, *map* 8
Papyrus, *105; books, 83
Paris, Roman origin of, *map* 8, *map* 66
Parthia, *map* 9, *map* 67
Parthians, 42, 142. *See also* Persian Empire
Pater familias, 12, 79-80, 121
Pater patriae, 12, 76
Patricians, 36, 39, 79, 80, 83; attitudes toward business, 13, 151; domination of *curiata* and *centuriata* by, 36; eligible for Senate, 36; way of life, 25, 116. *See also* Upper classes
Patron-client relationship, 83
Patron-freedman relationship, 65
Pax Romana, 63, 67-68
Peculium, 84
Penates, deities, 121, *122
Pergamum, *map* 9
Peristylium, 84
Perseus, King of Macedon, 38
Perseus and Andromeda, *112-113
Persian Empire, 143. *See also* Parthians
Persian Gulf, *map* 9, *map* 67
Pertinax, Emperor, 64
Perusia, *map* 37
Petilius Cerialis, quoted, 63
Petra, *map* 9, *map* 67; temple in, *26
Petrarch, Francesco, 164
Petronius, 60, 108; quoted, 109
Phalanx, Macedonian, *98-101
Pharmacy, *152
Pharsalus, *map* 9; battle of, 43
Philanthropy, 65, 67
Philip V, King of Macedon, 38
Philip the Arab, Emperor, 64
Philippi, *map* 9
Philippopolis, *map* 9
Philosophy, 14, 126; Epicurean, 105, 126; Stoic, 108, 126-127
Phoenicians, 37
Physicians, 152, *153
Picts, 33
Pirates, 42
Plague, 68, 141, 143
Plautus, 103
Plebeian assembly, 36
Plebeians, 36, 39, 79, 83
Pliny the Elder, 109; quoted, 61, 149
Pliny the Younger, 65, 147; quoted, 48, 59, 80, 128, 138, 151
Plow, *148-149
Plutarch, quoted, 41, 42, 98
Po River, *map* 8, *map* 37
Poetry, Roman: early, 103-104, 105; Golden Age, 105-106, 107-108, 112, 114-116; Greek myths as theme of, 107, 108, 112, 119; lasting influence of, 164; nature as theme of, 106, 114-116; Roman-Christian, 110; Silver Age, 108-109. *See also* Drama; Epic; Lyric poetry; Satire
Political reform movements, late Republic, 40-41
Political theory: Cicero, 104; Roman influence on Western, 160

Politics: alignments, 36, 39; First Century B.C., 41-44; a noble profession, 12, 83; support of patrons by clients, 83
Polybius, 15
Pompeii, *map* 8, 129, *130-139; murals, *29, *111-113, *120, *132, *134-135, *138
Pompey (Gnaeus Pompeius), 42-43, 44, 89
Pontifex maximus, 125, 172
Pontifices, 121
Pontius Pilate, 167
Pontus, *map* 67
Pope, 159, 172
Populares, 39, 40-41, 43
Porsenna, Lars, 15
Praetor, 40
Praetorian Guard: imperial office auctioned off by, 141; rebellion of 41 A.D., 60; rebellion of 68 A.D., 62
Prandium, meal, 86
Price increases, 143-144, 145; control legislation, 145
Princeps: Augustus as, 57; early Empire, 57-58, 59, 60, 63; discredited by Commodus, 141; problem of succession, 59, 60, 65; under Severus, 57-58, 63
Priest(s), 81, 121-122, 124-125, 126; Augustus as, *74-75; cultists, *120, 124; *fetiales*, 13
Prisoners-of-war, *59-60
Probus, Emperor, 64
Procession, triumphal, *58-61
Proconsul, office of, 40
Propertius, Sextus, 107; quoted, 16, 88, 111
Propraetor, office of, 40
Prose: Cicero and Caesar, 104-105; Golden Age, 106-107; Silver Age, 108, 109-110
Proserpina, deity, 122
Prostitution, 88
Provinces and provincials, 11, 17, 157; adminstration of, 40, 59, 60, 63, 65, 67-68, 71, 144; army rebellion of 68 A.D., 62; barbarian settlements in, 68; cities, 17, 21, *26-31, 60, 61, 65, 67-68; citizenship, 11, 60, 63, 68, 143; culture, 68, 157; economic decline, late Empire, 142, 143, 144; extension of Latin right to, 61, 63, 68; farmers of, 39, 40; fortifications in, *32-33, 63, 66, 144; grouped in dioceses, 144; at height of Empire, *map* 66-67; prosperity of early Empire, 65; religious tolerance in, 32; in Senate, 17, 27, 60, 68; taxation, 11, 29, 67, 144, *147
Prudentius, 110; quoted, 11-12
Ptolemaic Empire, 37
Ptolemy, King of Egypt, 43-44
Public baths, 86, *87, 88, 135
Public finance: administration of, under Augustus, 58, 59; currency devaluations, 142, 143; Egyptian revenues, 71; price and wage control laws, 145; problems of late Empire, 142, 143; property confiscations, 41-42, 142; strained by military needs, 68, 142, 143; strained by public welfare, 142; total collapse of Third Century, 143-144; use of commodities for payment, 143, 145; under Vespasian, 63. *See also* Currency; Taxation
Public libraries, 65, 83, *87
Public welfare, 67, 142, 152
Public works, 18, 30
Punic Wars; 37-39; origin of term, 37; mentioned, 16, 29, 124, 127
Pyrenees, *map* 8
"Pyrrhic victory," 37
Pyrrhus, King of Epirus, 37

Q

Quaestor, office of, 40

R

Rabelais, François, 160
Racine, Jean Baptiste, 164
Raetia, *map* 66

Ravenna, *map* 37; Ostrogoths in, *map* 158
Reading, 82-83, *129
Realism, 13-14; in art, 12
Red Sea, *map* 9, *map* 67
Reform: adminstrative, Caesar's, 44; franchise, 41; land- Gracchi proposals, 40; welfare, Trajan's, 67
Regulus, 67
Religion of Rome, 11, 121-128; character of, 121, 128; class restrictions, 36; cults, *120, 124, 127; early Rome, 121-125; Empire, 58, *74-75, 125-126, 127; Emperors' role, *76-77, 122, 125-126; Etruscan influences, 123-124; Greek influences, 124; images and statues, *122, 123; oriental influences, 126, 127; Republic, 125, 126; ritualism, 121-122, 123, 126; sacrificial offerings, *59, *74-75, 123; Sibylline oracles, 125; and Stoicism, 126-127; tolerance of foreign, 32, 124, 126, 128; Vestal virgins, 125. *See also* Christianity; Gods; Judaism; Mithraism; Shrines; Temples
Religious festivals, 118, 123; Saturnalia, 124
Remus, *10, 16, 123
Renaissance, 160; architecture, 161-162; poetry, 164
Rents, housing, 147, 154
Republic, 35, 36-44; class distinctions, 36, 39; end of, 44, 57; expansion in Italian peninsula, 36-37; expansion in Mediterranean, 36-37, 38; farmers of, 39, 40, 149; 14th Century restoration attempt, 160; government, 36, 39-40; late, political strife, 39, 40-44; law, 165-166; provincial administration, 40, 67-68; reform movements, 40-41; "restoration" in form, by Augustus, 44, 57, 73
Rhea Silvia, 16
Rhegium, *map* 37
Rhetor, teacher, 82
Rhine River, *map* 8; army insurrection of 68 A.D., 62; barbarian invasions across, 68, 143, *map* 158; Roman provinces on, *map* 66
Rhodes, *map* 9, *map* 67
Rhone River, *map* 158
Rienzi, Cola di, 160
Rights, individual, 166
Roads, 11, *17, 21, 28, 30, 63, *map* 66-67, 161, 163-164; markers, 163
Roma, goddess, *76; Temple, *18-19
Roman Catholic Church, 110, 157, 159
Roman character and values, 12-15, 16
Rome, city of, *map* 8, 17, *18-19, 25, 88, 147, 149, 167; baths of Caracalla, *87, 88; buildings, 11, *18-19, *23, 58, *72-73, 88, 154, *156, 162; decay, 162; early history, 16, 35; Etruscan kings of, 35-36; fire of 64 A.D., 61, 170; Forum Romanum, *18-21, *72-73, 88, 124, 125, 162-163; Gallic destruction of, in 390 B.C., 36; housing, 84-85, 147, 154; legend of founding of, *10, 16, 106, 123; origin of word, 35; population figure, early Empire, 147; public libraries, 83; retail business, *150-151; rise to Italian leadership, 36; slave revolt in, 84; streets and traffic, 88; superseded by Constantinople, 146, 157; urban problems, 147; Visigoths and Vandals in, 146, *map* 158; water supply, *162-163, 164
Romulus, *10, 16, 21, 22, 35, 123
Romulus Augustulus, Emperor, 64
Rubicon River, Caesar's crossing, 43
Russia, Church of, 159

S

Sabines, tribe, *map* 37
Sacrificial offerings, *59, *74-75, 123
Saguntum, *map* 8
St. Ambrose, 175
St. Augustine, 110; quoted, 122
St. Basil, 159
St. Jerome, 110
St. John, *177
St. Lawrence, 110
St. Luke, *176; quoted, 165

St. Mark, *177
St. Matthew, *176
St. Paul, quoted, 168
St. Peter, 168, *172-173
St. Peter's Basilica, Rome, 160
Salonae, *map* 8, *map* 66
Salvian, quoted, 110
Samnites, tribe, *map* 37
Sanitation, 161, 164; inspections, 152
Santa Costanza, Mausoleum, Rome, *175
Saragossa, *map* 8, 30, *map* 66
Sardinia, *map* 8, *map* 37, *map* 66; Vandals in, *map* 158
Sarmizegethusa, *map* 8, *map* 66
Satire, 103, 107, 108-109
Saturnalia, 124
Satyricon, Petronius, 108
Scales, merchant's, *151
Schools, 11, 82; of Gaul, 11, 164
Science, 109. *See also* Engineering
Scipio Africanus, 107
Scots, 33
Sculpture, *22, *34, *48-49, *140, *172; cameos, *69, *76-77; early Christian, *172-173; in homes, 84, 118; realism in, 12; relief, *30, *45, *56, *74-75, *139, *147-153; religious, 123
Segovia, *map* 8; aqueduct, *30-31, 164
Sejanus, 60
Seleucid Empire (Syria), 37, 38
Senate, and Senators, 21, 104, 125; and Augustus, 44, 57, 58, 71, 73, 76; *vs.* Caesar, 43, 44; Christian converts, 145; Curia, *18-19; declares war on Antony, 44; dress, 86; early Republic, 36; expansion of role under Vespasian, 63-65; *vs.* Gracchi, 40; in imperial household posts, 58, 63; *vs.* Marius, 40-41; membership, 36, 58, 60, 68; Nero's death sentence, 62; and Pompey, 42, 43; and principate, 57-58, 63; provincials in, 17, 27, 60, 68; strengthened by Sulla, 41, 42; Third Century loss of prestige, 144; and Vespasian, 62-63
Seneca, 61, 62, 108, 109, 127, 160; quoted, 86, 108, 109, 112
Septimius Severus. *See* Severus (Septimius)
Severan Dynasty, 143
Severus, Emperor, 64
Severus (Septimius), Emperor, *64, 141-143; Palace of, in Rome, *18-19
Severus Alexander, Emperor, 64, 143
Sewers, 161, 164; inspection, 152
Shakespeare, William, 108, 164
Shih Huang Ti, Emperor of China, 43
Shipping: merchant, *154-155; Punic Wars, 38, *39
Shoes, 86
Shrines, 116, *117, *123, 124
Sibylline oracles, 125, 127
Sicily, *map* 8, 25; Carthaginian colony in, *map* 37, 38; Greek colonies in, *map* 37; Romans in, 38, *map* 66; Vandals in, *map* 158
Siculi, tribe, *map* 37
Silver Age of Roman literature, 108-110
Sinope, *map* 9, *map* 67
Sirens' Rock, near Sicily, *112
Sirmium, *map* 8, *map* 66
Slaves, 84, 124; as business agents, 13; freed, 79; as gladiators, 48, 50; household, 80, 82, 84, *134; in imperial household posts, 58; Spartacus' revolt, 84
Smyrna, *map* 9, 63; marketplace in, *27
Social classes: early Empire, 79; late Empire regimentation, 146; loss of status through impoverishment, 142; and religious status, 36; during Republic, 36, 39; rigidity, 79, 146. *See also* Class war; Equestrians; *Nobiles*; Patricians; Plebeians; Upper classes
Social War, 41
Solidus, coin, *145
Spain, *map* 8; army rebellion of 68 A.D., 62; Caesar in, 43; cities, *map* 8, *30-31, 61, 63; extension of Latin right to, 61, 63; invasions by Germanic tribes, 143, *map* 158; Roman provinces and roads, *map* 66
Spaniards, in Senate, 17
Sparta, *map* 9

189

Spartacus, 84
Sports, 86, *87; children's, *52-53; women's, *25. See also Games; Hunting
Stoicism, 108, 126-127
Strabo, quoted, 161, 164
Suetonius, 14-15, 109, 110; *Lives of the Caesars*, 110; on Augustus, 58, 59, 69, 75; on Nero, 62; on Tiberius, 59-60; on Vespasian, 62, 63; quoted, 45
Suevi, 146; migration of, map 158
Sulla, Lucius Cornelius, 41-42
Sulpicianus, 141
Superstition, *124-125
Sybaris (Thurii), map 37
Syracuse, map 8, map 37, map 66
Syria, map 9, 62; cities, 17, 27; Persian threat to, 143; Roman law school in, 68; Roman province and roads, map 67; Seleucid Empire, 37; war with, 38
Syrus, Publius, quoted, 109

T

Tablinum, 84
Tacitus, 14-15, 63, 108, 109-110; on Augustus, 57, 69; on bloodbath of Cremona, 62; on Christ and Christians, 167, 170; on fire in Rome, 61; on invasion of Britain, 52; on schooling of boys, 33, 82; on 68 A.D. revolt, 62; on Vespasian, 62, 63; writings of, 109
Tacitus, Emperor, 64
Tarentum, map 37
Tarquin the Proud, King, 35-36
Tarquinii, map 37
Tarquinius, Sextus, 35
Tarraco, map 8, map 66
Tarraconensis, map 66
Tarsus, map 9
Taxation: early Empire, 60, 63, 67; forms of, 147; late Empire, 142, 143, 144, 145, 146; provinces, 11, 29, 67, 144, *147; Republic, 36
Teachers, 82
Temples, *22, 123, 124; in provinces, *26; in Rome, *18-19
Tenant farmers, 146, *148, 149
Terence, 103-104
Tertullian, 110
Tetrarchy, *140, 144-145
Thamugadi (Timgad), map 8, *28-29, map 66

Thapsus, map 8
Theater, 86, *136-137, 161-162; free admission, 67. See also Amphitheater
Thebes, map 9,
Theodosius I, Emperor, 64, 128, 175
Theodosius II, Emperor, 64, 146
Thessalonica, map 9; massacre, 175
Thrace, map 66, map 158
Tiber River, map 8, 16, 35, map 37; trade, 154
Tiberius, Emperor, 59-60, *64, *76, 109; mentioned, 108, 167
Tibullus (poet), 107
Tigranoceria, map 9
Tigris River, map 9, map 67
Timgad, map 8, *28-29, map 66
Tingis (Tangier), map 8, map 66
Tingitana, map 66
Tiro, freedman, 84
Titus, Emperor, 64, 65; Arch of, *156
Tivoli, 25
Toletum, map 8
Tolosa, map 158
Tomi (Constanta), map 9
Tools and utensils: of building trades, *155; farming, *148-149; hunting, 47; medical, *152; oil press, *150; scales, *151; writing, *105. See also Weapons
Trade, 11, 17, 27, 29, 30; imports, 29, 149, 154; routes, map 66-67; shipping, *154-155. See also Business
Traditionalism of Romans, 13, 79, 88
Trajan, Emperor, *56, *64, 65, 67-68; Arch of, scenes from, *58-61; correspondence with Pliny, 128; Forum of, *18-19; Temple of, *18-19; mentioned, 76, 163
Trajan's Column, 18, *56
Trapezus (Trebizond), map 9
Travel, map 66-67, 82, 88
Treasury. See Public finance
Tribes, in Italy: Etruscans, 35-36, map 37; Italic, 36, map 37; Latins, 16, map 37; prehistoric, 16, 35; representation in *centuriata*, 36
Tribunate of the Plebes, 36
Tribunes, 36; Drusus, 41; Gracchi, 40; powers of, 36; powers curtailed by Sulla, 42; powers restored by Pompey, 42; term of office, 36
Triclinium, 85
Tristia, Ovid, 108
Triumphal procession, *58-61
Triumvirates: First, 42; Second, 44

Troy, map 9, 14, 16, 106
Twelve Tables, 165-166
Tyre, map 67
Tyrrhenian Sea, map 8, map 37, map 66

U

Ulpia Traiana, map 8
Umbrians, tribe, map 37
Unemployed: in city of Rome, 147, 149; games for, 45; work procurement, 30, 44
Upper classes, 13, 79; code regarding occupations, 13, 83, 151; in imperial household posts, 58, 63; impoverishment of, in late empire, 142; office holders, 36, 39-40, 79; political alignment, 39; and slaves, 84; way of life, 25, 79-86, *129, *132-135. See also Aristocracy; *Nobiles*; Patricians
Urban migration, 147, 149
Usus, marriage, 81
Utensils. See Tools and utensils
Utica, map 8, 68

V

Valens, Emperor, 64
Valentinian I, Emperor, 64
Valentinian III, Emperor, 64
Valerian, Emperor, 64, 170
Vandals, 146; migration of, map 158
Vaults, barrel and groined, 162
Vegetius, quoted, 89, 99
Veii, map 37, 123
Velleius Paterculus, 59
Veneti, map 37
Venus, 16, 124; mural, *118-119
Venus and Roma, Temple of, Rome, *18-19
Vergil, 105-106, 107, 111, 160, 164; *Aeneid*, 14, 15, 75, 106; *Eclogues (Bucolics)*, 106; *Georgics*, *102, 106, 114; quoted, 15, 106, 109, 114-115
Verona, map 8
Vespasian, Emperor, 18, 58, 62-65, 157
Vesta, deity, 121, 125
Vestal Virgins, 125
Vesuvius, Mt., 129, *138
Veto power: consuls, 36; tribunes, 36

Vetulonia, map 37
Via Appia, *17, 164
Viaducts, 22
Vicar (*vicarius*), office of, 144
Vicenza, Teatro Olimpico, 161
Vida, Jerome, 164
Villas, 84-85, *132, *134-135; Hadrian's, *24-25, *116; murals, *114, *118-119
Viminacium, map 8
Vindobona (Vienna), map 8
Visigoths, 146; migration of, map 158
Vitellius, Emperor, 62, 64
Vitruvius, 161-162, 163; quoted, 161
Volaterrae, map 37
Volsci, tribe, map 37
Vulgate Bible, 110

W

Wage controls, 145
Warfare: battlefield, *98-101; border, late Empire, 68, 142, 143, 146; declarations of war, 13; naval, 38, *39; siege, *89-97; tactics, 89, 98. See also Army; Civil Wars; Expansion; Gallic Wars; Punic Wars; Weapons
Washington, D.C., architecture, 163
Wax tablets and styli, *105
Weapons, 89, 90, 93; artillery, *91-95; assault machinery, *89-93, *96-97; assault, naval, 38, *39; field, *98-101; gladiators', 48, *50-51; hunting, 47
Weddings, 81
Welfare, public, 67, 142, 152
Wine, 30
Women: in business, *150-151; education of, 82; fashions, 29, *80-81, 86, *132; leisure, *129, 132, *133; married, rights of, 80-81; naming of, 80; role in society, 80, 83-84; in sports, *25
Writing tools, *105

Z

Zama, map 8; battle of, 38
Zeno, Emperor, 64
Zeno, philosopher, 127
Zeus, 124
Zoroastrianism, 127
Zosimus, quoted, 144